World
Food
Unlimited

John (Jack) L. DeWitt
Agronomist & Farmer

In memory of my

Father and Mother,
who taught me by example,

&

W. L. (Shine) Minnick,
who gave me the opportunity to
shine in my profession

IN APPRECIATION

I wish to acknowledge the help and support of my wife and family during research and writing of this book, and for the help of friends, specifically:

Dr. Stewart Wuest, USDA-ARS soil scientist at Columbia Basin Agricultural Research Center, Pendleton, Oregon, who edited the entire work and gave helpful suggestions;

Dr. Fred Crowe, Emeritus Professor of Botany & Plant Pathology, retired and living in Dayton, Washington, who also edited the work and gave helpful suggestions;

Dr. Robert E. Allan, retired plant geneticist and club wheat breeder, USDA-ARS, and Adjunct Scientist, Crop and Soil Sciences, Washington State University, Pullman, Washington, who carefully reviewed Chapter 5;

Dr. Stephen O. Duke, Research Leader, Natural Products Utilization Research Unit, USDA-ARS, University of Mississippi, Oxford, Mississippi, who reviewed Chapters 5 and 6;

Sterling Allen, Agri-Times Northwest publisher, who reviewed the manuscript and gave helpful publishing advice;

Farmer friend and fellow agronomist, *Larry Coppock* of Adams, Oregon, who read the manuscript and gave helpful comments;

Farmer friend *Robert McKinney* of Walla Walla, Washington, who also carefully read the manuscript and gave helpful comments;

And helpful suggestions from my nephew, *Ronald Kuka,* English Professor at the University of Wisconsin, Madison, WI.,

PREFACE

Why do farmers use pesticides, fertilizers, and GMOs? How can their use be sustainable? Why can't all food be produced organically? Will there be enough food for everyone in the future?

If these questions cross your mind, you need to read this book. Discover the basics of soil health and plant breeding. Understand why farmers use pesticides, fertilizers and GMOs. Discover how farmers have changed their practices over the last 70 years in order to tame soil erosion and grow more food sustainably and safely with less resources.

This book has been gestating in my mind for 50-plus years. I'm in my early 80's now, and it's time to let it all out. I have tried to describe the many facets of agricultural production in terms the general public can understand, but if you don't have an agricultural background, allow time to absorb some new words and consider new concepts. Set aside for now the constant internet and media litany denigrating modern farming methods and demanding we all eat organic food and grass-fed beef. This book is for the reader who is not afraid to have his or her beliefs challenged.

John (Jack) DeWitt, author, agronomist (MS), and life-long farmer.

AUTHOR'S BIOGRAPHY

Mr. DeWitt, born in 1936, has been a farmer for 50-plus years following a brief stint working as an agronomist for Lamb-Weston, Inc. He graduated from the University of Idaho in 1958 with a Bachelor of Science degree in Agriculture and from Washington State University in 1960 with a Master of Science degree in Agronomy.

During his farming career he has served as President of the Washington Association of Wheat Growers (1973), the Washington State Crop Improvement Association (1984-85), and as a Washington Wheat Commissioner for six years, Chairman in 1990-91. He is a graduate of the Washington Agriculture and Forestry Education Foundation's Leadership program, Class I, 1980.

He and Geraldine have been married for 62 years and have four children—Jay, Julie, Janet, and Jeana—and eleven grandchildren.

TABLE OF CONTENTS

CHAPTER 1.
AUTHOR'S LIFE LESSONS

"Agriculture is our wisest pursuit, because it will in the end contribute most to real wealth, good morals, and happiness." –Thomas Jefferson

It was the middle of the Depression, 1936, when my mother gave birth to me, her fourth and last child. A cold winter day in Moscow, Idaho, a small town on the eastern edge of the Palouse Country, a fertile area of rolling hills occupying much of eastern Washington and Northern Idaho. My Dad's farm (actually my Grandfather's farm) was East of Moscow, where the prairie soils of the Palouse transition to the timbered country that covers much of northern Idaho. Farms were much smaller then, and Dad's was smaller than most. Sixty acres of cropland and 60 acres of timber and brush. But Dad gave his family a decent living and paid Grandfather his share. He supplemented his farm income with a custom threshing operation, and mechanical work for neighbors in the winter. His three boys all earned college degrees, and his daughter married well. I never thought our family poor, though I knew some in the neighborhood were more affluent, but also many were much worse off.

It was on organic farm, because that's all there was in those days. Commercial fertilizers and carbon-based pesticides didn't come along until after World War II. Nitrogen is the nutrient that most often limits yields, and farmers had to rely on whatever nitrogen nature provided. Sources of natural nitrogen include atmospheric nitrogen (N_2) and oxides of nitrogen (NO, NO_2, NO_3) that enter the soil dissolved in rainfall; nitrogen released from the breakdown of organic matter reserves in the soil; and nitrogen from whatever leguminous crops in the rotation might capture from the atmosphere with the help of *Rhizobium* bacteria living in nodules on the plant's roots (which convert nitrogen gas, N2, to nitrate, NO3, called "fixing" nitrogen). Most farms had some livestock, of course, and made use of whatever manure was available. (More on all this in following chapters.)

In the Palouse Country of Eastern Washington and adjoining lands of the Idaho Panhandle, a farmer could expect a yield of 30-50 bushels of wheat from these natural nitrogen sources, providing annual rainfall was at least 18 inches.[1] If too much nitrogen was available, say from an application of manure, or from a perennial leguminous crop, such as clover or alfalfa, that had been plowed under for a "green manure" crop, the wheat varieties of the day would grow too tall and fall over before maturity. Called "lodging", grain that falls over makes harvest more difficult, and the stems are often damaged so that nutrients and water cannot reach the developing kernels, resulting in little or no yield. Even though tall crops were in danger of lodging, farmers of that time period generally judged the health of their crop by how tall it was, while plant breeders of the day were selecting for shorter straw to combat lodging.

---

[1] People unfamiliar with the topography of Washington State tend to associate Seattle climate with the whole state, and are surprised to learn the center of the state is a desert, though some of it has been transformed to very productive irrigated farmland with water from the Columbia river. Seattle gets nearly 40 inches of rain yearly, while cities in central Washington get approximately 8 inches per year. The Cascade Mountains that divide Western Washington from Central and Eastern Washington provide a barrier to moisture heading inland from the Pacific, causing clouds to rise and dump their moisture, leaving Central Washington in a "rain shadow". As clouds continue east, they rise again as they approach mountains near the Washington-Idaho border, allowing farmland in the Palouse Country to receive 16-30 inches a year. Rainfall is very important to farmers that don't irrigate. It takes approximately four inches of soil-stored rainfall to grow a wheat plant to heading stage, and each additional inch will produce (theoretically) seven bushels of grain.

Many farmers devoted one-third of their cropland to "growing" their nitrogen. Wheat grown one year would be followed the next year with peas seeded with a companion crop of sweet clover. Sweet clover is a biennial plant, meaning it makes a small amount of growth the first year and major growth, including seed production, the second year, after which it dies. So the second year the sweet clover would grow to a height of four-six feet by June, and then the farmer would plow it under and let the land lie fallow the rest of the summer, seeding wheat in the fall. This "green manure" provided adequate nitrogen for a good wheat crop, and added to the organic matter stores in the soil. Leaving the land fallow also provided some control of troublesome weeds.

In the 1930's and early 1940's the transition from horses to tractors was not yet complete, and some farmers had to devote over one-quarter of their cropland to providing hay and grain (fuel) for their horses.[2] Many also had other livestock to feed. Thus hay was a necessary part of their crop rotation. In other words, farmers prior to WWII had to devote a substantial portion of their cropland to non-cash crops in order to fertilize their crops and feed their livestock. Cattle, of course, provided cash income, but horses only provided power, and, unlike tractors, they required "fuel" and care every day of the year.

Horses could, however, do some things tractors can't, at least until recently. Grandfather described his method of harvesting corn in Ohio in the late 1800s. He would walk between two rows, pulling the ears off by hand and tossing them over his shoulder into a wagon drawn by his horse. The horse would stop and go as needed to keep close behind.

Farming with horses today is romanticized by today's

---

[2] In 1915, before the conversion to tractor power gained momentum, U. S. farmers devoted 97 million acres (out of a total of 344 million crop acres) to growing hay and oats for their horses. Horse population on farms at that time was estimated to be over 25 million, or about one horse for every 13 crop acres [7].

media, and viewed with nostalgia by those removed two or three generations from the farm. The young farmers of to-day who choose to farm with horses—walking behind with the reins in hand-- and fill niche markets with "sustainable, organic foods" are idealized in magazines and newspapers. (These markets will be analyzed in future chapters.) But an old friend of my family who lived through the era of horse farming and walked miles every day behind a team of horses described to me what a happy day it was when the machinery dealer delivered a new plow with a seat on it.

Going back even further in time, I have in my personal library four large books hand bound by my great- grandfather John DeWitt. They are full of clippings he collected and pasted onto 8 by 12-inch sheets of paper. They are a precious insight into events and opinions of the late 1800s and early 1900s, and also an insight into the opinions and feelings of my great-grandfather. Though he died before I was born, I feel a special attachment to him because I am a clipping saver also. Following is a clipping from around 1880 that was written by a young farmworker tired of following horses around the field:

"If you raise much corn you must plow a great deal. Many years ago men hitched up their wives to the plow and tended their corn that way. But if any man around here should try that way I'm pretty sure it would cause a revival (sic, revolution)…Some men plow with oxen—they are good for breaking prairie…some men like to plow with mules, but others are afraid of their heels… Some men plow with a shovel, others plow with a hoe—a hog plows with his nose, and a hen with her toes. But if I had my way, I would use a steam (engine to pull my) plow, with cushioned spring seat, with brackets for holding (an) umbrella over my head, with patent fan always in motion, to cool my heated brow, as the wheels revolve a hand organ attachment that plays one hundred tunes, would be set in motion, and as I turned the furrows brown and bare, the music would float out on the summer air..." This poor guy was born 130 years too soon, as everything he dreamed about, plus much more, has come true.

I will never forget the first time I drove a tractor with an air-conditioned, dust-proof cab. It was such a good feeling to breathe clean air while watching the dust stirred up by my implement roll by. I was also reminded of a comment in a book critical of modern farms (circa 1975) in which the author declared that "modern farmers in air-conditioned cabs lose the intimate touch with their land." It angered me that the author felt farmers didn't deserve a comfortable, air-conditioned, dust free work environment, one the author no doubt enjoyed every day.

Farm work was hard for my Dad, even though he was among the early adopters of tractors. Tractors in those days were not so easy to drive. I remember a comment from an old farmworker who had farmed with both horses and tractors. "With horses," he said," you got to rest when you stopped to rest the horses. When driving a tractor you were expected to keep it moving all day long."

Peas were a new crop in the Palouse country in the 1930s, and equipment to harvest them efficiently had to be invented. Dad told how he took a temporary job harvesting peas in the middle of the Great Depression. The job required crawling on one's knees between two rows of peas, pulling the plants by hand and stacking them in a continuous pile, called a windrow, so they could be forked onto a wagon and hauled to a thresher. He was paid 50 cents a day.

By the 1940s, pea harvesting was mechanized by mounting a cutter bar, similar to the "header" long used to cut wheat for threshing, on the back of a wheeled tractor and driving the tractor in reverse. As with the wheat "header", a rotating reel above the cutter bar pulled the cut vines onto a moving platform constructed of canvas (called a draper) that moved the vines to one side and dumped them in a windrow.

The whole process was called "swathing".

Weed control before modern herbicides was hit and miss. Farmers delayed planting in the spring in order to allow weeds to germinate and be tilled under. Delayed seeding reduces yields, and excessive tillage exacerbates erosion from wind and/or water. Fields were sometimes left fallow (without a crop) and tilled every couple of weeks during the summer just to reduce the weed population. If a green manure crop was not plowed down first, these fields were particularly erosion-prone. Small patches of weeds, particularly new weed invasions, were sometimes hand-weeded. I spent many hours pulling Jim Hill (tumbling) Mustard from my father's fields when it first appeared in our neighborhood. But mostly farmers just tilled, planted, and lived with whatever invaded their fields. Sometimes the weeds choked out the crop, and the harvest was abandoned. Even a small population of weeds reduces yields by using precious moisture and nutrients, and sometimes robbing the crop of light by growing tall and shading the plants. It was a great day for wheat and corn farmers when the broadleaf weed killer 2,4-D became available in the late 1940's.[3] Grassy weeds could not be controlled with 2,4-D, but many of the most troublesome weeds could be controlled with one spray application costing less than a dollar per acre.

Diseases and insects sometimes destroyed crops. There weren't many tools to fight them. Compounds containing sulfur or copper were sometimes used against rust--fungus diseases that turn leaves and stems a rusty color and sap the life out of the plant. Smuts, (named long before pornogra-

---

[3] 2,4-D has received a lot of bad press in past years due to its association with Agent Orange. Agent Orange was a 1:1 mix of 2,4-D and 2,4,5-T, the latter being a potent brush killer sometimes contaminated with a very poisonous dioxin. It was the dioxin contaminate in Agent Orange that sickened troops and civilians. 2,4-D does not contain dioxin. It has been extensively tested many times over the past 60 years and its safety repeatedly proven. More on 2,4-D and other chemicals in the chapter on pesticides.

phy became "smut"), especially one called "stinking smut", could also be devastating to wheat crops. A fungus whose spores inhabit the soil, stinking smut would germinate with the newly seeded wheat and then penetrate the seed, growing benignly inside the plant until maturity. But instead of producing kernels of grain, the infected head would be home to smut spores, millions of them packed into the space reserved for the kernels. Combines at harvest time would sometimes appear to be on fire, black "smoke" emanating from the rear of the combine as billions of spores, released from the confines of the wheat head, floated away on the breeze,[4] re-infecting fields nearby and hundreds of miles away. It's a scene no one has seen since the 1960s, as effective seed treatments plus resistant varieties were developed which virtually eliminated the fungus. Organic farmers of today are able to grow smut-free wheat only because seed treatments used by conventional farmers for 50-plus years has lowered the smut spore level in the soil to near zero.

Except for the use of lead-arsenate on expensive fruits and vegetables, insect control before the mid-1940s was dependent almost entirely on natural predation, and farmer's crops were sometimes wiped out by grasshoppers, aphids or other insects. In another of my great-grandfather's clippings from the 1870's, a reporter for a Kansas newspaper, the Atchison Champion, described a sudden grasshopper invasion: "Yesterday we were thunderstruck with amazement, to see the air filled with countless millions of these grasshoppers on the wing, and taking a general direction toward the northwest. Any description of the sight is impossible. The vast number almost cast a shadow over the sun, and they reached as high in the heavens as the eye could see, and at the highest point they seemed the thickest. Like flakes of snow they seemed,

---

[4] High concentrations of smut spores sometimes caused explosive fires. My Father nearly lost his threshing machine to a smut-caused fire. Mini-explosions coming out of the back of a combine often set fields on fire.

only a thousand times more dense. As the day progressed they seemed to increase in numbers, the great body slowly moving to the northwest, a monstrous, fatal plague, that, naught but the interposition of Providence can withstand, and that now bids fair to once more lay waste and destroy the growing crops, so promisingly abundant all over our State."

Disastrous hordes of grasshoppers often plagued farmers in the Plains states through the Great Depression of the 1930s. "Some of the people who survived the 1930s on the Plains have told stories of how swarms of hoppers descended on them, eating entire fields and even (wooden) farm implements and household items. Fields of corn or alfalfa or oats could be destroyed in hours. The grasshoppers would eat anything. The conventional wisdom was that hoppers liked salt, so they would eat the shirt off your back or wherever else sweat landed" [6]. Modern insecticides can now control grasshoppers when they threaten crops, but local infestations can still be severe, especially in dry years. In June of 2014 the National Weather Service in Albuquerque, N.M., reported a swarm so dense it appeared like rain on their radar. Moving into the city because of a lack of food in the drought-stricken rangeland, the 'hoppers were devouring people's gardens and flowers [5].

Most insecticides used before 1945 were based on metals such as mercury, copper, lead and arsenic—all very poisonous if ingested. Two made from plants, rotenone and pyrethrum, were also quite poisonous to humans, but rapidly degraded in sunlight. Metals-based insecticides could poison the soil if repeatedly applied. Some orchard land in Washington is still unusable for any purpose other than fruit orchards because of high levels of lead and/or arsenic. Children could be harmed by soil resides of these metals if the land is used for housing or playgrounds. Vegetable crops grown on such land could take up harmful amounts of lead or arsenic.

Home gardeners before 1950 routinely used lead arsenate

to kill potato bugs and other insects. One of my earliest memories is of my Mother heading to the garden with a gallon can half filled with lead arsenate and a paintbrush in her right hand. She would walk down a row, dipping the paintbrush in the can and shaking it over the vegetables. The vegetables were washed before eating, of course, but I'm sure some residue remained. No ill effects as far as I know, but I suppose those who know me might disagree.

With the introduction of DDT after WWII insect control became cheap and effective. And, even though DDT has been devastatingly criticized, it is actually quite safe to mammals. It does interfere with calcium metabolism in birds, thus affecting eggshell thickness. What sounded DDT's death-knell was not its toxicity: It was its longevity in soil and water, and its universal use. It was used on nearly every farm and every urban household, sprayed everywhere by municipalities, falling on pavement and then into storm drains, carried in soil from eroding lands, washing into rivers, lakes and ultimately the oceans from every continent. Because of public response to Racheal Carson's book, Silent Spring, pesticide manufacturers were forced to find alternatives. Today's pesticides are short lived and regulations guard the safety of the environment and our food supply. (More on pesticides in Chapter 6.)

My dad rotated wheat with dry beans. The beans, being a legume, provided enough nitrogen to adequately nourish the wheat crop the following year. They also served the same purpose as a fallow field in controlling weeds. The beans were seeded in rows and cultivated when weeds appeared. Weeds in the row were hand weeded. I spent many hours with my dad and brothers hoeing beans.

Dad and his Father bought a threshing machine and a steel-wheeled Rumely Oil Pull tractor for power, and started a custom threshing operation in the early 1920's. Wheat in those days was first cut and bound in bundles with a horse or tractor-pulled machine appropriately called a "binder" (a descendant of Cyrus McCormick's "reaper"). The bundles were accumulated on the binder and dumped in rows by the binder operator. Two or three workers would then take the bundles and stand them upright in "shocks" of eight or more bundles. There they would stand, sometimes a month or more, until the thresher crew arrived.

When the threshing machine arrived, it would be "set" in a central location in the field, and the steam engine or other power source (such as Dad's Rumley Oil Pull) would be linked to the thresher by means of a long belt. "Set" refers to the process of leveling the machine, sometimes by digging holes for one or more of the wheels to drop into. If the field was large, two or more "sets" might be required to prevent long travel times for the bundle wagons.

Using pitchforks, the field crew would throw the bundles on a horse-drawn wagon which was then taken to the thresher. The bundles were then "pitched" into the threshing machine with a pitchfork. The threshing machine separated the straw from the kernels of grain, blowing the straw into a big pile, called the "strawstack". The threshed grain would be put in sacks and piled next to the thresher to be loaded onto wagons and hauled to a warehouse sometime after the thresher left. A crew of 15 or more men, plus three or four women to cook meals, could thresh 30 or so acres a day. Counting also the men who bound and shocked the bundles, and those who hauled away the sacks, 20 or more people were involved in harvesting 30 acres with a total output of 1000 or so bushels for the day's work. Today that 30 acres could yield 3000 or more bushels, and a crew of three could harvest all of it in three hours: One person driving a $500,000 combine and two more hauling the wheat to storage. And the combine computer can give a steady readout of the yield and store the data so the farmer can have a map of how each area of the field yielded. This map becomes a tool to customize fertilizer applications to soil type. And, with the punch of a button, the driver can flag spots to closely examine after harvest using his GPS. Some critics of modern agriculture charge that "farmers that farm more and more land with increasingly bigger and better machinery lose their intimacy with the land" [1, p.32]. Not so. Farmers just have more technological ways to stay in touch with their land.

Dad used his threshing machine for over 30 years, long after everyone else had converted to combines. By the 1940's though, his customers were very few, and finally just his own crops. By the time I was 11 years old, I was riding the binder. Dad's other boys now worked summers away from home. Dad and I did all the binding, shocking, and threshing on his 30 acres of grain. We would load the wagon (now tractor-drawn) with bundles, park by the thresher, start it up, pitch that load into the thresher, shut it off, go get another load. The threshed grain now went into a truck parked next to the thresher, and when it was full we drove to the home-built granary (which I helped to build) and emptied it.

When I was 14 and old enough to get a full-time summer job away from the farm, Dad bought a combine.[5] Not a new one, of course. One the neighbor had used for 20 years. I had ridden that combine with my Dad while still a little boy. It took a crew of four—one to raise the header up and down as the height of the plants changed (called "punching header"), one to throw the leveling mechanism in and out of gear (to keep the machine level on the hillsides), one to sew the 140-pound sacks of grain, and one to drive the tractor that towed it around the field. The sacks of grain would be left in the field for a crew of 2-3 men to bring them into storage on

---

[5] The word "combine" comes from combining two machines, the "header" and the "thresher". The header, which cuts the stalks and conveys them into the thresher, was first used as a separate machine with horses pushing it through the grain. The cut stalks were conveyed into a horse-drawn wagon pulled alongside. When the wagon was full it was taken to the thresher.

a wagon sometime after harvest. Since Dad didn't have any boys at home to help him anymore he devised ways to punch header and level the machine from the tractor. Threshed grain was stored in a bin on the combine, and emptied into the truck when full.

From the time I was a little boy I knew I wanted to be a farmer. As soon as I was old enough to hang on I spent hours riding on the hood of Dad's old tractor, my legs hanging over the sides of the motor as if I was riding a horse. (OSHA would be aghast). Facing rearward from my "saddle", I watched how he did everything—how he turned corners, how he tilled sometimes around and around, sometimes back and forth, what kind of implements he used and when he used them. I built my own tractor in the backyard out of old boards and spent hours on it, tilling fields with my mind's eye while mimicking engine noise with my vocal chords. Sometimes I would get in Dad's old truck and, again in my mind's eye, take a load of grain to town, shifting like I'd watch Dad do. All this practicing helped when I got my first job.

Doing field work on time is critical to getting the most out of a farmer's land resource. Today's farmers often keep their tractors rolling 15-16 hours a day, or maybe all night if they have enough help. Getting crops in as early as possible in the growing season is a crucial part of getting a good crop. And often they have to work around rainy or windy weather to complete their tasks: it's therefore important to have enough horsepower and manpower to get field work done in a timely manner.

But in my Father's day, things were a little more relaxed. Farmers who used horses had to stop often to rest them, and working them more than 10 or 12 hours would classify as animal abuse. And the importance of getting a crop in early took a back seat to making sure as many weeds as possible had a chance to germinate and grow so they could be killed with tillage before seeding the crop. (Synthetic herbicides changed this priority. More on this in later chapters.)

So when my Father and his neighbor found themselves working fields just across the fence from one another, it was time to stop the tractors and visit a while, even though it may have been only a few days since their last visit. Somehow, even at my young age, my sense of urgency in getting the crop planted was greater than my Father's, and after 20-30 minutes of wasted time I had to restrain myself from urging Dad to get the tractor rolling. (I've never seen farmers stop their tractors to visit with a neighbor in my 50-plus years of farming. A quick wave as one tractor passes the other across the fence is the most interaction that happens when field work is pressing.)

Beginning with my 14th summer I worked June and July on my brother-in-law's crew harvesting green peas. Nowadays green peas are harvested with a machine that strips the pods from the vine and threshes them (called vining) in the farmer's field. The peas are then hauled to the processing plant where they are frozen or canned. But in the 1950s they were first cut from the ground and deposited in windrows (swathed). The windrows were then picked up by a machine that elevated them into a truck to be hauled to a vining station. It was my job to drive the tractor pulling the loading machine.

In August I would drive a tractor pulling a wheat combine. (Most combines in the hilly Palouse Country were pulled by tractors, as self-propelled combines were not yet equipped to remain level on hillsides.) This was my pattern through high school and the first two years of college. Then I married my college sweetheart, Geri, in the fall of 1955, and took the spring semester off to work full time for a farmer near Moscow. Geri quit her studies and began working full time to financially support my eventual return to college. I did return, part time, the following fall semester. In the fall of

1957, our first child was born, and I returned to school full-time, earning my Bachelor of Science degree in Agriculture from the University of Idaho in June, 1958.

Although I always knew I wanted to farm I also knew there was no place for me on Dad's small farm. And getting a start in farming without start-up money was nearly impossible. That's why I went to college in the first place, planning to get a job in agricultural business. Upon graduation, however I found jobs in my field scarce due to a mini-recession. So I applied for a half-time assistantship with Washington State University's graduate program in Agronomy, and was accepted for the fall term. My wife and I moved to student housing, and I spent the next two years researching harvesting methods for the production of turf and pasture grasses.

My research project was to find out at what moisture content a grass seed crop could be swathed into windrows to let dry without harming the germination ability of the seed. For most grass species, if one waits until the seed is ripe enough to store without spoilage due to high moisture, much of the seed has fallen out of the seedhead onto the ground (called "shattering"). The research turned out to be of practical use, and was published in the *Agronomy Journal* [2]. In the spring of 1960 I had my Master of Science degree and went to work immediately for a green pea processing company where I had worked summers for my brother-in-law, Mel Lyon, who had a contract to harvest their peas. The company, Lamb-Weston of Weston, Oregon, was a family owned business just expanding into potato french-fry processing in southern Idaho.[6] I took charge of developing a new green pea growing area 50 miles from Weston in The Grand Ronde Valley of Oregon. It was a great experience recruiting growers and guiding them through seeding to harvest. I learned a lot of good practical lessons from those farmers, and used

---

[6] Lamb-Weston was sold to food giant, Con-Agra in the 1970s.

my agronomic knowledge to great advantage also.

After three years, a large farmer near LaGrande, Oregon, asked me to be his farm foreman and crop manager. Wanting to be a farmer, I accepted. After a year, however, I became disillusioned with how the job was working out, and fortunately another offer came my way. A stockholder in Lamb-Weston who controlled a large amount of family farmland in Walla Walla County, Washington, offered me the job of managing the farming operation. The land had been his father's, and his grandfather's before that, but it was currently leased to an area farmer who was retiring. It would be my job to make decisions on all aspects of the farm--fertilizing, weed and pest control, labor, tillage, crops and crop rotations, etc.—in consultation with Mr. Minnick, the family patriarch, who was busy with a successful law practice. I accepted. I now was in charge of the farm of my boyhood dreams: 1500 acres of rolling dryland with adequate rainfall for annual cropping, 1000 acres of almost flat irrigated land, and a 500 acre dryland lease in a wheat- fallow rotation— about 3000 acres in all. Not the biggest farm in the county, but way above average. I would be there for 40 years, 20 as manager and 20 as lessee in partnership with my wife, my son, my brother-in-law, and the Minnick family. Eventually the farm would grow to nearly 5000 acres.

While others drove the tractors, I spent many hours walking fields, sometimes 10 miles per day, monitoring the growing crops for signs of diseases or insects, mapping areas needing weed control, and looking for signs of nutrient or water stress. Every year there were lessons to be learned. The growing plants "talk" to you if you know how to listen. Though a farm may be large, a good farmer never loses "intimacy "with his/her land, crops or livestock. Farmers now often use all-terrain vehicles (ATVs) or drones to stay in touch with their crops and livestock.

Soil conservation was always a priority when making

cropping and tillage decisions. Topsoil (the top foot or so where all tillage is done and most organic matter resides) is a precious asset, one that has taken thousands of years to build. One pounding rainstorm can wash away thousands of tons per acre if the soil is not protected by vegetation or other conservation methods. One of the first things I did, at the urging of Mr. Minnick, was to divide the slopes so that the upper-half of a slope was always in a different crop than the lower half. Some crops are more erosion-prone than others, so water that starts to run from the upper slope may be slowed or stopped in the lower half. Or, if the most erosion vulnerable crop is on the lower part of the slope, at least the erosive force of downhill water is significantly reduced.

It was a common practice in the 1960s to moldboard plow after each crop. The moldboard plow turns the soil upside down, burying most of the surface residue to a depth of six to ten inches, depending on how the plow is set. When most writers refer to the "plow" they are referring to the moldboard plow. The practice of turning the soil with a plow as the first step in preparing a seedbed goes back centuries. But until the early 1800s plows were not much more than a curved stick. The first plow to do a really good job of turning the soil was made of cast iron and invented by Charles Newbold of Burlington County, New Jersey, in 1797. According to Mary Bellis, writing about the history of the plow, "early American farmers mistrusted (Newbold's) plow. They said it 'poisoned the soil and fostered the growth of weeds'" [3]. Initial rejection has often been the pattern when new technologies are introduced, right up to the present day.[7] (See chapters 5-8.)

The steel plow, still used today, was invented in 1837 by John Deere, a blacksmith living in Grand Detour, Illinois. Deere's strong, efficient plow was just what was needed to break prairie sod, and within a few years he was selling thousands of them. It was the foundation of a giant machinery manufacturing company.

As indicated earlier, plowing after every crop was a common practice. Getting the crop residue below the surface made it easier to prepare a seedbed for the next crop. Seed needs a "bed" that is firm without excessive residue next to the seed that will prevent good seed-to-soil contact. (But not too firm. A person walking across the "bed" should leave distinctive footprints.) Plowing also buries weed seeds, some of which will die before being returned to the surface in the next tillage cycle. Burying crop residue, however, has negative consequences for soil erosion. Surface residue is a prime barrier to both wind and water erosion. I therefor chose to use tillage methods that would leave as much residue on the surface as possible and still be able to prepare a seedbed. In low-residue situations I would start with a chisel plow, an implement that will work the soil as deeply as a moldboard plow, but leave 90 per cent of the residue on the surface. A chisel plow consists of rows of "C" shaped shanks that penetrate the soil and stir it rather than rolling it over. In medium-residue situations I would first use a disc, an implement consisting of rows of concave-shaped discs two or more feet in diameter pulled through the soil at a slight angle, turning the soil, but less severely than a moldboard plow. A disc buries about one half of the residue. The

---

[7] Norman Borlaug, Father of the Green Revolution, faced this same problem in Mexico in 1945. After persuading a large farmer to provide him with an acre of land for a demonstration plot, Borlaug and his crew began plowing the soil with a steel plow. The farmer, who had used a wooden plow all his life, "exploded in protest. 'No! No! Only wood must be used on my soil. You must not touch the land with metal. It will take away all the warmth, all the life! Without warmth, the soil will be dead.'" At length, Borlaug and his helpers pacified the man, and they planted the plot. The next day they returned "to thank the farmer for allowing them to use the land. The acre of land over which they had labored was being trampled under the hooves of a small herd of cows. The farmer shook his fist at the men. His voice trembled with conviction: 'You have stolen the heat from my land; only the animals can put it back!'" [4, p.144].

moldboard plow was used in heavy residue situations, such as would follow an eighty bushel or more wheat crop. As the years went by, I would till less and less as machinery improvements allowed it. This kind of tillage practice is now called "minimum tillage" or "conservation tillage", and it is very effective in reducing erosion.

In the 1980s some farmers began experimenting with no-till, a practice that disturbs the soil just enough to get fertilizer and seed into the ground with one pass. It takes specialized machinery, both heavy and expensive, to penetrate untilled soil through sometimes copious residue and get the fertilizer and seed placed correctly. Seed and fertilizer need to be separated by at least two inches, with the fertilizer best positioned below and to the side of the seed. This kind of placement results in more efficient use of the fertilizer by plants, thus increasing yields and reducing fertilizer losses due to leaching.

Stymied by trying to seed through huge amounts of residue, farmers resorted to burning the residue in order to get the seed into the ground. The roots of the previous crop were still in place, so this helped reduce erosion, but burning year after year leads to significant reductions in soil organic matter. So that was not a long term solution. Eventually farmers and equipment companies devised equipment to deal with most of the problems. No-till is now widely practiced in all parts of the country and in many countries around the world. Where it is practiced erosion has been reduced to near zero.

With this book I hope to enlighten the general public on issues affecting our food supply from the perspective of one who has lived through great change, and (I think) understands the challenges of the future. Now that you are familiar with my background, let's dig in.

CHAPTER ONE REFERENCES

1. Dan Barber. The Third Plate. The Penguin Press, New York, 2014

2. DeWitt, J. L.; Canode , C.L.; Patterson, J. K. "Effects of Heating and Storage on the Viability of Grass Seed Harvested with High Moisture Content". Agronomy Journal, Vol. 54, pp. 126-129, 1962.

3. Bellis, Mary. "History of the Plow". http://inventors. about.com/od/pstartinventions/a/plow.htm

4. Bickel, Lennard. Facing Starvation. (Biography of Norman Borlaug). Reader's Digest Press. Distributed by E. P. Dutton & Co., Inc., New York. 1974.

5. "Grasshopper Swarms so Dense They Show up on Radar." Yahoo-ABC News Network, June 2, 2014.

6. Reinhardt, Claudia and Ganzel, Bill. "The Grasshoppers are Coming". Farming in the 1930s. Wessels Living History Farm. York, Nebraska. http://www.livinghistoryfarm. org

7. Ganzel, Bill. "Horses Finally Lose Their Jobs". Farming in the 1940s. Wessels Living History Farm. York, Nebraska. Undated. http://www.livinghistoryfarm.org

INDUSTRIAL FARMS, ORGANIC FARMS, CONVENTIONAL FARMS & THE ISSUE OF SUSTAINABILITY

"A farmer's most important business partner is the earth." [8]

DEFINING A FARM

Industrial farms are a favorite topic of pundits critical of modern farming methods. But what is an "industrial farm"? If you ask that question of a farmer, most would give you a blank stare. An organic farming enthusiast might answer "anyone who uses non-natural fertilizers and pesticides" A farmer who uses synthetic (non-natural) fertilizers and pesticides would consider himself a "conventional farmer". An urban person might reply "corporate farms" as opposed to "family farms". But what is a family farm and what is a corporate farm? Some of the largest farms in America are controlled by members of one family, and may employ hundreds of workers, be incorporated, and consider themselves a family farm. Truly corporate farms, owned by many stockholders and managed by hired professionals is the exception, not the rule, in rural America.[9] The "industrial "moniker, it seems, is the purview of the agricultural critic.

There are good reasons why big corporations generally stay out of actually growing crops and livestock. Returns on capital are low in agriculture, historically around two per cent. Big corporations can't satisfy their stockholders

---

[8] Amanda, thefarmersdaughterusa.com. Earth Day, 2017.
[9] According to the 2012 Census of Agriculture (table 64), 1136 farms (0.054 per cent) fit this category.

with such low returns. People in agriculture production are there because they love what they do, and are willing to take low returns, punctuated by the occasional period of bumper crops and high prices. When returns become negative, they hunker down, take pay cuts, work longer hours, and hope their savings account will last until things turn around. Another reason corporations avoid farming is that economies of scale level out at a very small size. A farm that employs just the owner and part time help can be just as efficient as a farm 10 times as large if the owner is well capitalized and employs the latest technologies. (This is not necessarily true in countries with political systems that fail to protect individual rights and discourage corruption and cronyism.)

A dairy farmer in Iowa sums up the issue quite well in the "Illinois Farm Family "blog. Jessica Zobrist writes, "While the term 'industrial' seems cool, pressured, and unfeeling, the term 'family' invokes warmth, understanding, and passion. I'm not sure farms can always be clearly divided into one of these categories. Oftentimes, family farms are farms which have been passed on from generation to generation by people who have a deep passion for raising animals, growing crops, and carrying on the family name. This passion is reflected by how much they care about their livestock and the concerns about the ways they work their ground...They are environmentalists to their acreage and caregivers to their livestock."

She continues, "If the family farm is such a beautiful, caring entity, then is the Industrial Farm the bad guy? Not in my opinion. Industrial farms are often run by people who also care about their livestock and their crops. They have just taken a different path and ended up at a farm owned and operated as a company versus a family-owned farm [1]. (Jessica is obviously conflating "industrial" with "large" in this instance).

Many large farms started out as homesteads. For example,

Burk Davis of Adams, Oregon, farms 10,000 acres with his brother Roger. They are fifth generation farmers, growing mostly wheat followed by peas. Burk lives on the land his great-great grandfather homesteaded in 1880. Over the generations, farmland was accumulated through marriages and land purchases. At one time the extended family owned two pea canneries to market their crop and those of other area farmers. But the canneries were sold when markets changed and canning became uneconomic. The accumulated land was divided among the fourth generation, and Burk and Roger now farm what their Father had accumulated. And they farm in a sustainable way, converting all their cropland to no-till in 2005. (More about no-till and other sustainable methods in succeeding chapters.)

Wikipedia takes a very inclusive and implied negative view of modern agriculture. Under the heading, "Industrial Agriculture" the writer states "Industrial agriculture is a form of modern farming that refers to the production of livestock, poultry, fish, and crops. The methods of industrial agriculture are techno-scientific, economic, and political. They include innovation in agricultural machinery and farming methods, genetic technology, techniques for achieving economics of scale in production, the creation of new markets for consumption, the application of patent protection to genetic information, and global trade...Most of the meat, dairy, eggs, fruits, and vegetables available in supermarkets are produced using these methods of industrial agriculture." The article goes on to say, "The birth of industrial agriculture more or less coincides with the Industrial Revolution in general."[2]

In another section the writer equates industrial agriculture with intensive farming techniques "designed to increase yield" involving "increased use of fertilizers, plant growth regulators, pesticides and mechanization, controlled by increased and more detailed analysis of growing conditions, including weather, soil, water, weeds, and pests. Smaller intensive farms (e.g., organic) include higher inputs of labor and use less intensive methods that are claimed to be more sustainable." [3]

The bias of the Wikipedia writer is subdued, but is clear that he/she intends to include all farms that are not organic as "industrial". It is clearer in the next few samples that the term "industrial farming" is a pejorative term used, not by conventional farmers, but by those writers and pundits who idealize and romanticize the agricultural methods of the early 1900's.

"Good soil is precisely what low-impact, low-input, local agriculture builds, and precisely what industrial farming destroys" [Bill McKibben, 4].

"The industrial model, where most of our food comes from now, is dead". [Dan Barber, 5] Dan Barber also says in his book *The Third Plate*, [6, p. 329] "Large-scale agribusiness...has helped bring about ecological problems of unparalleled scope and significance. The costs to soil fertility alone are too great to sustain in the long term."

Writers that malign modern farming methods have one theme in common: The soil is being ruined by fertilizers, pesticides, excessive erosion, monoculture, etc., and current practices are therefore not sustainable. To them the term organic means sustainable, and industrial (i.e. conventional) equates with destructive. They do this without any mention of backup research, or any apparent knowledge of what transpires on a modern conventional farm. The organic method is always glorified and the conventional method is always vilified. One of the best descriptions of their rhetoric was stated by a past president of the Oregon Wheat Growers League, Jerry Marguth, in the League's newsletter, "Oregon Wheat" Feb, 2014. "Some people will refer to 'sustainable agriculture' as being different from mainstream agriculture without understanding anything about conventional food and fiber production systems, yet secure in a belief that conventional ag needs to change. They can't actually articulate those differences, but they are absolutely certain they exist."

Low chemical input and high labor input combined with intensive tillage is how land in the U.S. was farmed before 1940. The critics of modern agricultural methods describe this kind of farming as "low input, low impact", and therefore sustainable and more desirable. They are wrong. Those methods were not sustainable. As a young boy growing up near Moscow, Idaho, I was concerned about the soil erosion I saw around me year after year. Big, deep diches would often appear in my father's fields and those of our neighbor's after winter rains or after a summer cloudburst. Sometimes they were too deep and too wide to cross with harvest machinery, and considerable tillage would be required to fill them in. I became a soil conservationist very early in life.

There was a drainage draw near our house, covered with grass and sheltered with pine trees, where I often played. One summer, when I was around 8-10 years old, I decided a channel for the water to flow in would be a good idea, and I spent a good deal of time and energy digging a ditch about two feet wide and a foot deep through the grass. I had constructed about 100 feet, complete with wooden dams to slow the water and collect silt about every 20 feet, when my Grandfather noticed what I was doing. He was very upset, confronted my Father about my project, and I received a lecture from Dad on how grass protects the soil, and what I was doing would now allow the moving water to cut a deeper channel. It was my first lesson in stopping soil erosion.

A friend of mine, Eric Thorn of Dayton, Washington, told me about the excessive erosion on his grandfather's farm, and how it was eventually controlled. Eric's great-grandfather homesteaded 160 acres East of Dayton, Washington, in 1871. Native vegetation included a mix of trees, grass and shrubs on steep slopes, vulnerable to erosion when left bare, but capable of growing good wheat crops. By the 1920s the farm had grown through land purchases to about 800 acres, and Eric's grandfather was doing the farming. These were depression years for agriculture, and Eric said his grandfather neglected conservation in order to maximize cash crops to pay the bills. Eric's grandfather died in 1927 when his dad, Wilford, was a senior in high school. In 1928, Wilford enrolled in college (Washington State). The hired man was plowing up and down some deep ditches eroded into the hillsides during the previous winter, filling them in so they could be crossed with the combine, and he became very concerned about the excessive erosion. He called Wilford and told him if he didn't get home and take over the farm soon there was not going to be anything farmable left.

Wilford Thorn did take over the farm, but he also finished his college education, getting a degree in Ag Economics. He had a strong conservation ethic, and implemented a rotation for the farm that kept 20 percent of the farm in grass, plowing it out after 4 years and growing wheat and other crops. The Family thought he was going to bankrupt the farm by taking so much of it out of production, but he held fast and eventually prospered. In 1950 he was named conservation farmer of the year for Washington State.

1950 was also the first year nitrogen fertilizer was used on the farm. Before that, a green manure crop of sweet clover grown in rotation every third year was the source of nitrogen for the following wheat crop. Applying commercial fertilizer meant one-third of the farm was no longer needed to provide nitrogen, and, in addition, the amount of nitrogen applied could be fine-tuned to the needs of the crop. Also, the land in sweet clover had to be left fallow all summer following the late-spring plow-down, thus leaving the soil vulnerable to summer cloudbursts. Commercial nitrogen fertilizer, therefore, was another conservation tool.

In 1969 Eric began farming with his father. In 1971 they

began experimenting with no-till, but it would be 30 years before the practice became mainstream in The U.S. Wilford passed on in 2003, still an active farmer at age 93. His sons, Eric and Jim, continue their father's legacy. Every acre on the Thorn farm is no-till seeded and erosion is a thing of the past. From the original 160 acre homestead, the farm has grown to 5000 acres as neighbors retired and sold to three generations of Thorns. Another example of how large family farms are built.

Before the introduction of modern herbicides farmers were forced to till too much in order to control weeds. The moldboard plow was the standard method of beginning seedbed preparation, because it buried weed seeds and troublesome plant refuse. It was also considered necessary in order to mix air into the soil to encourage good root growth. Most farmers of the day just accepted erosion as a necessary consequence of growing cash crops. That attitude prevailed among many farmers even into the 1970s. I once hired a neighbor to come help me harvest after he completed his. The wheat crop was especially good for those days, 90 bushels plus, and a rain had knocked much of it flat. My neighbor was amazed that I could grow such a high yield without any erosion. He was of the notion, as were many farmers, that exceptional crops were only produced in years of excessive rainfall that resulted in troublesome diches on the slopes.

The introduction of the selective weed killer, 2,4-D, in the late 1940s reduced some of the need for excessive tillage. Following decades saw the introduction of more sophisticated herbicides, and fertilizer use became widespread. Breeders at land grant universities churned out higher yielding varieties at a steady pace. All of these factors resulted in more plant refuse to restore organic matter.

With the need for tillage reduced, farmers used the moldboard plow less and used chisels and discs more, leaving plant refuse on the surface to protect the soil from erosion by wind and rain. By the 1980s, many farmers were experimenting with methods of disturbing the soil under the refuse just enough to get the seed in contact with the soil, and at the same time inject fertilizer near to the seed. Dubbed "no-till" farming, new machinery had to be developed to accomplish this task, much of it invented and built in farmers' shops. By the turn of the century equipment manufacturers had turned farmers' ideas into practical implements, and no-till farming became mainstream. According to the 2012 Census of Agriculture 278,290 U.S. farmers practiced no-till on 96.5 million acres, most of it in corn, soybean and wheat country [7]. No-till farming virtually eliminates erosion, builds soil organic matter, sequesters carbon,[10] and saves diesel fuel and other inputs. Another 195,738 farms used conservation tillage (tillage methods that leave 30 percent of the soil surface covered with residue) on 76.6 million acres. To say that our soils are being destroyed by modern farming methods is just plain wrong.

PLANT AND SOIL BASICS

To understand how and why farmers use various methods to protect and maintain the productivity of our soils one needs to understand the basics of soil tilth and plant nutrition. First of all, soil consists of a mineral fraction derived from the weathering of rock, and an organic fraction. The organic fraction includes plant material in various stages of decomposition and an extensive biota of bacteria, fungi, algae, and animal life ranging from large (worms) to microscopic. The mineral fraction is by far the largest, accounting for 90 per

---

[10] A one percent rise in organic matter will sequester about five tons of carbon per acre. An average coal-fired power plant will spew about 0.8million tons of carbon (3 million tons of CO2) into the atmosphere per year. One hundred million acres of no-till could sequester 500 million tons of carbon for each one percent rise in organic matter, enough to offset the carbon production from 100 power plants for 6.25 years. Caveat: The sequester is only good as long as the farmer continues to practice no-till. (For a complete explanation, see note 2-1)

cent, more or less, of the soil weight when air-dried. Tightly held water will account for approximately three per cent of air-dried soil, and the remaining fraction, which can vary

Photo 1. A no-till grain drill (seeding-fertilizing machine). Note the thick residue protecting the soil surface after the drill has passed by. (Photo by Author.)

widely, is the organic matter. The water remaining when soil is air dried is tightly held by the soil particles and is unavailable to plants.

The mineral fraction is categorized according to particle size, clay being the smallest size, sand the largest, and silt the intermediate size. The relative proportions of these particles determine the soil type. (See figure one). Soils with a high clay content require more power to till because the particles cling together tightly, and tend to form large clods. Such soils are termed "heavy", not because they weigh more, but because of the relative difficulty in preparing a seedbed. Clay soils are highly weathered, and are found mainly where forests once predominated or in floodplains where fine soil particles have been deposited during floods. Sandy soils are on the opposite end of the soil spectrum, being easily tilled and difficult to coax into forming and maintaining clods (which are an erosion deterrent). They are referred to as light soils. Sandy soils are found in arid and semi-arid areas.

Soils with a significant silt fraction are medium textured, relatively easy to till, easily form clods of optimum size, and are generally very productive.

Organic matter is a very important portion of the soil, even though under natural prairie conditions it accounts for only about five per cent of the soil by weight. Organic matter holds mineral particles apart in small, crumbly clumps, creating voids for air and water. But it also provides the "glue" to hold particles together in a crumbly manner when tilled, providing "good tilth" in the presence of prodigious amounts and "poor tilth" when present in scarce amounts. Organic matter is a must-have for soils high in clay. Without a generous amount such soils can be very difficult to till, akin to tilling bricks. That is one definition of poor tilth. Clay soils are very prone to puddling after a heavy rain, thus sealing the surface and slowing or preventing water penetration. This is another indicator of low organic matter and/or poor tilth. Silty soils are also prone to surface sealing if organic matter is low. Course, sandy soils rarely suffer this condition, but low organic matter makes them vulnerable to erosion by wind.

Besides promoting good tilth and helping to control erosion, organic matter is a storehouse for plant nutrients, which become available to growing crops as it decomposes. When plant refuse is mixed with the soil, about one-half will decompose in the first year, one-quarter in the second year, one-eighth in the third year and so on providing the soil is warm, moist, and enough nitrogen is available in the refuse or in the soil to supply the nutritional needs of the organisms doing the decomposing. If nitrogen is limiting, decomposition will slow, and growing plants will also suffer (see Note 2-1). Humus is the end product of plant decomposition, or I should say "near end" as it continues to decompose at about one-two percent per year, depending on temperature and rainfall. Humus is the only storehouse in the soil for the plant nutrients nitrogen and sulphur. Humus is composed mainly of plant lignins that are difficult for soil microorganisms to dismantle. In its most decomposed form, it is said to be "mineralized" and functions as a clay particle does, absorbing and later releasing plant nutrients. It also absorbs moisture for later release to plants, and binds soil particles together to resist erosion by wind and water.

Note 2-1. Carbon and nitrogen are the nutrients in highest demand by soil microorganisms. Their cells require a carbon to nitrogen (C:N) ratio of about 8:1. Carbon is their source of energy for growth and maintenance. About 2/3 of the carbon they consume is respired and the rest is incorporated into cell structure. Nitrogen is a major component of DNA and plant proteins. If the C:N ratio of plant refuse is higher than 24:1, microorganisms must scavenge nitrogen from soil sources for decomposition to proceed normally. If lower than 24:1, carbon must be sourced from other residue to complete decomposition. Wheat straw will have a C:N ratio of about 80:1, requiring a significant soil source of nitrogen in order for decomposition to rapidly proceed. Pea straw, on the other hand, will have a ratio of about 29:1, and decomposition will proceed rapidly if moisture and temperature conditions are favorable [16].

Beginning no-till farmers often experience a rapid rise in soil organic content because mixing of refuse with the soil is significantly reduced, drastically slowing decomposition. This fact can mislead farmers and others to conclude no-till permanently increases organic matter levels when the increase, in reality, can rapidly reverse if the farmer later incorporates the residue. As explained in footnote 4, the organic matter increase can be considered a carbon sink so long as the farmer continues to no-till. Farmers who grow cover crops and return large amounts of refuse to the soil are truly increasing organic matter and providing a more permanent carbon sink (see note 2-2).

Can crops be grown in soils lacking organic matter? Of course. Plants can even be grown hydroponically without soil, circulating a nutrient solution through gravel that serves as an anchor for the roots.[11] The sandy soils of deserts, which are very low in organic matter, grow great crops as long as nutrients are supplied. When desert soils are irrigated and intensively cropped, organic matter builds until an equilibrium is reached whereas the organic matter returned equals the amount being decomposed each crop cycle.

How much organic matter is enough? For the conventional farmer, if the tilth is good and the residue adequate to control erosion, the supply is adequate. For organic farmers, high amounts of organic matter is crucial in order to supply nutrients for their crops. Plowing down green manure--plants grown and plowed under while green for the sole purpose of recycling nutrients for the next crop—and/or animal manure has to be a regular practice. The effect of these practices on the world's future food supply will be discussed in the next chapter.

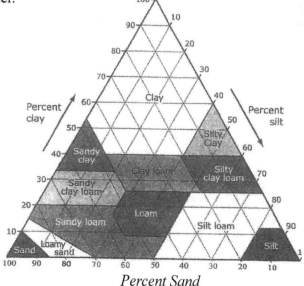

Percent Sand

Figure 1. Soil texture chart, identifying soil types by sand, silt, and clay content.

ESSENTIAL PLANT NUTRIENTS

Nitrogen is the plant nutrient that most commonly limits growth and yield, and the nutrient most commonly supplied from outside sources, either organic or inorganic. It is an essential component of protein, and proteins are the workhorses of the cell, involved in all facets of plant metabolism. Nitrogen supplies in the soil can come from many sources and plants don't care what the source is as long as it's converted to nitrate (NO_3), a job soil bacteria are eager to do. Natural sources include rainfall. Rain will absorb nitrogen in the many forms it may exist in the atmosphere and carry it into the soil. Bacteria in the soil will then convert any of these forms to nitrate. About five to ten pounds of nitrogen finds its way into the soil each year in this manner. The amounts are highest where electrical storms are frequent. Lightning will "fix" nitrogen gas (N_2), combining it with hydrogen to form ammonia (NH_3) or with oxygen to form nitrogen oxides (NO, NO_2, NO_3) in the same manner as some commercial nitrogen fertilizer manufacturing methods. Near big cities cars and trucks spew out oxides of nitrogen from their exhaust pipes which then enter the soil through rain.

Some bacteria in the soil, such as *Azotobacter*, can fix nitrogen gas found in the soil air. As with all forms of bacterial conversion, the amount fixed is dependent on favorable soil temperature and moisture supplies. Thus high rainfall, warm climates will produce the most, but such fixation is not a significant source in any soil. In rice paddies, however, nitrogen-fixing blue algae can be a significant nutrient source for the rice.

A third natural source is bacterial decomposition of organic matter. This can be substantial to nil, depending on several

---

[11] It is interesting to note that hydroponic vegetables are considered "organic" if nutrients are "naturally sourced". The emphasis of organic farmers centers on a naturally healthy soil "full of worms and microbiota". There is nothing natural about growing plants in gravel.

conditions. Climate is one factor. Soils in arid climates, usually sandy, are naturally low in organic matter, often less than one percent. Silt loam soils in climates with moderate to heavy rainfall may have three to five percent organic matter. Crops and tillage methods will affect organic matter. If the crop grown leaves more residue than the microbes decompose, organic matter rises. If the reverse, organic matter content falls. The rate of decomposition is determined by moisture and temperature conditions.

Unless copious amounts of manure are applied, all cropping systems will result in organic matter degradation to a level of 50 per cent or less of that found in virgin soils. That is to be expected as virgin prairie had 10,000 years or more of unharvested growth to contribute to organic matter build-up. Degradation is not a serious problem until organic matter levels fall far enough to significantly compromise tilth and erosion control. What is that level? That depends on the soil type, the topography (slope), rainfall, etc. Many people are concerned that much of our farmland is at that point now. I do not think that is generally the case. I have data collected from farms within 50 miles of my home [8] confirming that annually cropped soils are stable, with the amount of residue returned equal to the amount decomposed each crop cycle as long as excessive tillage is avoided. Long-term research at some experiment stations support that conclusion [9, p.50], others do not [10]. That is why no-till research and promotion is so very important. No-till builds organic matter supplies under continuous cropping regimes, but not always under crop-fallow rotations [10]. Tillage is detrimental to organic matter maintenance because air is regularly mixed with the soil. The extra air stimulates biological activity. It's like opening the draft on a wood stove: The fuel (organic matter) "burns" faster.

Manure, of course, is an excellent source of plant nutrients and organic matter. Like any fertilizer, however, it can be overdone. Add too much to soil and the nitrogen will leach away as with any other fertilizer [11, p. 1572]. And too much will cause plants to become "obese", growing too much vegetative matter and running out of moisture before making seeds or fruit. Farmers call this "burning up the crop". Also, too much nitrogen can cause weak stems, causing plants to lodge (fall over) before maturity, damaging the stems and cutting off nutrients and moisture to the maturing seeds. Manure is also high in potassium and phosphorus, and repeated application can cause these elements to build up too much in the soil solution, resulting in their leaching into groundwater, or reacting with other nutrients and rendering them unavailable to plants.

There is one other point that needs to be made about manure. The nutrients in manure come from some farmer's cornfield or pasture. The cow is only recycling the nutrients, not making new supplies. So when a person buys a bag of manure for their vegetables or shrubs they are moving nutrients from some farmer's field to their property. Manure is a great way to recycle some nutrients back to the soil, but manure is not an environmental free lunch.

Soil organic matter content is one of the tests I take on my fields every year. It generally runs about three percent. The furrow slice of an acre of soil will weigh about 2,000,000 pounds. (A furrow slice is the depth of soil a moldboard plow turns over, defined as being six inches.) If three percent of that is organic matter, then the organic matter in a furrow slice of soil weighs 60,000 pounds per acre. About ten percent of that will be nitrogen, or 6,000 pounds [12]. In my climate zone I would expect about one percent of that will become available to the crop each year, or in this case, 60 pounds. Assuming ten pounds from other natural sources, about 70 pounds will be available to my wheat crop without adding anything. It takes about 2.3 pounds of nitrogen to grow a bushel of wheat, so that means I have a crop potential of 30 bushels per acre without additional nitrogen if no other limiting factors are present, such as drought, diseases or insect damage. This yield is in line with an unfertilized continuous wheat study at the Columbia Basin Research Station at Pendleton, Oregon, that was begun in 1931 and continues to this day [9, p.10,14].

Besides nitrogen, the other major nutrients are phosphorus (P) and potassium (K). Both are inherent properties of the mineral portion of soil, with some amount of each becoming available each year. The amount of P and K stored in the soil depends on the concentration of those elements in the rocks from which the soil formed, and the amount extracted from previous plant growth and stored in the humus. Potassium and phosphorus are positively charged ions in soil and are attracted to and held by the negatively charged soil and organic matter particles. They therefore resist leaching unless added to soil in amounts so large that all the available negative charges are occupied. This can happen in sandy soils, but mainly these nutrients are only removed by crops or soil erosion. Manure contains generous amounts of P and K, and excessive use on sandy soil can result in leaching of these nutrients into waterways.

Sulfur is also needed by plants in moderate amounts and is usually included in a fertilizer mix. Gypsum is a good source of sulfur (S) and is used by organic growers, not as a fertilizer but as a soil "amendment". As with P and K, S comes from the rock the soil originated from, plus some in rainfall (especially around large industrial sources), but the main soil storage is in the organic matter, from which small amounts become available to plants each year. Sulfur and nitrogen exist in the soil as negatively charged ions, and therefore are rejected by the negatively charged soil and humus particles. As with nitrogen, that portion not taken up by plants can leach away.

The other nutrients needed in moderate amounts are calcium and magnesium. Besides being nutrients, these two elements are the chief buffering agents in the soil, reacting with free hydrogen ions which helps keep the soil solution from becoming too acid for good crop growth. Arid and semi-arid soils are usually well supplied with these elements while soils that developed under conditions of heavy rainfall (Eastern U. S.) are generally deficient, leaving soils too acidic to grow nutritious, high-yielding crops unless lime is added to raise the pH of the soil solution. Acid soils are also becoming a problem in some arid and semi-arid areas of the West because most nitrogen fertilizers leave an acidic residue that, over many years, has reduced soil pH to undesirable levels. Liming of cropland in the West will become more common in the near future.

There are seven other nutrients needed by plants in very small amounts and are therefore called micronutrients. The amounts of micronutrients in soils, as with all other nutrients except nitrogen, depend on the rocks from which they came, and most soils are adequately supplied. Availability of all nutrients can be tested for by soil labs, and trained agronomists are well aware of symptoms of deficiency when and if they occur in growing plants. Additions to soils can be made as needed. There is no justification, I repeat, no justification for charges by pundits that "industrial farming" has exhausted the nutrient supply of our soils, and therefore the nutrient quality of the food grown. There is also no justification for the charge that our soils are being destroyed by unsustainable farming methods. That was true before 1940. Since then, advances in erosion control techniques have eliminated erosion in some areas and greatly reduced it in the rest. The introduction of fertilizer and high-yielding varieties have increased the amount of residue returned to the soil, and as a result organic matter decline has generally been arrested, and even reversed under some no-till regimes.

UNDERSTANDING SUSTAINABILITY

In his book *The Third Plate*, Dan Barber charges that "shorter straw means less to plow back into the ground to become food for soil microorganisms" [6, p.366]. His intuitive conclusion is wrong. The tall varieties of 75 years ago that Barber idolizes grow (under ideal conditions) five feet tall and fall flat to the ground if yield is higher than 50-60 bushels per acre. They are inefficient grain to straw producers, producing 2 pounds of straw for every pound of grain. That means a 50 bushel crop (3,000 pounds of grain) will produce 6,000 pounds (3Tons) of straw. Modern short-strawed wheat varieties require only 1.7 pounds of straw to produce a pound of grain. Now here's the catch: If you grow a modern variety side by side with an old, tall variety, with just enough nutrients to produce 50 bushel in the old variety, the modern variety will yield up to 27 percent more, or 63 bushels (based on data from long-term, unfertilized plots at the Columbia Basin Agricultural Research Station) [9]. The modern short-strawed varieties have a straw to grain ratio of 1.7:1, meaning a 63 bushel (3,780 pound) yield will produce 6,400 pounds of straw, five percent more than the old varieties from the same nutrients. Now for the argument clincher: 50 bushels is near the maximum for the old, tall varieties. With extra fertilizer and water, modern varieties can yield 140 bushels or more—producing 14,000 plus pounds of residue to enhance soil organic matter. Conclusively, shorter straw can mean over twice as much food for soil microorganisms. And, importantly, less soil needs to be put under cultivation to produce a given amount of food.

Barber further charges, vacuously, that "modern varieties depend on chemicals now more than ever. To get them to work, you need the chemicals: once the chemicals are in use, soil organic matter falls off, and the soil is less able to transport nutrients to the plants efficiently. The result is that

more chemicals are needed to get the same kick [6, p.365]."
These are mythical claims, supported not by research, but
by anecdotal biases of the organic movement. Modern varieties do not "depend "on chemicals: they will perform just
fine if planted on an organic farmer's field alongside older
varieties, and likely will have improved yield and disease
resistance. Since they are bred to take advantage of extra
nitrogen if its available, without falling flat on the ground,
farmers that have enough moisture to support more yield
can get more yield. They don't need weed killers any more
than older varieties. But if you want maximum yields you
have to control weeds, old varieties or new ones. And as
I have pointed out, organic matter does not fall off when
yields go up: the truth is just the opposite. The notion that
more and more chemicals are needed to get the same "kick"
is preposterous. It takes three pounds of nitrogen to produce
a bushel of high-protein wheat, and 2.3 pounds to produce a
bushel of low-protein wheat. It takes 1.2 pounds of nitrogen
to produce a bushel of corn. These averages are well supported by agronomic research. Farmers routinely test their
soil for the major nutrients and plan their fertilizer application according to researched formulas for maximum yield.
I always test for available nitrogen and moisture to a depth
of six feet (yes, fall planted wheat will draw nutrients and
moisture from that depth, even deeper if growing conditions are favorable) before planting my wheat in the fall.
Factoring in expected rainfall and nutrient availability from
natural sources, and also considering the yield potential of
the variety I am growing, I make my fertilizing decision.
Farmers in all developed countries do this: No farmer con-
sciously throws money away on fertilizer he doesn't need.

Barber also charges that "wheat breeders select for higher protein and stronger gluten" to satisfy the needs of the
packaged bread industry [6, p.340]. This is an unfair and
erroneous charge. Breeders must tailor their varieties for

the intended market. For cookies and cakes, a baker wants weak gluten and a protein of eight per cent. For noodles, the preferred protein is 10-11 percent. For breads, the protein required is 12-14 percent. Spaghetti needs a wheat with about 18 percent. Every breeder has access to a bread lab that tests their selections for the particular end use intended. Varieties do not get released until the desired end-use quality parameters are met.[12]

Barber wants breeders to breed for taste, and he found a "kindred sole" in Steve Jones, wheat breeder and Director of Washington State University's Mount Vernon experiment station in the Skagit Valley, one hour north of Seattle. Jones specializes in breeding varieties for local climates, with special attention to taste and other attributes artisan bakers may want. He has become famous among chefs, artisan bakers, and writers that love to denigrate the wheat varieties that feed the masses. Jones is a breeder deserving of praise, and I do not begrudge him his accolades. What I don't agree with is the elitist writers that accuse the modern wheat and milling industry of producing flour that is void of nutrition because the germ,[13] where the vitamins reside, is removed in the milling process. Oils in the germ will turn the flour rancid in a short time if not removed. After milling, the vitamins lost are added back, creating nutritious "fortified" flour with a long shelf life. This is a necessary step for millers to take if flour is to be supplied to the population in large quantities at a reasonable price. It is a marketing problem, not a breeding or variety problem.

Grinding the whole grain, including the germ, is the preferred method for artisans, who charge two-four dollars more per loaf, and sometimes make specious claims of supe-

---

[12] Protein is not the only factor that determines the end use of a wheat variety, but it is one of the most important.

[13] The germ is the embryo from which the new plant will develop. It is a small portion of the seed. The rest of the seed is starch--food for the embryo.

rior nutritional qualities. This works for the customer more concerned with process than with price. It is not a necessary procedure to supply the general public with nutritious flour. Ground flour has a short shelf life.

MONOCULTURE

Another indictment of modern agricultural methods is that of "monoculture", which is defined by critics as the practice of growing the same crop, such as corn, on the same land year after year. (Some critics expand the definition to include a two-year rotation of corn and soybeans, which is an agronomically sound rotation.) Conventional farmers define this practice as "continuous cropping". Critics charge that this practice ruins soil productivity, but the charge is without merit when good conventional farming practices are followed. In the first place, most farmers rotate their crops on regular basis. Some farmers may continuously crop to wheat or corn for a few years if market signals portend to make it more profitable than other options. But, as I will elaborate on later, this practice, even if continued for a decade or more, has no permanent negative effects on the soil so long as nutrients hauled away at harvest are replaced by organic or inorganic means and sufficient organic matter reserves are maintained. Many farmers now grow "cover crops" to build organic matter and protect the soil during the winter months when the soil is normally barren (see note 2-2).

Some rice paddies in the Orient have been in continuous rice for thousands of years, growing two, sometimes three, crops per year. Closer to home, an orchard or a vineyard is a monoculture that can last a hundred years or more. (If a cover crop is grown between the rows that changes the dynamic, but it is the same crop that is extracting nutrients that are hauled away each harvest). And consider a native prairie. For 10,000 years or more the same grass species may dominate vast areas without interruption. For thousands of years rain delivered small amounts of nitrogen to the soil bacteria which then converted it to a form the grass could use. And every year the weathering of the soil particles released small amounts of other nutrients. The grass went unharvested, the old stems and leaves falling to the ground, and slowly decomposing. Rainfall moved some of the products of decomposition into the soil. Worms, rodents, insects and the trampling of animals and birds gradually mixed the decomposing residue into the upper layers of soil. Decomposing roots added to this growing reserve of humus. By the time the plow arrived, some soils had bankrolled 12000 pounds of nitrogen per acre in the furrow slice (6 % organic matter), enough to supply good crops for the pioneers for decades [13].

Corn is a grass. Wheat is a grass. They are at home on the former prairie. If they were grown year after year and a harvest never taken, the soil supporting these plants would also slowly accumulate nutrients in humus. But, of course, there would be no point in such a practice.

Note 2-2. Cover crops are seeded following harvest of a cash crop, such as corn, or sometimes seeded into the ripening crop. The purpose of cover crops is to (a) protect the soil from intense winter storms that can wash soil and nutrients away, (b) scavenge nutrients left behind by the cash crop, thus reducing loss due to leaching and making those nutrients available to the next crop when the cover crop decomposes, (c) provide a mulch that reduces moisture loss during the summer and also supply some weed control benefits, (d) supply live roots for beneficial soil mycorrhiza to interact with between cash crops, and (e) break up layers of compacted soil from various causes such as passage of heavy equipment. A mixture of seeds is usually grown depending on the goals the farmer has in mind. Sometimes one goal is winter pasture for livestock. Before planting the cash crop in the spring, the cover crop is terminated with herbicides, or sometimes destroyed by rolling over it with

---

a crimping machine. The cash crop is then usually no-till seeded into the residue. For farmers who have enough late summer or early fall rainfall or irrigation water to make this practice feasible, cover cropping is a very effective sustainability practice.

Long-term plots at experiment stations in the U. S., Canada, and Great Britain support my contention that monoculture is not necessarily "evil". The Agricultural Experiment Station at the University of Illinois at Urbana-Champaign has plots, named the Morrow Plots that have been in continuous corn since 1876. One plot has never received any nutrients except those provided by nature. Yields, as expected, have dropped off continually as organic matter is used up. Beginning organic matter is unknown, but native soils close by average six per cent. By 1903, organic matter was 3.7 per cent, and by 1955 it was 2.3 per cent. Yields had dropped from the high 40s (bushels per acre) to the 20s. Then in 1955 the plot was split and lime, nitrogen, phosphorus, and potassium were added yearly to one portion. Yields more than doubled in the first year, and had nearly tripled by the third decade of treatment to a respectable yield of 121 bushels. By 1973, organic matter had risen to 2.9 per cent, demonstrating that bigger crops producing more refuse will gradually build soil organic matter. Incidentally, the yields in the untreated portion rose to the 40s in the decades following 1955, demonstrating that improved hybrids were more efficient at using the limited amounts of nutrients naturally available. [13].

Similar results have been obtained at another set of long-term plots at the Rothamsted Research Station in England. Plots there have been growing wheat continuously since 1843 on land that had been farmed for centuries prior to that. Plots now receiving high amounts of nitrogen exceed yields of plots that have received 16 tons of manure yearly, in spite of the fact that manure treated plots contain double the organic matter of the fertilizer treated plots. The best yields now exceed 166 bushels per acre, and organic matter is increasing where these big crops are being produced [14]

The Magruder Plots at Oklahoma State University, Stillwater, Oklahoma, have been growing continuous wheat since 1892. A yield summary of the plots was posted on the internet in 2005. After 112 years of continuous wheat without fertilization (1892-2004), the yield was 18.5 bushels per acre. Plots receiving 238 pounds per acre of nitrogen as manure every four years (equivalent to 60 pounds per acre per year) yield 39.5 bushels per acre, and plots receiving 60 pounds of inorganic nitrogen per acre per year yield 41.7 bushels per acre [15]. All plots have lost organic matter, but data from other long-term experiments suggest that stable levels are near at hand. The prairie sod the plots were created from contained 3.58 per cent organic matter. In 2002 the manured plot had lost 55 percent of the original amount, the inorganic nitrogen plot had lost 59 per cent, and the check plot (no fertilizer) 67 per cent [11].

There are other examples. Researchers at the Columbia Basin Agricultural Research Center at Pendleton, Oregon established some long-term management plots in 1931 [9]. The average rainfall at the experiment station is 16.75 inches, most of which falls in the winter months. Sixteen inches of yearly rainfall in that part of the State is considered the dividing line between growing a crop every year and letting the land lie fallow every other year in order to accumulate moisture. Therefore the researchers established plots of continuous (every year) wheat, and plots in a continuous wheat-fallow rotation. The wheat fallow rotation was, and still is, the preferred rotation of farmers surrounding the experiment station. Quoting now from the Station Bulletin 675 which summarizes the first 56 years of the plot results, wheat yield of the wheat-fallow plots using standard conventional practices rose "steadily from 45 bushels per acre in the 1930's to 83 bushels in the 1980's. The increase results from both varietal improvement and the application of adequate nitrogen to meet crop need. The yield advantage of fallowing over annual cropping is significantly less today than it was 50 years ago because **drought stress has less impact on semi-dwarf wheats than on older, taller varieties.**"[9, p. vii, my emphasis]

In a wheat-fallow plot where no nitrogen was applied the average yield from 1937-1966 was 36 bushels per acre, just what one would expect with only natural sources of nitrogen. Beginning in 1967, high-yielding semi-dwarf varieties were planted on this plot, and the yield over the next two decades (1967-1986) averaged 46 bushels per acre (a 27 percent increase), demonstrating the ability of the short-strawed modern varieties to use available nitrogen more efficiently [9, p. 17, table 7]. Other plots in this study received 10 tons of manure in the fallow year, and the yield from 1937-1966 was 52 bushels per acre, and from 1967-1986 the yield from semi-dwarf varieties was 80 bushels. The 10 tons of manure supplied 99 pounds of nitrogen to the following wheat crop. Another plot received 80 pounds of inorganic nitrogen yearly beginning in 1967, and it yielded an average of 76 bushels per acre, almost as much as the 10-ton manured plot. The researchers concluded "Long-term addition of organic residues to wheat stubble have increased wheat yield in almost direct proportion to the nitrogen added..... **There appears to be little difference in yield enhancement between inorganic and organic forms of nitrogen**" [9, p. 17, my emphasis].

Soil organic matter in the annually cropped plots has stabilized at 69 per cent of the level in permanent pasture. Organic matter in the wheat-fallow plots was 55 per cent of permanent pasture in 1986 and still declining, except where manure was applied [9, p. 50.]

I do not site these examples to promote monoculture. Rotation is the preferred practice to guard against root diseases, and to allow the rotation of weed control practices so that weed resistance to herbicides or tillage practices can be minimized. I just want to point out that it is not the soil-killing practice railed against by critics. When world supplies of a crop that is important to world food supplies, as corn and wheat are, falter for some reason, it makes sense to rebuild supplies by engaging in monoculture for a few years.

To emphasize the point that monoculture is not a soil-killing practice I personally sampled 21 different sites within 50 miles of my home farm and sent the samples to Brookside Laboratory in New Bremen, Ohio. From a combination of five different tests on the biological properties of each sample they arrive at a soil health level from one to ten, ten being the best possible. I chose sites from farmer friends where continuous cropping had been practiced for many years next to patches of grass, some that had never been farmed. I also took samples from some long-term plots at the Pendleton Experiment Station. Here are some of the results [8]:

(First four samples—See Photos 2 and 3)
Soil health rating (highest possible=10)

Conservation Reserve Grass 15 years—   5.7
Continuous wheat for 45 years, adjacent to above, conventionally tilled—   5.4
Three year rotation, wheat-wheat-pea, no-till last 10 years—   5.3
Native grass prairie adjacent to above—   4.5
Continuous no-till wheat last 10 years—   3.9
Native grass adjacent to above—   3.9
Experiment station continuous wheat-fallow rotation since 1931, fertilized with nitrogen—   4.2
Experiment sta. simulated prairie since 1931—   4.0

Scientifically valid conclusions cannot be drawn from this data without resampling the same areas in future years, but trends can be noted. The first four samples are from a rainfall zone of 18-22 inches per year. The last four are from semi-arid fields of 16-17 inches rainfall per year. These trends are worthy of note:

1. Soil biological activity is determined by moisture, temperature, and food supply. Higher rainfall results in higher health scores, likely due to more refuse (food) produced yearly and longer periods of favorable soil moisture.

2. Continuous cropping to wheat or similar grains (adequately fertilized) results in soil health comparable to that of native soil.

Photo 2. Left side is wheat, 45th continuous year. Right side is Conservation Reserve Grass—15 years.

Photo 3. Left side is native prairie, never been cropped. Right side—Three year rotation, wheat-wheat-peas. (Photos by Author.)

So what is soil health, really? Is a healthy soil a soil that supports a healthy crop? Hydroponics can support a healthy crop growing in gravel devoid of microbiota. Or a healthy plant can be grown in a growth chamber by misting the roots with a nutrient solution. So producing a healthy crop is not necessarily the domain of a healthy soil. So why worry about soil health, or try to define it?

First of all, we need soils that resist erosion by wind and water, and soils with good tilth to allow water penetration and prevent crusting. Otherwise the human race of the future will be growing everything hydroponically, not a healthy, sustainable or economic prospect. Controlling erosion requires a good supply of organic matter, mostly in a raw state. For the conventional farmer, this is more important than how well the biota is doing. Nutrients can be supplied from the "bag" as needed.

The organic farmer, however, is dependent on the soil to provide most of the nutrients for his/her crop. To do that, the soil biota must be fed a regular and copious amount of organic refuse from which nutrients can be extracted (see note 2-3). So soil health means different things and requires different things depending on how you farm, and in what type of climate your farm is located. To my eye, all of the growing crops I sampled were on their way to producing an excellent crop for their respective rainfall zones, with the exception of the Experiment Station plots that received no added nitrogen, and even those plots looked healthy considering they had not been fertilized in 84 years. Nutrients, organic or inorganic, and an adequate supply of raw material for the soil biota are the keys to productive and, therefore, healthy and sustainable soils, From these samples and hundreds of plots on experiment stations around the world it should be self-evident that this can be accomplished through crops that are rotated or continuous, and fertilized organically or inorganically.

It is time to stop criticizing farmers who are meeting market demands by growing crops in large fields in a "monoculture" manner. Most of the farmers in America are trying to meet the needs of a burgeoning world population in an efficient and sustainable way. If that population wants to switch from corn, rice, and wheat to quinoa, amaranth and teff, farmers will figure out how to do that, but not until the market demands it and will pay for it. Returning to the farming methods used 100 years ago would not be in the best interest of the environment, the consumer, or the farmer. It is time to embrace the new technologies available to farmers, technologies that will enhance nutrition, be easy on the environment, conserve our soils, increase yields, and provide food at reasonable prices for consumers while providing the farmer with a comfortable income.

Note 2-3. Organic farmers love to demonstrate the health of their soils by turning over a shovelful of soil and displaying the earthworms. Worms are especially dependent on a good supply of plant refuse. If a soil is high in organic matter, they will come. Whether a field is farmed organically or conventionally makes no difference to the earthworms so long as a plentiful supply of raw organic matter is present. My field that has been in continuous wheat for 45 years (second one of the fields listed previously)—fertilized with ammonia-based fertilizer every year--has an organic matter content of about three percent and a good supply of earthworms.

Earthworms have been called "soil engineers" because of their many benefits: Mixing plant residues with the soil by pulling surface residue into their burrows and consuming it, thus releasing nutrients in their castings; improving drainage with their network of burrows; improving water-holding capacity by fragmenting organic matter; and stimulating microbial activity by excreting partially digested organic material for attack by microorganisms.

Soils, however, can develop just fine without earthworms. The glaciers that covered Canada and the northern U. S for thousands of years exterminated any earthworms underneath them. Yet the forests and grasslands that emerged after the glaciers retreated grew just fine. Earthworms were not reintroduced until Europeans arrived, apparently carrying them unknowingly in potted plants from the homeland. Since that introduction, earthworms have become too abundant in some northern forests, consuming so much surface residue that forests soils lose their protective patina of leaf litter. Some long-term no-till farmers in high rainfall areas have also built up earthworm populations that destroy erosion shielding surface residue between crops [17,18,19].

CHAPTER 2 REFERENCES

1. Jessica Zobrist. Illinois Family Farm Blog. Jan. 19, 2012. http://www.watchusgrow.org/illinois-farm-families-blog

2. Wikipedia "Industrial Agriculture". Dec.,2015.

3. Wikipedia "Farming Techniques". Dec., 2015.

4. Interview with Bill McKibben in Scientific American, April 2010, p.67.

5. Barber, Dan, as quoted in Time magazine, Oct. 5, 2010, p.38.

6. Barber, Dan. See chapter 1, reference 1.

7. Internet search: 2012 Census of Agriculture. No-till.

8. DeWitt, J. L. "Soil health of Selected Fields in Columbia and Walla Walla Counties, Washington, and Umatilla County, Oregon. May 27, 2015. Unpublished, available from author.

9. Rassmussen, P., Collins, H. P., Smiley, R.W. "Long-term Management Effects on Soil Productivity and Crop Yield in Semi-arid Regions of Eastern Oregon." Station Bulletin 675, Columbia Basin Agricultural Research Center, Pendleton, Oregon. 1989, reprinted 1994.

10. "Long-Term Agricultural management Effects on Soil Carbon." USDA Soil Quality—Agronomy Technical Note. No. 12, August, 2001.

11. Davis, R. L., et al. "Nitrogen Balance in the Magruder Plots Following 109 Years of Continuous Wheat." Journal of Plant Nutrition. Vol. 26, No. 8, pp. 1561-1580. 2003.

12. Author's Agronomy Notes.

13. University of Illinois Agriculture Bulletin 775, 1982, revised 1984. Pages 12, 19-21.

14. http://www.rothamstead.ac.uk/long-term-experiments-national-capability/classical-experiments. Feb. 7, 2015.

15. http://www.nne.okstate.edu/Long-Term-Experiments/Magruder-Plots-Yield-Summary.htm 3/29/15.

16. "Carbon to Nitrogen Ratios in Cropping Systems." USDA Natural Resources Conservation Service, East National Support Center, Greensboro, NC. Jan., 2011. http://www.soils.usda.gov/sqi.

17. Burton, Dennis, Director of Land Restoration, at The Schuylkill Center for Environmental Education. "The Trouble with Worms." Undated.

18. Edwards, Clive A. Soil Biology, Chapter 8, "Earthworms." University of Illinois Extension at Urbana-Champaign. 2017.

19. Holdsworth, Andy; Hale, Cindy; Frelich, Lee. "Contain Those Crawlers." University of Minnesota Center for Hardwood Ecology. March2003, updated July 2017.

CHAPTER 3.

CAN ORGANIC FARMS
FEED THE WORLD?

"Farming looks mighty easy when your plow is a pencil and you're a thousand miles from the corn field."—Dwight Eisenhower

In 1980 I was privileged to visit China with 29 fellow agriculturalists, all members of the first leadership class sponsored by the Washington Agriculture and Forestry Education Foundation. China was just beginning to open its doors to the world, and making vast reforms to its economy. Food was still produced mostly on communes, and we visited several. A typical commune in the wheat-growing north could encompass 20,000 acres, and have a village with a population of 20,000 to work the land, feed the pigs, grow the vegetables, make the charcoal briquettes to fuel their stoves, etc. In other words, self-sufficient units. Night soil (untreated human feces) and livestock manure was their fertilizer, but there was not enough for the vast fields of wheat, so they went unfertilized unless some inorganic fertilizer could be procured from the state bureaucracy. On the highways near Beijing, every fifth truck (and there were a lot of trucks) would be loaded with a 1000 gallon tank of night soil from the city's latrines, transporting it to holding tanks in the countryside.

One morning, as my group was waiting to eat breakfast at a commune's dining hall, a young woman carrying two 3-gallon buckets hanging from ropes on the ends of a stick held across her shoulders, trotted up to a tank near where I was standing. A man opened a spigot and brown night soil filled the buckets to the brim. Putting the stick behind her neck and splaying her arms across it to steady her load, she took a few slow steps and then broke into a trot, the contents of the bucket undisturbed as she headed for her plot of land. On another occasion I observed a man carrying ashes to his plot in the same manner. (Ashes are a source of potassium and phosphorus.)[14]

Food production in China in the 1980's was very labor intensive. Eighty percent of the population was engaged in growing food as it had been for centuries. A billion people were being fed almost exclusively by organic means, though not adequately by western standards (see Note 3-1). Today, employing modern seeds and adequate fertilizer, Chinese farmers are keeping the country well fed. At the turn of the century, China was a net exporter of food, and remained that way for much of the first decade. By 2010, rising demand for meat and dairy fueled extra demand for feed grains, shifting China to the list of net food importing nations.

Note 3-1. From 1958 to 1961, during Mao Zedong's Great Leap Forward, an estimated 31 million Chinese died of starvation as agricultural production collapsed under the harsh policies that put all independent farmers into communes and banned private garden plots. In 1962 private plots were restored and food production recovered enough to prevent massive starvation. Still, when President Nixon visited china in 1972, meat was a luxury and most Chinese subsisted on rations of rice and scarce vegetables. Mao knew his communes needed fertilizer, and his first large transaction with the West after Nixon's visit was to buy "thirteen of the world's biggest, most modern Haber-Bosch fixed-nitrogen plants" [1, p.269]. It was the beginning of a "green revolution" for China. Subsequently, many more plants were built, the right to farm individually was restored (beginning in 1978) and "today, China is both the world's largest producer and the world's largest consumer of synthetic fertilizer" [1, p.269,270, and Wikipedia, "Agriculture in China"].

Could the world be fed organically today? A lot of writers and pundits seem to think so. And a lot of organic farmers feel that way too. But it's just not practical in today's world. In the first place, there is not enough manure to feed our crops, even if all human waste was used. Most animal manure is recycled to the soil now, and about one-half of the biosolids from municipal sewage treatment plants is applied to cropland or gardens. And, as pointed out in Chapter 2, animals don't create nutrients; they only recycle a portion of what they eat.

Nitrogen is the plant nutrient most often in short supply, and thus the chief limiter of yields. Its importance to plants and animals is crucial. It is a constituent of every protein and is in every plant and animal cell as a major constituent of deoxyribonucleic acid, more commonly known as DNA. When we harvest a crop we pack off copious amounts of nitrogen, and the amount removed must be restored to maintain productive soils.

In addition to animal manure, organic farming promoters say we can use green manure crops to restore nitrogen supplies in the soil, and to recycle other nutrients in forms readily available to growing plants. That is true, but there are considerable downsides to that program when applied universally. First, land occupied by a green manure crop is not producing food. Therefore, more land must be put into cultivation in order to produce enough food for the current population of 7 billion, and much, much more to feed the projected population of 9.5 billion by 2050. Even now we are approaching the limits of land available for production of crops. To grow good grain crops, a farmer would have to

---

[14] Manure was precious in China. Traveling a busy highway one day our bus suddenly swerved to avoid something in the road. I glanced out a window and saw an old man in the middle of the lane calmly sweeping a pile of horse manure from the pavement into a dustpan. Risking his life for a gallon of manure for his garden.

devote at least one-third of his land to green manure. Even then, judging from my experience with leguminous (nitrogen fixing) green manure crops, the nitrogen supply would not be near enough to get the high yields farmers now get with modern varieties. We would also have to cultivate all marginal lands now reserved for wildlife and recreational uses, and we would still not have enough to adequately supply the world with food.

In his book *The Alchemy of Air*, Thomas Hager states that "If we all ate simple vegetarian diets and farmed every acre of arable land as wisely as possible using the best techniques of the late 1800s, the earth could support a population of around four billion people [1, p,xiii.]" The other three billion-plus people presently (2015) living on this planet owe their existence to the Haber-Bosch nitrogen fixing process invented in the early 1900s and commercialized by the German chemical giant BASF. Haber-Bosch combines nitrogen from the air with hydrogen from natural gas to make ammonia (water can also be used as a source of hydrogen if cheap electricity is available for electrolysis). From ammonia, many other nitrogen-containing fertilizers can be made—urea, ammonium nitrate, ammonium sulfate, ammonium phosphate, etc.

The importance to the world's peoples of Haber-Bosch is totally lost on today's population. In June of 2015 Discover magazine asked subscribers, "What scientific advancement, from any point in history, are you most thankful for today?" Twenty-three percent said "surgery/organ transplants". Nine percent said "birth control", 10 percent said "the internet" and one percent, having a long term view of history, said "fire". No one mentioned anything about food supply [2].

Some people argue that Haber-Bosch was the worst invention ever made because it enabled the population of the planet to expand. But when it came along in the early 1900s intellectuals praised it for saving the world from eventual starvation. Fritz Haber received the Nobel Prize in chemistry in 1919 for his world-changing process (Bosch was the BASF engineer that made it work). Europe had long since used up the bird guano deposits in Peru for fertilizer, and it was feared the Chilean supply of sodium nitrate, the primary source of nitrogen for European crops, would soon be depleted also. North American farmers were still mining the organic matter of the prairies and used little fertilizer except on the oldest fields along the Eastern seaboard.

Sodium has negative effects on soil structure and is of no value to growing plants. After World War II it was generally replaced with ammonium nitrate, which is wholly used by plants and leaves no harmful residue except for a slight increase in soil acidity after many years of use. This increase can be corrected by an application of lime. Ironically, organic farmers can legally use sodium nitrate mined from Chile because it is "natural", whereas they cannot use the superior synthetic sources of nitrogen such as ammonium nitrate.

The nitrogen fixing power of legumes (peas, beans, clover, and alfalfa) is over-rated by organic enthusiasts (and more than a few agronomists). Annual legumes, such as peas and beans, spend the first two-thirds of their lifespan using more nitrogen from the soil than from the air. It takes that long for the nitrogen-fixing bacteria (*Rhizobium spc.*) to establish themselves on the roots of the legume. Annual legumes therefore end up using more nitrogen from the soil than is returned from nitrogen fixation. In other words, they deplete soil nitrogen supplies as do other crops, just not as fast.[15]

Biennial and perennial legumes do contribute net increases in soil nitrogen, especially alfalfa that is allowed to grow three years or more. Grain crops grown after alfalfa can "burn" (excessive growth, resulting in lodging and

---

[15] For example, soybeans need four-five pounds of nitrogen per bushel produced, and nodule bacteria will only supply 50-60 percent of the total [16].

64

sometimes complete crop failure) from too much nitrogen. Nitrogen fixation by legumes is not always a 100 percent environmental benefit. Leaching into groundwater can occur the same as can happen when too much synthetic nitrogen fertilizer is applied.

Another fact about nitrogen fixation by legumes is that approximately ten percent of the plant's carbohydrate production is used to support the *Rhizobium* bacteria. In other words, ten percent of the yield potential of the legume is consumed by the *Rhizobium.*

The second reason why organic farming is not a good universal concept is that too much tillage is required. Weed control is one of the worst headaches for organic farmers, and tillage is the first line of defense. Bury the seeds with a moldboard plow. Prepare the ground for seeding, then wait 10 days for weeds to sprout so you can kill at least the first flush with another tillage pass before seeding, meaning optimum planting time may be compromised. With crops that have wide enough row spacing to permit it, cultivate between the rows, and budget big dollars for hand weeding. Use more seed than is optimum for solid stand crops, such as grains, so as to provide more competition for weeds. These practices can depress yields, increase erosion by wind or water, and accelerate decomposition of organic matter and the concurrent release of CO_2 to the atmosphere.

A third reason organic farming won't work universally is because it requires the integration of livestock and rotations of crops, not as the market may demand, but as the suppression of weeds and diseases and the nutritional health of the soil may demand. This can result in crops being grown where they are not well adapted to the local environment, resulting in inefficient production. And it can also cause a shortage of crops with a large market demand and a corresponding surplus of minor crops with limited demand.

Consider the possibility of growing more vegetable crops,

as some activists advocate. According to the 2012 Census of Agriculture, there are 389 million acres of cropland in the U.S. Just 4.5 million acres (1.2 percent) is devoted to the production of vegetables (including melons). Potatoes account for 26 percent of that total, and sweet corn another 12.7 percent. Add tomatoes, lettuce and snap beans to the total and the top five vegetables account for 60.7 percent of the acreage devoted to vegetables.

Some people say vegetable farmers should be subsidized so more will be grown and retail prices will fall. There are two good reasons why this is a bad idea. First, over 50 percent of vegetables are grown on contracts for delivery to canners and freezers. Subsidizing these acres would just lower the price the contractor pays, so it would be the canner or freezer, not the farmer, who gets the subsidy. Second, fresh vegetables are grown to match the market--local, national or export. This market is relatively inelastic (demand not responsive to price changes), so stimulating production through subsidies might lower the retail price temporarily, but lack of extra demand would cause unsold production to be plowed under, possibly bankrupting some growers. The ultimate result would be wild swings in prices as farmers moved in and out of the market. During the long history of subsidies to grain farmers, the vegetable lobby has fought subsidies for vegetable growers for these reasons, and also successfully prevented, through farm bill legislation, growers of subsidized crops from switching to vegetable crops unless they could prove a history of growing them. Activists who call for the growing of vegetables to be subsidized should instead direct their efforts to subsidizing low income consumers.

Now consider the acreage devoted to wheat, corn and soybeans. In 2012, these three crops occupied 229.8 million acres-- 59 percent of total U.S. cropland. To expect any significant amount of this vast acreage to be devoted to a vegetable rotation is economic nonsense. Some people will say "Why not rotate to quinoa, amaranth, or teff, alternate grains with added nutritional benefits." The answer is, when market demand and economic feasibility presents a farmer with a profitable opportunity, it will be done and is being done. But these grains are a long ways from being mainstream due to low yields, high costs of production, and, as a consequence, high retail prices that severely limit demand.

And what about growing more hay and integrating livestock with grain farming so as to utilize manure to fertilize the grain? A lot of farmers do do that, especially dairy farmers, and grain farmers who elect to market some of their corn and soybeans through beef or hog feeding operations connected to their farm. But here again, switching large amounts of corn, soybean or wheat acres to forage production makes no economic sense. In 2012, 15 percent of cropland was devoted to forage production, and another 3.3 percent was devoted to pasture. This amount of cropland therefore is all that is needed to support the country's various livestock operations. Much of this land is in pasture or forage production because it is unsuitable for other crops. And fertilizing with manure is not a universal environmental plus (see Note 3-2).

Note 3-2. Livestock (including poultry) in the U.S. excrete over one billion tons of manure per year, with one source estimating 1.3 billion tons [3]. Most of that is dropped haphazardly by animals on pastures or rangeland. About 335 million tons is produced by animal feeding operations (AFOs) and most of that ends up in lagoons or dry storage mixed with bedding [4]. The manure on pastures and rangeland stays there, but that in dry storage or lagoons is available to be spread on cropland. How many acres of corn would 335 million tons fertilize?

The nutrient content of manure will vary depending on

---

the moisture content, the bedding materials mixed in, the kind of animal, and what storage conditions it has been subjected to. Phosphorus, potassium and minor nutrients are not affected by exposure to air, but portions of the most important nutrient, nitrogen, will rapidly volatilize. Under the best conditions, such as daily gathering and injecting into the soil or storing in a covered lagoon, 15-35 percent of the nitrogen will be lost to the atmosphere. Packed into bedding, 20-40 percent will be lost, and left on the surface of a pasture or feedlot 40-60 percent will be lost [5].

Fresh manure will generally contain about 12 pounds of nitrogen per ton. If handling is "best practices" about 10 pounds could be injected into a corn field per ton applied. General recommendation for a corn crop in Iowa is 180 pounds of nitrogen per acre, so that would require the application of 18 tons of manure per acre—a costly undertaking, even if the transport distance is small. Bottom line, 335 million tons of animal waste could theoretically fertilize 18.6 million acres of corn, or nearly 20 percent of the national crop. Put another way, if it were spread evenly over the 389 million acres of cropland in the U.S., it would supply 8.6 pounds of nitrogen to every acre, about the same amount as nature supplies from rainfall and microbial fixation in the soil. By now, it should be evident to the reader that manure from livestock will never be sufficient to fertilize the nation's cropland. Even if all human waste, estimated to be over 10 million tons per year [3], could all be spread evenly across the U.S. cropland it would provide only another one-quarter pound of nitrogen per acre.

Finding enough nearby land to absorb the manure from AFOs can be difficult, especially the largest two percent, called concentrated animal feeding operations (CAFOs), which account for 40 percent of all animals fed [4]. Spreading or injecting 18 tons of manure to an acre of land is an expensive operation, and becomes prohibitive if it must be transported more than a few miles. Some AFOs elect to cover their lagoons and collect methane produced as the manure is digested by microbes, burning the methane to furnish some of their energy requirements.

Fertilizing fields with manure on an annual basis can cause unexpected problems. The nutrients in manure are not well balanced. In order to meet crop requirements for nitrogen, phosphorus and potassium will be over-supplied. After several years of application, phosphorus can build up to the point that it begins to tie up other needed nutrients. It can also become leachable in sandy soils.

Copper in some manures can also build up to toxic levels in soils with repeated applications. Copper sulfate is used in some dairies to spray cow's feet to cut down on infections. The wash water ends up in manure lagoons. A university of Idaho researcher found repeated applications of dairy waste to sandy soils can inhibit root growth in potatoes due to copper toxicity [6]. Hog manure can also contain excessive copper. Hog rations sometimes include copper sulphate to help fight intestinal infection, and most of the copper ends up in the feces. Copper is an essential nutrient for plants, but only in very small amounts.

Heavy metals other than copper (zinc, nickel, lead, cadmium, arsenic, chromium, mercury) are also found in manure and biosolids, as well as pharmaceuticals fed to humans and livestock. Biosolids also contain household products [7, 8, 9]. The ubiquitous presence of these contaminates together with the over-supply of some nutrients raises the question of how much and how often manure should be applied to cropland. This question prompted one writer to ask, "Is organic agriculture polluting our food with heavy metals" [10]. All soils contain a background level of naturally occurring heavy metals, and plants take

> them up and our bodies (and livestock) eliminate them. So they concentrate in manure and we add them back to the soil. **When this is done over and over on the same field, toxicity problems to plants or the humans and animals that eat them can be expected at some point. "It is something organic advocates are aware of, but do not publicize"** [10]. (My emphasis.)

Our country is blessed with a wide variety of climatic environments that make possible the efficient production of a wide variety of crops. Corn and soybeans dominate in Iowa, Illinois, Indiana and Ohio because the climate endows the area with generous late summer rains and heat which these crops love. And the soils are deep and naturally productive. In the southern plains hard red winter wheat dominates, because that crop demands dry, hot weather during the ripening stage in order to produce the 12 percent protein necessary to make bread flour. In the northern plains, winter kill of fall-seeded wheat can be a problem, so these states excel at producing high protein spring-planted wheat varieties that result in even higher protein, 14-18 percent. Flour from these wheat varieties is used in spaghetti and other pastas.

When wheat is grown east of the Mississippi it is a soft red variety because these states get too much rain to produce high protein kernels. Soft wheat varieties are used for pastries and cookies. West of the Rocky Mountains, white wheat (color of the bran) prevails. Millers prefer a white bran because they can mill closer to it and still get a white flour, thus increasing their flour yield. So why isn't wheat with white bran grown everywhere? Because white wheat varieties sprout easily if rained on after maturity but before harvest. West of the Rockies significant sprout-causing rains at harvest time are a low risk: East of the Rockies they are a high risk. Wheat varieties with red-colored bran are relatively resistant to pre-harvest sprouting.

The Mediterranean climate of southern California is ideal for efficiently growing many kinds of fruits, vegetables, and nuts. California provides the nation with 50 percent of these foods. This may change in the future if climate change denies California sufficient irrigation water. The center of production for these items would then shift to the Southeast where water is more plentiful.

California is a long ways from the big population centers east of the Mississippi, and that fuels a lot of the sentiment among consumers to "buy local". This notion is misguided. The Economic Research Service (ERS) of the USDA did extensive research on local and regional food growing and marketing systems for the U.S. Congress in January of 2015. The researchers found that "Contrary to some perceptions, the literature suggests that the provision of local foods may actually result in a larger transportation 'footprint', in terms of greenhouse gas emissions and energy consumption, than foods marketed through commercial outlets due to transportation inefficiencies" [11, p.44]. To understand why, consider this hypothetical scenario. Twenty farmers each haul a ton of produce 20 miles to a farmers' market. They get 15 miles to the gallon and collectively, round trip, they use 53 gallons of gasoline. The shoppers each travel, on average, 10 miles extra on their shopping trip to get produce from the market. They each carry away 30 pounds, so it takes 1333 shoppers to carry away the 40,000 pounds brought by the vendors. Getting 25 miles to the gallon, the shoppers use an extra 533 gallons of gasoline they otherwise would not use on their shopping trip. A total of 586 gallons of gasoline has been consumed to deliver 40,000 pounds of produce to the consumer. In a worst case scenario, a refrigerated van hauling 20 tons (40,000 pounds) of produce from San Diego to a New York distributor will travel 2800 miles in about 50 hours, and use about 450 gallons of diesel. The distributor may use another 25 gallons distributing to grocery stores, for a total of 475 gallons vs. 586 for the local food.

People buy from farmers' markets, roadside stands (myself included) and other local Direct to Consumer marketing entities (DTCs) and Community Supported Arrangements (CSAs, where customers pay ahead for weekly deliveries) for various reasons [11], one of which is perceived transportation savings explained above. People erroneously feel they are reducing transportation emissions. Some also feel they are supporting local farmers, and they are. It is a good strategy for small beginning farmers, completely eliminating the middleman. Some consumers want the freshest food possible, and they may or may not be getting it, as some farmer market venders cover several states with their offerings. Shoppers may or may not secure price savings over the supermarket, but that's no concern to affluent shoppers. Some also come to get, in their worldview, safe organically grown local food, and again they may or may not be successful. For those on welfare, discounts are often offered through state sponsored programs to encourage purchases from farmers' markets. And some come, most likely, purely for the social interaction and entertainment that is a part of all farmers' markets. In summary, DTCs and CSAs offer a feel-good venue for those shoppers concerned about the environment, about being "socially and politically correct," and desiring to bypass the "industrial" manner in which most of the nation's fruits , grains and vegetables are grown. That their feelings are justified, particularly in the "earth friendly" category, is debatable.

A fourth reason organic farming will never be mainstream is that it is too labor intensive. Before the modern technological farming methods took hold in the last half of the 20th century, 25-30 percent of the U.S population was engaged in growing crops. Today it is about two percent. Some people estimate it would take 70 million people just to provide weed control—22 percent of the 2014 population--in order to feed our nation organically [15]. This, I believe, is not an exaggeration. Would we empty our cities or bring in 70 million foreign workers? Trying to comprehend all the adjustments that would then be needed in our society would take another book. One thing is certain: Food would get very expensive and consume a large portion of the average family's income, which would then depress markets for other consumer goods, stifle innovation, and lower the standard of living for everyone.

Sure, the market for organic food is currently rising every year, but when the overall market share is five percent a 20 percent yearly increase doesn't get consumption to a high mark very fast. I will be very surprised if the total market share of organic food ever rises much above 10 percent. And those who count on bigger supplies bringing down the price stand to be disappointed. For the reasons stated previously, organic production costs are always going to be higher than conventional costs, and yields are generally lower.

I'm not against growing and eating organic food, but consumers will vote with their pocketbooks, and those willing to pay the extra cost for a perceived, not proven, health benefit are in the minority (see Note 3-3). Eventually the market will be saturated: 20 percent yearly increases will not go on indefinitely.

Note 3-3. A quick internet search will provide research-supported arguments on both sides of the nutrition issue, and both can be right. The supply of minerals available to a growing plant will affect the nutritional quality for people and animals without necessarily affecting plant health or yield, since nutritional requirements of plants are not the same as those for people and animals. William Albrecht, Chairman of the Department of Soils at the University of Illinois in the mid-1900s, continually harped on the notion that soil fertility affected protein and other nutritional factors important to human and animal health. Writing and lecturing in an era before the widespread use of synthetic fertilizers to correct soil deficiencies, he maintained the health of people in the Midwest and arid West was better than those in the East, particularly the Southeast, the reason being that heavy rainfall in the eastern portion of the nation had leached minerals, especially calcium, from the soil. Lecturing in 1944, he stated that "the more able bodied selections for the military service of whom seven out of ten are chosen (from the northern Midwest) in contrast to seven rejected out of ten in one of the southern states where the soils are more exhausted of their fertility" [14, p.278]. He also states that calcium is in such short supply in southern soils that "southern mothers tell you that each childbirth costs two teeth" [p.293]. In another section of the same lecture [p.283] he says humans cannot be labeled as to "the particular soil that nourished him" because human food comes from many different soils. This is truer today than in 1944 when more food was locally grown. The modern supermarket can have vegetables and fruits--at certain times of the year--from many states, many countries, and two or three continents. Modern farmers are well attuned to correcting nutrient deficiencies in their soils, and we need not worry about the nutritional quality of organic or conventionally grown foods.

Before leaving the subject of organic farming, Dan Barber's vision of the future of food production described in his book *The Third Plate* [12] deserves comment. Dan Barber is the owner and chef of the Blue Hill at Stone Barns farm to-table restaurant in New York City. He also owns the Stone Barns farm where much of the food for the restaurant is organically grown. And he buys the rest of his meat and produce from local (when possible) organic or "sustainable" producers. ("sustainable" is in quotation marks because what qualifies as sustainable is often in the eyes of the beholder.) Barber writes about this farm and restaurant extensively in his book. It is his premise that "our country's indomitable and abundant food system, for so long the envy of the world, is unstable, if not broken."[p.9]. He continues, "Fixtures of agribusiness such as five-thousand-acre grain monocultures and bloated animal feedlots are no more the future of farming than eighteenth-century factories billowing black smoke are the future of manufacturing."

Mr. Barber's vacuous view of our country's agriculture that provides its people with the most varied, most affordable, most nutritious food in history is insulting to the modern American farmer. He proposes we go back to the way food was produced 100 years ago, from small farms that provided vegetables, fruit and grain for nearby cities. His proposal is fatally flawed. Nearby farms, even the farms in nearby states, cannot supply the food needs of the burgeoning population of the east and west coasts and other high population centers. California supplies 50 percent of the nation's fruit, fresh produce and nuts. The Midwest supplies the wheat for the nation's bread and the corn to produce our meat and a plethora of food and industrial by-products.

When I was a young boy growing up on the farm near Moscow, Idaho, watermelon and strawberries were only available in grocery stores in season. It was the same with most other fresh fruit and vegetables. Vegetables and fruit in the winter came from cans. Today, people who live in the Northern states can buy watermelon and strawberries at reasonable prices year around, and most other fruits and vegetables also. Nutritious food for American families has never been more diversified or more reasonably priced than it is today. This is because crops are efficiently grown where they grow best, and efficiently shipped to where the people live. Containerized shipping allows the world's farmers to make their perishable crops available to customers worldwide at reasonable off-season prices. It is because we are so well supplied with nutritious, cheap food year around that we can afford to complain about the way it's produced, and wish for a more romantic era. Dan Barber's vision of nearby farms supplying our nutritional needs by using production methods of 100 years ago would narrow our food choices, and make them much more expensive. Barber celebrates the fact that he makes do with what is locally available to his restaurant. And I am sure the great chef he is makes his creations delicious. Curious, I looked up his menu on line: It costs $218 per person to "graze" [13, May 4, 2016]. If Dan Barber and other advocates are successful in returning our food system to the early 20th century, or even the mid-20th, only the wealthy will be able to eat nutritious, diversified meals.

Small organic farms close to cities that supply some of the people's needs will always be welcomed by some consumers. Farmers' markets and retail stands supply a niche, but the economic truth is that the bulk of our food will always be supplied by large fields of grain, fruit and vegetables. And just because fields are large and sometimes very distant from the end consumer doesn't mean the crops are being grown in an unsustainable, uneconomic or unsafe manner.

CHAPTER 3 REFERENCES

1. Hager, Thomas. Alchemy of Air. 2008. Three Rivers Press, www.crownpublishing.com.

2. Discover Magazine, June 2015, p 20.

3. Pew Commission on Farm Animal Production. http://www.ncifap.org/issues/environment/.

4. National Program 206: Manure and Byproduct Utilization FY 2005 Annual Report. http://www.ars.usda.gov/research/programs/programs.htm?np_code=206&docid=13337 .

5. Schmitt, Michael and Rehm, George. "Fertilizing Cropland with Beef Manure" University of Minnesota Extension. 2002. http://www.extension.umn.edu/agriculture/manure-management-and-air-quality/manure-application/docs/AG-FO-5882-C-1.pdf .

6. O'Connell, John. "Scientists Warn of High Copper Levels in Manure". Capital Press story on research by Amber Moore, University of Idaho extension soils specialist. Feb. 3, 2012, p. 18.

7. Kinney, Chad, et al. "Bioaccumulation of Pharmaceuticals and Other Anthropogenic Waste Indicators in Earthworms from Agricultural Soil Amended With Biosolid or Swine Manure." University of Nebraska, USGS staff, paper 65, 1-1-2008. http://digitalcommons.unl.edu/usgsstaffpub/65 .

8. USGS. "Biosolids, Animal Manure, and Earthworms: Is There a Connection?" USGS Environmental Health—Toxic Substances. Aug 4, 2015. http://toxics.usgs.gov/high-

lights/earthworms.html .

9. Nicholson, F. A.; Chambers, B. J.; Williams, R. J.; Unwin, R. J. "Heavy Metal Contents of Livestock Feeds and Animal Manures in England and Wales". Bioresource Technology 70 (1999) 23-31. Elsevier Science LTD.

10. McWilliams, James E., professor of history at Texas State University. "Rusted Roots. Is Organic   Agriculture Polluting Our Food with Heavy Metals?" Sept. 8, May 2008.

11. Economic Research Service Administrative Publication 068, "Trends in U.S. Local and Regional Food Systems." Report to Congress, January, 2015.

12. Barber, Dan. See reference 1, Chapter One.

13. www.bluehillfarm.com/dine/stone-barns .   May 4, 2016.

14. Albrecht, William A. Albrecht's Foundation Concepts. Volume 1. Acres U. S. A., Austin, Texas.1975. Edited by Charles Walters.

15. Wheat Life, Oct 10 2010, p. 33.

16. Unglesbee, Emily. "The Nth Degree: Do soybeans need a nitrogen nudge?" The Progressive Farmer. Mid-February 2016, p.35.

CORN—VILLAIN OR HERO?

"This corn will teach you, should you peel away the husk, and be willing to open your ears."—Anthony Liccione

Trashing corn and the growing of corn is a favorite topic of thousands of media people. They regularly accuse corn of ruining our soils, causing an obesity epidemic, causing air and water pollution, emptying our small towns, and colonizing every nook and cranny of our supermarkets.

Michael Pollan, author of the best-selling book, *Omnivore's Dilemma,* devotes 25 percent of his book to trashing corn [1]. First he gives corn anthropogenic qualities (I assume tongue-in-cheek) and accuses it of changing it's genes to seduce humans into making it one of mankind's most important food sources. Instead of humans domesticating corn, Pollan says "corn has succeeded in domesticating us" [p.23]. This would be funny, except that what he is really saying is that farmers and researchers have been stupid to allow one plant to take over so much of our food supply. The truth is, South America's native peoples recognized the important food qualities nature gave this crop (South America is corn's native home)   and selected for natural improvements over the millennia they cultivated it before the Spanish arrived. Improvements have continued ever since, making a big leap in the 1930s with the introduction of hybrids. Breeders have become more ingenious as the decades have advanced to the present. A plant that once yielded 20 bushels per acre for native peoples averaged a record 171 bushels per acre nationally in 2014 [USDA, January, 2014].

The corn plant is capable of much more. The National Corn Growers Association [12] sponsors a yield contest each year. In 2014 a farmer in Valdosta, Ga, set a new record for irrigated corn--503 bushels per acre—and it was a continuous corn field. The non-irrigated winner from Jarrettsville, Maryland, made 353 bushels per acre. You might think they put on excessive amounts of nitrogen to do that, but they didn't. Corn on average requires 1.2 pounds of nitrogen per bushel. The irrigated farmer applied 500 pounds of nitrogen, or less than one pound per bushel produced. He did not apply it all at once. He applied it throughout the growing season as soil and tissue tests showed the growing corn required it. No wasteful use here. The dryland winner applied 400 pounds of nitrogen per acre, or 1.13 pounds per bushel produced. No wasteful use here either.

Pollan's thesis is that that corn has been so successful at manipulating it's genes that it has become ubiquitous in our food supply. He claims [p.19] that "there are some forty-five thousand items in the average American supermarket and more than a quarter of them contain corn". He goes on to say that corn is in the toothpaste, disposable diapers, trash bags and a host of non-food items that include plastics and adhesives. He is right, but corn farmers need not apologize. Besides being a principal source of feed for our beef, dairy cows, pigs, and chickens, corn provides important ingredients at a reasonable price for the food processing industry and many other industrial sectors, especially the ethanol industry. In Pollan's words, corn starch can be made into "adhesives, coatings, sizings, and plastic for industry: stabilizers, thickeners, gels, and viscosity-control agents for food ". To him that's a problem, but I don't see it that way. If these items were not made from corn, they would be made from some other starch source, because industries of all kinds demand them. Why not use a starch source that is plentiful and has been efficiently (and sustainably) gathered from sunshine?

Corn is extremely well adapted to growing conditions in America's heartland, and it is an efficient gatherer of sunshine. Corn is a C4 photosynthesizer, an invention of Nature endowed on only three percent of known plant species, only a few of which are important food crops—corn, sugar cane, millet and sorghum. C4 plants capture carbon more efficiently and use less water doing it than C3 plants, especially in hot, sometimes dry conditions. Despite accounting for only three percent of plant species, C4 plants account for 30 percent of terrestrial carbon fixation [2]. C4 plants can withstand high temperatures better than C3 plants, so C4 species abound in the tropics [3]. For more about C4 and C3 plants, see Note 4-1.

Note 4-1. Photosynthesis in C4 plants results in compounds containing four carbon atoms whereas C3 photosynthesis results in compounds with three carbon atoms. C4 plants use both water and carbon dioxide (CO_2) more efficiently than C3 plants. Though all plants grow best when water and carbon dioxide are plentiful, C4 plants are better able to withstand dry, hot conditions, making corn a good fit for the hot, wet, but sometimes dry, farmland known as the U.S. "corn belt".

C4 plants make good use of the carbon 13 that comes their way while C3 plants tend to discard it. This is one reason C4 plants capture carbon more efficiently. (The carbon atom normally contains six protons and six neutrons, giving it an atomic weight of 12. A small percentage of carbon (1.1 percent) in the atmosphere has an extra neutron, giving it an atomic weight of 13.) The other reason is that C3 plants lose some 25 percent of their captured carbon in photorespiration (respiration in the presence of light) before it is incorporated into plant products, a process C4 plants bypass[2]. (All plants respire at night, releasing some of the CO_2 captured during the day.)

C4 plants growing in 86 degree (Fahrenheit) weather use only 277 molecules of water to fix one molecule of CO_2 while C3 plants require 833 molecules of water, a 300 percent increase in water use efficiency [2].

Pollan says early on in his book [page 45, paperback edition] that it takes 1/4 to 1/3 gallon of (crude) oil to grow a bushel of corn or "about 50 gallons per acre". I have no argument with that statistic, but he goes on to say it takes a Calorie of fuel energy to produce a Calorie of food, and it's "too bad we can't simply drink the petroleum directly". Here is where I begin to argue. That figure may be correct for some foods, but certainly not for corn. A large field of corn is a gusher of an oil well in terms of captured energy through photosynthesis. Let's do the math.

First, a definition. A calorie is defined as the energy needed to raise the temperature of one gram of water by one degree Celsius (1.8 degrees Fahrenheit). This is sometimes called a "small-c" calorie. Capital "C" calories listed on food labels are 1000 small-c calories (also called one kilocalorie, or kcal), and sometimes authors distinguish them from "small-c" calories by capitalizing the "c," as in "Calorie". Other energy units, such as British Thermal Units (BTUs) or joules (J) can be converted to Calories. For example, a gallon of diesel contains approximately 137,000 BTUs [11] or 34,500 Calories (BTUs X 0.252). Since Calories are a familiar unit to most people, that is the unit I will use to put oil energy and photosynthetic energy on equal terms in the following discussion.

University of Iowa researchers [4] calculated the energy cost of growing corn using a gallon of diesel as the energy unit. An acre of continuous corn requires 175 pounds of nitrogen, which uses the energy equivalent of 21 gallons of diesel to manufacture. Nitrogen fertilizer is made by taking nitrogen from the air and combining it with hydrogen from natural gas to form ammonia (NH_3). Ammonia can then be injected into the soil directly, or it can be made into ammonium nitrate, urea, or other fertilizers. Manufacturing ammonia requires high heat and high pressure, with the energy coming from electricity (which the Iowa researchers converted to gallons of diesel). Most farmers also add phosphorus and potassium which come from deposits that are mined. Mining, processing, and distributing these fertilizers costs another 2 gallons of diesel energy.

A no-till growing system uses 2.5 gallons of diesel for planting, spraying and harvesting. Manufacturing a pound of pesticide (active ingredient) requires the equivalent of one gallon of diesel [4]. The no-till farmer may make three applications of a pesticide using a pound or less of active ingredient, so add three gallons of diesel for pesticide manufacture and distribution. Growing, processing and distributing seed, (1/4 to 1/3 bushel) consumes about another gallon of diesel, and we should allow about 2 gallons for machinery manufacture and ongoing repairs.

So far we have used 31.5 gallons of diesel to produce a crop with an expected yield of 160 bushels per acre. Add in drying costs, as most corn requires drying from an average of 22 percent moisture to a storage-safe moisture of 15 percent. Diesel equivalent to dry a bushel of corn equals 0.09 gallons, or about 14.4 gallons for a 160 bushel per acre crop [5]. Add all these together and the total diesel equivalent to grow an acre of Iowa no-till corn and put it safely in storage comes to nearly 46 gallons.

The energy in a gallon of crude oil is roughly equivalent to that in a gallon of diesel [11]. A barrel of crude oil is 42 gallons, so the energy required to grow one acre of corn is equivalent to 1.1 barrels of crude oil. The oil industry says (rule of thumb) it takes one barrel of crude oil to extract, transport and refine 10 barrels of crude oil [6], so we need to add 0.1 barrel to our total energy cost, making the total crude requirement to grow an acre of 160 bushel corn to 1.2 barrels, or 50.4 gallons, or 0.32 gallons per bushel. A barrel of crude oil contains approximately 1,460,000 Calories, and multiplying that figure by 1.2 means growing an acre of corn consumes 1,752,000 Calories, or 10,950 per bushel, or 195 per pound.

Now, how much sun energy did that 1.2 barrels of crude capture? A pound of corn kernels contains 1550 Calories. There are 56 pounds in a bushel and we have 160 bushels for a total of 8960 pounds. Pounds multiplied by 1550 gives a total Calorie production from an acre of corn: 13,880,000. Dividing Calories of corn produced by Calories in a barrel of crude oil (1,460,000) equals the equivalent barrels of crude oil captured by sunshine: 9.5! But wait, there's more. It takes a pound of stover (foliage and cobs) to produce a pound of corn and the stover contains as much energy per pound as the grain, so double the output to 19 barrels. And for every pound of stover, add a quarter pound of roots—another 2.3 barrels of captured energy. So the 1.2 barrels of expended energy captured a total of 21.3 barrels! Or, in terms of Calories, 1.75 million Calories of oil energy enabled the capture of 31.1 million Calories of energy from photosynthesis, an output-input ratio of 17.8 to one! Or in terms of oil, one thousand acres of no-till corn, genetically modified to use less pesticides, will capture 21,300 barrels at a cost of 1200 barrels—a real gusher! And in terms of food Calories, one Calorie of oil energy produced 9.5 Calories of food energy (grain only) and 11.8 Calories of refuse energy (roots and stover) to feed the soil biota.

The net energy from the grain, 8.4 barrels (12.3 million Calories) per acre, can now enter the economy as new wealth to be exploited by food and manufacturing industries for the benefit of consumers. Applying that energy gain to the 90 million acres American farmers normally grow means a whopping energy input into the economy equal to 756 million barrels of oil. New wealth, sustainably produced, to be used in over 10,000 different products.

The energy in the stover and roots will be incorporated into the soil to feed the biota who will release the nutrients contained in the stover for future crops. Nutrients in a ton of stover averages 17 pounds of nitrogen, 6 pounds of phosphate (P2O5), 28 pounds of potassium oxide (K2O), plus secondary and minor nutrients [7]. So, the stover from a 160 bushel (4.48 ton) crop will return 76 pounds of nitrogen (43 percent of the amount applied), 27 pounds of phosphate, and 121 pounds of potassium to the soil. About 50 percent of these nutrients will be released in the succeeding crop year. Approximately ten percent of the stover (one-half ton per acre) will eventually be added to the soil stores of humus. This doesn't sound like much, but it is about the same amount that a natural grass prairie would add yearly. People who say continuous corn is ruining our soils and promoting erosion are 100 percent wrong. What I have described here is an average, no-till Iowa corn crop, and it's building soil organic matter and controlling erosion so long as the stover is returned to the soil (see Note 4-2).

At this point, people who are familiar with the very extensive work of David and Marcia Pimentel [8] in calculating energy use in agriculture worldwide will point out that the output-input ratio I have calculated is much higher than their calculated ratio for U.S. corn production: 3.84 to one. There are several reasons for this difference. First, their figures include all U.S. acres in all kinds of environments and soil conditions, and all kinds of fertilizing, tillage and technology condition, and they ignore the energy contribution of stover and roots to soil health. I am showing what a typical Iowa farm using the best technology available is capable of. This is the future of farming. The Pimentels are describing the status quo in 2008.

Secondly, they show diesel requirements for field work to be 9.4 gallons, much higher than the 2.5 gallons required for no-till operations. Third, they say machinery manufacture and repair requires 435,000 Calories per acre vs. 69,500 in my calculations (12.6 gallons of diesel vs. 2 gallons). I justify the lower figure because, one, the Pimentels use a 10-year life with 25 percent of the machinery value expended yearly for repairs, figures much too high; and two, no-till farming takes much less equipment than full-tillage farming,

Machinery is not scrap metal after 10 years. Some farmers may trade every few years, but that is mainly to take advantage of new technologies. Much of the equipment used by farmers is 20 or more years old. I don't farm much acreage any more, but I'm still using tractors I bought in the 1960's, and most of my other equipment is 30 or more years old. The custom harvester that threshes my wheat uses combines that are 20 or more years old. And, expending one-fourth of a machine's value each year for repairs is ridiculous. I have over 50 years of experience with machinery repair bills, and five percent of a machine's original cost per year is a more reasonable figure.

Another major difference is the amount of energy allocated to fertilizer manufacture and distribution. The Pimentels allocate nearly twice as much energy to this segment of corn production as researchers at the University of Iowa. They also allocate some to soil liming and some to irrigation, both of which I ignored. Not all farmers need lime, and only 10 percent irrigate their crop.

The Pimentels use a yield of 138 bushels for output, which is low for the period when their Third Edition was published (2008). U.S. average yield for the three years 2006-2008 was 151 bushels per acre. U.S corn growers now average over 160 bushels per acre most years.

Note 4-2. Farmers who sell or give away their stover or straw in order to earn more income, or burn it to simply make it easier to no-till the next crop need to be aware that they could be affecting soil reserves of organic matter in a negative way. In warm, wet climates (eastern one-half of the U.S.) about two percent of the soil organic matter will decompose each year, or about 800 pounds (soil containing two percent organic matter in the top 6 inches). About 10 percent of the straw or stover returned to the soil will eventually become humus, the portion of soil organic matter that is very resistant to decomposition. The nutrients in the rest will be released over several years while most of the carbon will be lost to the atmosphere through microbial respiration. So to return 800 pounds of humus the farmer needs to leave 8000 pounds (4 tons) of crop residues. That would be the roots and stover from a 114 bushel per acre corn crop or the roots and straw from a 70 bushel wheat crop. Farmers in more arid climates that lose less organic matter per year would need to add proportionally less plant refuse to maintain soil organic matter

High Fructose Corn Syrup

High fructose corn syrup is the corn product anti-corn activists love to hate. I wonder if any of them understand basic chemistry. Table sugar, sucrose, is a disaccharide built from two simple sugars--50 percent fructose and 50 percent glucose. Corn syrup, which is made from corn starch, contains only glucose. Glucose is not as sweet as fructose, so food engineers figured out how to convert some of the glucose to fructose with an enzyme in order to make a sweetener as sweet as sucrose. Hence, high fructose corn syrup was born, essentially a liquid form of table sugar containing approximate equal amounts of fructose and glucose. The only difference is that in table sugar the fructose and glucose are bound together, forming a disaccharide, sucrose. In the modified corn syrup, they exist as free monosaccharides. This makes no difference to the body that consumes them, as sucrose is broken into its constituent monosaccharides by saliva and stomach acids long before they reach the gut [9]). The moral to this story is this: Everything you have read about high-fructose corn syrup being a villain in our diet is wrong. It is no more a villain than common table sugar [10].

Corn the Destroyer?

Pollan says "the corn plant's population explosion in places like Iowa is responsible for pushing out not only other plants but the animals and finally the people" [1, p.38]. There is a definite nostalgia for the "good old days" among the activists who want to change how our food is produced, and even among some farmers. The bucolic Image of the family farm with its cows grazing in a green pasture, the chickens running around the farmstead chasing bugs and scratching in the dirt, the pigs happily rooting up their pasture, and the farmer, ever working at something, and never a vacation or a complete day off. For most of us farmers those days are, thankfully, gone. Activists who want to bring them back would not think of returning to the days of rotary dial telephones, tiny black and white televisions, typewriters, slide rules and manual calculators : A world without computers, cell phones, music and movies arriving on demand in our households, streamed over amazing technology unimagined in the 1940s.

I remember those "good old days". Dad got rid of his last two horses in the early 1940s. We never had milk cows in my memory—we went every few days to a neighboring farmer who sold us raw milk. Sometimes we would arrive in the evening before the milking was done. Dad would visit with our neighbor, Otha, and I would play with my best friend, Orrin. When the milking was done and the mewing barn cats fed, I would sometimes sample the warm, fresh milk, a delicious taste one never forgets. We brought the milk home and kept it in the icebox in the cellar, retrieving some as needed. The milk never made us sick, but I would never take a chance on raw milk today. With so many antibiotic resistant bacterial strains in the environment, people who buy and drink raw, unpasteurized milk are playing Russian Roulette with their health, risking infectious agents that can cause paralysis, kidney failure, stroke, and even death.

We had chickens and a chicken pen, but most of the summer they were allowed to run wild, and I was constantly forced to dodge their excrement while playing in the yard. Gathering eggs was my chore, and some hens chose to forgo the henhouse nesting box and sneak their nest far under the barn in hopes of raising a family. So I would drag my small body under the barn floor, and, when finding a secluded nest, the procedure was to put the eggs in a bucket of water. If they sank, they were good to eat. If they floated, throw them away.

We eventually built a better chicken house and pen, and I got to sell a few eggs. I even raised fryers a couple of years, chopping off their heads, plucking them and disemboweling them for customers. And I raised pigs a year or two. My Dad, who didn't like dealing with livestock, was nonetheless very patient and helpful with my entrepreneurism.

But technology advances in agriculture as in every other industry. Tractors replaced horses, and now the farmer could grow cash crops where he once had to grow fuel for the horses. Then tractors got bigger, and the young farmer rented or purchased the land of his retiring neighbor. Cash crops are a more productive use of land, so pastures disappeared and meat production moved to more confined quarters or to land ill-suited for cash crops. Farmers became specialists, some growing only cash crops, some only involved in dairy, beef, hogs, or chickens. Specialization, combined with modern farming methods, meant each farmer could produce his crop or animal product in the most efficient manner possible, and without sacrificing sustainability. This has kept food prices low for consumers. If we were still farming the way we did in the 1940s urban America would be paying 18 percent of their take-home pay for food instead of six percent [13]. And there would be way less people available to invent and produce new products and services our society has been so privileged to experience. Sure, small towns have dried up as a result of advancing technology in food production, and that is sad. On the other hand, everyone's standard of living has been lifted because of the efficiency of our farm sector. And all kinds of farmers can, as Pollan puts it somewhat pejoratively, "take the weekend off, and even think about spending the winter in Florida" [1, p.40]. To me, corn is a hero of modern agriculture.

CHAPTER FOUR REFERENCES

1. Pollan, Michael. The Omnivore's Dilemma. 2006. Penguin Group (USA) Inc, 375 Hudson Street, New York, New York 100014.

2. Adapted from Wikipedia, "C4 Carbon Fixation", July 6, 2015, version.

3. Watkins, Thayer. "The Direct and Indirect Effects of Increased Carbon Dioxide on Plant Growth". July 23, 2015. www.applet-magic.com/CO2plants.htm .

4. Hanna, Mark; Sawyer, John E. and Peterson, Dana. "Energy Consumption for Row Crop Production". Iowa State University Extension and Outreach, PM2089W, June 2012.

5. Uhrig, J. William; Maier, Dirk E. "Costs of Drying High-Moisture Corn". Grain Quality Fact Sheet #3, Oct. 1, 1992. Purdue University Cooperative Extension Service. https://www.extension.purdue.edu/extmedia/gq/gq-3.html

6. Margolis, Jason. "The Energy costs of Oil Production". Nov. 2, 2012. http://www.pri.org/stories/2012-11-02/energy-costs-oil-production .

7. Vagts, Todd. "Nutrient Content and value of Corn Stover". Iowa State University Extension, Jan. 26, 2005. https://www.extension.iastate.edu/nwcrops/corn_stover.htm

8. Pimental, David and Pimental, Marcia H. Food, Energy, and Society, Third Edition, 2008. CRC Press, 6000 Broken Sound Parkway NW, Suite 300, Baca Raton, FL 33487-2742.

9. White, John S. "Straight Talk About High-Fructose Corn

Syrup: What it is and What it Ain't." The American Journal of Clinical Nutrition. Vol 88, No. 6, pp.1716S-1721S. Dec. 2008.

10. "High Fructose Corn Syrup". Wikipedia, July 31, 2015. https://en.wikipedia.org/wiki/High_fructose_corn_syrup

11. U.S Energy Information Administration. EIA.gov. July 29, 2015.

12. National Corn Growers Association, 632 Cepi Drive, Chesterfield, M, 63005. 2014 corn yield contest results.

13. USDA Economic Research Service. Food expenditures by families and individuals, Table 7, 1929-2014.

CHAPTER 5.

Gmos—WHY WE NEED THEM, WHY THEY ARE SAFE

"Gmos are scientifically sound, nutritionally valuable and morally noble"—Michael Shermer[16]

Years ago, in the mid-1970s, I was attending a National Wheat Growers convention and listening to a speech by the director of USDA agricultural research. He was talking about what we can expect in the future in wheat breeding. I was calmly listening when he suddenly got my full attention. My mind's eye can still clearly see him at the podium as he declared, "what if, in the future, we get the wheat plant to make its own nitrogen? Think it's impossible? Hang on to your hat!" I had no idea what he was talking about, and it sure seemed like pure fantasy to me.

Well, I'm still hanging on to my hat, but I long ago quit thinking it was impossible. Legumes (peas, beans, clovers,) make some of their own nitrogen with the help of symbiotic bacteria, *Rhizobium* species, which infect the plant's roots. With genetic engineering, why not wheat? And corn? And cotton? Think of what that would mean for our planet. Nitrogen supplied to the plant on an "as needed" basis. No more

---

[16] Michael Shermer, publisher of *Skeptic* magazine and author of *The Moral Arc*, commenting on GMOs in *Scientific American*, April 2015, p. 78. He continues, "GMOs have become to be treated more like moral categories than biological entities...Moreover, the elevation of 'natural' foods to near mythic status, coupled with the taboo many genetic-modification technologies are burdened with—remember when in vitro fertilization was considered unnatural?—makes GMOs feel like a desecration. It need not be so."

large expenditures of energy to take it from the air, convert it to a form plants can use, distribute it and spread it on fields.

Of course that would be a big blow to the fertilizer industry, and maybe that is why no company has yet seriously pursued the possibility.[17] And now, with the war on GMOs making no exceptions it seems unlikely that we will see such a development in the foreseeable future, if ever. The take-no-prisoner attitude of the anti-GMO, environmentally conscious NGOs (Non-governmental Organizations) completely ignores the health and environmental benefits that genetic engineering can bring to the world's food supply. "Greenpeace 'demands the complete elimination (from) the food supply and the environment' of biotech products'" [40, p. 44]. That would eliminate such products as chymosin, an enzyme produced by genetically engineered bacteria and used as a clotting agent since 1990 to produce hard cheese. Chymosin substitutes for rennet, an enzyme scraped from the stomach lining of calves, and is considered to be much safer. It would also eliminate over 100 drugs and vaccines derived from genetically engineered organisms, drugs that "include life-saving therapies for anemia, cystic fibrosis, hemophilia, hepatitis, organ-transplant rejection, and leukemia and other cancers." Millions of diabetics inject themselves daily with insulin derived from genetically engineered bacteria, insulin much safer than that purified from cow and pig pancreas [40, p. 9]. Greenpeace, a public opinion powerhouse with a $360 million budget [2], should be careful what it wishes for.

The primary ammunition of the NGOs is emotion. There

_____

[17] Several efforts to accomplish this feat by academia were made in the 1980s, but were eventually abandoned as too difficult. In June of 2012, the Bill and Melinda Gates Foundation awarded $10,674,606 to the John Innes Centre in Norwich, Norfolk, England, to study the feasibility of enabling cereal grains (wheat, corn, rice) to fix at least part of their nitrogen requirements. No significant progress reported so far. Google: John Innes Centre Bill and Melinda Gates grant. New attempts are now being advocated using the newest genetic engineering techniques [60,61].

is no large body of credible science that supports their radicle position. Their position relies heavily on a few questionable studies which spawn hypothetical consequences, anecdotal experiences, specious theories, and sometimes, outright lies (see Note 5-1 for two examples). I hope in this chapter to use science to slice through the emotion and convince the reader to embrace the promises inherent in GMO technology.

Note 5-1. A few studies, poorly done or without biological significance, are repeatedly cited by anti-GMO activists nullifying, in their view, the thousands of studies that show GMOs to be safe. One commonly cited is a feeding trial coordinated by Arpad Pusztai, a protein scientist working at the Rowett Institute in England. The feeding trial was intended to be a pre-commercialization safety test of a potato variety engineered by John Gatehouse of Cambridge Agricultural Genetics. The potato contained a lectin gene taken from a *Galanthus* (snowdrop) plant, a plant known to be toxic to some insects. Lectins are toxic proteins produced by many plants, including major food plants, presumably to defend against insects. A very poisonous one is produced by the castor bean, from which the potent poison ricin is made.

Some rats were fed the genetically modified potatoes, both raw and cooked, and a control group was fed potatoes that were (supposedly) substantially equivalent except for the lectin gene The varieties were not equivalent, however, as the three lines (two modified and one control) varied in starch, sugar and protein content by as much as 20 percent. Pusztai admitted these differences were enough to throw the results in doubt. The results after 110 days of feeding showed significant deleterious changes in the digestive tract of the rats fed the transformed potatoes, but not in rats fed control potatoes spiked with the toxin. Pusztai concluded the effects were the result of the genetic engineering procedure and not the toxin per se, perhaps resulting from the cauliflower mosaic virus used as a promoter in the transformation procedure.

Because of the negative results the potato was never commercialized. But on June 22, 1998, Pusztai was interviewed on television, and revealed his research findings with the caveat that the testing techniques were questionable. Nevertheless his results were sensationalized by the press, fueling paranoia about all GMOs, even though this one would never have been released because of questionable safety. The feeding trial has been unjustifiably cited by those opposed to GMOs ever since. (See Wikipedia, "Pusztai affair.")

Another study that has caused much controversy was led by Professor Gilles-Eric Seralini at the University of Caen, France [47]. This study examined the effects of feeding rats (1) Roundup Ready corn, (2) Roundup Ready corn plus Roundup, and (3) low levels of Roundup in their drinking water, over a two year (lifetime) period. Seralini used the Sprague-Dawley strain of rats, a strain that is especially prone to develop tumors, even when fed normal food. An experiment in 2001 demonstrated just how easily this strain of rat succumbs to tumors. Nakazawa, et al, observed untreated rats over a lifespan of 1.7 to 2.1 years, and found that 70-77 percent of females and 87-97 percent of males developed tumors [46].

The standard industry practice is to feed such rats for 90 days to test for toxic effects. Since these rats develop tumors so easily, the 90 day test is considered adequate. Seralini found more tumors in the treated rats than in the control rats, but not enough to be significant considering the small number of rats in each treatment [48]. This was the principal criticism of the feeding trial by his peers around the world, who vigorously objected to the publication of the results. The paper was published in *Food and Chemical Toxicology* in September of 2012 and retracted 13 months later due to objections by other scientists to the methodology. It was republished without peer review in *Environmental Sciences, Europe*, an open source journal, on June 24, 2014. The republished paper included all original data, but did not receive a review from peers any more favorable than the first publication. The data revealed that "some of the rats fed GM corn outlived the control group, further confusing the picture" [48]. ("Open Source" journals are criticized by many researchers because the author pays to have his/her paper published, and critical peer review before publishing is often absent, allowing "junk science" to be easily circulated.)

"Other long-term studies, which were public, had uncovered no health issues with GMO corn or the herbicide glyphosate. The Japanese Department of Environmental Health and Toxicology released a 52-week feeding study of GM soybeans in 2007, finding 'no apparent adverse effect in rats.' In 2012, a team of scientists at the University of Nottingham School of Biosciences released a review of 12 long-term studies (up to two years) and 12 multi-generational studies (up to 5 generations) of GM foods... concluding 'there is no evidence of health hazards'" [48].

The slander of Golden rice is a prime example of the paranoia the NGOs spread. Rice, a staple for half the world's population, is totally devoid of vitamin A in the grain (the leaves contain the vitamin, but production is turned off in the grain). Among the world's poorest of the poor, who rely on this grain for most of their calories, 1-2 million people die each year from vitamin A deficiency, and 500,000 suffer irreversible blindness [1]. Golden rice, a genetically modified variety that produces enough beta-carotene (Vitamin A precursor) in the grain to meet most of the vitamin A needs of these poorest of the poor, is available for widespread introduction in Asia and Africa, but has been vehemently opposed by Greenpeace and other anti-GMO groups, such as Friends of the Earth, who view anything genetically modified as unhealthy. These NGOs have lobbied government bureaucracies in the undeveloped countries of Asia and Africa, claiming GE crops are inherently dangerous, and attempts by big agricultural firms such as Monsanto to introduce GE seeds should be viewed as a form of industrial imperialism. Such governments, often scientifically illiterate and hostile to U. S. exceptionalism, are easily influenced by such arguments.

As an example of the above, in 2002, 14 million people in Southern Africa were in danger of starvation because of drought, floods, and bad government policies [49]. Swaziland and Lesotho accepted GMO corn donations from the U.S. without restrictions. Mozambique Malawi and Zimbabwe insisted the corn be milled into flour, afraid farmers would plant some of the seeds the next year and introduce GMO genes into the local environment, endangering African export markets to Europe if crops cannot be certified GM-free. Zambia rejected the aid in any form, and kept aid that had already arrived locked in warehouses, refusing to distribute any of it. Even though the World Health Organization certified the corn for human consumption, Zambia's president declared, "Simply because my people are hungry, that is no justification to give them poison, to give them food that is intrinsically dangerous to their health [50]." Desperate people soon broke into some of the warehouses and carried off the corn.

These NGOs and the activist groups they have spawned ignore the fact that we have been genetically modifying plants and animals by manipulating genes for over 100 years. Anytime a plant is crossed with a close (or a distant) relative new genes are introduced that produce proteins the target plant never had before. The problem with traditional breeding is that all kinds of genes are transferred that are not useful, or even toxic, which must then be eliminated by backcrossing for several generations until the undesirable genes are eliminated. (Backcrossing involves crossing the progeny of the original cross to the parent variety the breeder is trying to improve.) Genetic engineering only introduces the desired genes, thus significantly shortening the time to transfer desirable traits. And it allows traits to be introduced that would be impossible with traditional breeding methods.

Why this method of plant breeding garners so much fear in the general public is hard for me to understand. One reason, I suppose, is that we tend to fear things we don't understand. When I was a young boy I slept in an upstairs room that had a passageway to the attic covered by a curtain. My young mind envisioned ghostly monsters coming from that dark and mysterious place and hovering over me as I slept. I slept with my head completely covered by the blankets in order to feel secure, a habit I kept long after I lost my belief in ghosts and monsters.

Fear of new technology is not a new phenomenon. "Skeptics predicted that Jenner's immunizations against smallpox would cause grotesque, homunculus-like growths at the injection site; that telephones would electrocute their users; and that if humans traveled in trains at speeds faster than a horse could run, their rib cages would collapse" [40,p.27).

Genetic engineering is the modern day monster that is feared by a public that does not understand the basics of plant breeding. The notion that manipulating genes in a laboratory petri dish is somehow more likely to produce poisonous proteins than if they are manipulated conventionally using another plant's pollen is unfounded. It often takes 10 years or more of backcrossing to remove the undesirable genes resulting from a traditional cross. Results from laboratory gene manipulation can be achieved much sooner. However, to insure safety to the environment and to people and animals, government agencies require years of testing. The U. S. Department of Agriculture (USDA) through its Animal and Plant Health Inspection Service (APHIS) regulates field testing, first deciding if field testing can be conducted with safety to the environment and people. If testing is allowed, several years of data are required before unregulated release is granted. The applicant is then free to commercialize the plant or product.

If the plant is engineered to produce its own pesticide to kill or repel insects or diseases, it must also pass Environmental Protection Agency (EPA) rules concerning pesticides before commercialization is allowed. In addition, the Food and Drug Administration (FDA) must approve its release if products from the plant will end up in the food supply.

Interestingly, none of these agencies (USDA, EPA, FDA) get involved if a plant is conventionally bred to resist or kill an insect or disease. Plant breeders have been roaming the world for decades, going to places where a particular crop originated (for example, the Middle East for wheat, barley, garbanzos: South America for corn, potatoes, tomatoes) to search for related plants that might have resistance that could be transferred to desirable varieties. And with great success, I might add. As I said before, proteins in our food crops have been changing for over 100 years. Or, more accurately, the last 10,000 years or so, as ancient farmers selected for superior mutated plants they observed growing in their fields.

In the book *Tomorrow's Table: Organic Farming, Genetics, and the Future of Food,* Pamela Ronald recites an example of unintended consequences of the conventional breeding of celery. Celery "produces toxic compounds called psoralens to discourage predators and avoid being a snack too early in life. Breeders have selected celery with relatively high amounts of psoralens because farmers prefer to grow insect resistant plants and consumers prefer to buy undamaged produce. Unfortunately, workers who harvest such celery sometimes develop a severe skin rash" [3, p.92].

She also relates that potatoes produce glycoalkaloid solanine, a toxic compound, but produce it in very small amounts
and its presence is considered nonhazardous to animals, including humans. However, if a potato is exposed to light
bright enough to produce the green pigment chlorophyll, the
amount of solanine produced can be very poisonous. Do not
eat green potatoes!

Incidentally, I highly recommend Pamela Ronald and her
husband Raoul Adamshak's book. Raoul teaches organic
farming at the University of California, Davis, and Pamela is
Professor of Plant Pathology at the University of California,
Davis, and is also a genetic engineer. Raoul writes pragmati-
cally about organic farming, and Pamela makes a gentle but
compelling argument for the use of genetic engineering.

BASICS OF PLANT BREEDING

So that the reader might better understand why doubts
about the safety of genetic engineering is unjustified, let's explore some basics.

I am sure most readers have heard of DNA and how it carries the blueprint for life, and have seen pictures of the double helix that carries that blueprint. And they understand that
genes are the units of heredity. That's probably as far as most
people have pursued the subject, and it leaves them open to
the "merchants of doubt[18]" who sow the myth that genetic
engineering produces "seeds of destruction[19]". Having a basic
understanding of what goes on in a plant every time genes are
passed to the next generation is crucial to understanding why
the "merchants of doubt " are so misguided.

To explain this rather confusing and esoteric subject to
laypersons, I wrote an article for *Wheat Life* in 1990 [6] that I

---

[18] Title of a book by Naomi Oreskes [4]. Her book deals with doubters of
global warming, acid rain, tobacco, etc. She does not deal with GMOs, but her
principles apply to this issue.

[19] Title of a book by F. William Engdahl [5]. More about his book in succeeding
chapters.

think is appropriate to repeat here:

"If genetics is not your bag, chances are the abundance of lectures and articles on genetic engineering these days leave you scratching your head. The vocabulary is intimidating and the concepts can be mind-boggling. Everyone knows that a gene is a unit of heredity, but what is it really? And those other words—genome, DNA, chromosomes, base pairs, nucleotides, etc.—how do they fit in? Maybe drawing a few analogies with things that are familiar will help.

"Let's start with the concept of the genome. Think of a genome as a library. This library contains all the information necessary to build and maintain a plant or animal. Every cell of an organism, whether it has one cell or a billion, contains this complete library. Libraries have books, and the books of the genome are the chromosomes. The wheat plant has forty-two books, barley's has fourteen, and the human genome has forty-six. In a real library, books are made of paper. The paper of the genome is deoxyribose nucleic acid, or DNA for short. The DNA molecule varies in size, but is generally very large. DNA subunits are linked together in a long chain—a double helix—and protected by a protein sheath, the "cover" of the chromosome "book"

"The construction of a DNA double helix is boringly repetitious—like laying thousands of concrete blocks in a long line. Each block in this instance is a sugar compound of five carbon atoms, called 2-deoxyribose. The blocks are "cemented" together on the ends by a phosphate compound. Attached to one side of each block is a molecule called a base.

"There are four kinds of bases (and only four) that may attach here—adenine, thymine, cytosine, and guanine, usually referred to as bases A, T, C, and G. Each block (sugar unit) with its attached base and its phosphate 'cement' is called a nucleotide. The bases attached to the nucleotides constitutes the letters, analogous to letters written on paper. Since there are only four letters in the genetic alphabet (A, T, C, and G), genetic prose can seem rather unimaginative. The vocabulary is also small. Experimentation has determined that the code is "read" in three-letter units only, so three bases equal one word (called a "codon"). Codons (words) say, "make this amino acid". For instance, the base sequence (codon) G-C-A says, "make alanine", and the sequence C-A-T says, "make histidine". There are 20 amino acids essential for making proteins, so there are 20 words (codons) in the vocabulary of DNA. If you are wondering how so much information can be stored with such a small alphabet and vocabulary, just remember that any message of any length can be conveyed with the dot-dash of Morse code, or the on-off code used in computers. It is the sequence of the letters and words that count.

"The words are organized into sentences that convey a complete instruction—a gene. A gene will vary in length, from perhaps a few hundred words to 10,000 or more. Like a sentence in a book, a gene occupies whatever space it needs to express a complete thought. A complete thought in this case means complete instructions detailing the arrangement of amino acids that comprise a specific protein (see Note 5-2). Special "start" and "stop" codons mark the beginning and end of a gene.

Note 5-2. The instructions, or "template", can be used to make more than one protein. After making a copy of the instructions, RNA (ribonucleic acid) can modify the copy by removing some portions, resulting in a different protein. And not all genes code for proteins, some code for various types of RNAs [7].

"So there we have the basics—basics that hold true for every plant and animal. Genome = library. Chromosomes = books in the library. DNA = paper. Bases = letters. Three bases = one word. Five thousand or so words = one gene.

Viruses, bacteria, oak trees, human beings—all living things on earth share this same basic genetic code.

"Chromosomes normally come in pairs, so that the wheat genome of forty-two chromosomes is said to have twenty-one pairs. (One member of each pair is contributed to the cell by the female parent, and one member by the male parent). The chromosomes in each pair are like two versions of the same book—for instance, the King James Bible compared to the Revised Standard Version. When you line up the same verses side by side, they may or may not be worded exactly the same, but they will address the same subject. Genes on paired chromosomes are similarly matched. Geneticists have a term for paired genes—they are called "alleles". In most cases, one allele will be dominant over the other, so that the recessive allele is expressed only when the alleles on both chromosomes are identical or, as a geneticist would say, homozygous. Heterozygous is the term used when alleles are not identical, therefore conveying a slightly different message, such as short beards vs. long beards that adorn a head of wheat.

"Actually, we should think of a chromosome more as a scroll than a book. There are no pages, just one long continuous sheet, with the message beginning at one end and proceeding to the other. In order to more exactly visualize the structure of a chromosome, picture again the cement blocks with the bases sticking out to one side. Arrange the blocks in two long, parallel rows, separated by a distance about two blocks wide. The row of blocks on the right side has its bases poking to the left, and the row on the left has its bases poking to the right. The bases touch each other and thus connect the two strings of blocks like rungs on a ladder.

"It might help at this point to draw a ladder on a piece of paper. Make the sides of the ladder about half an inch apart, and use a different color for each side. Space rungs about a quarter inch apart. Divide each rung in half, and label the right half randomly with the letters A, C, T, and G. Now label the left half, but follow this rule: A always matches T, and C always matches G. (Yes, that's the way it always happens in the real world of DNA, the significance of which will be explained later). The rungs of your ladder can now be referred to as base pairs—and wheat has about eighteen billion of them! Now, cut the ladder down each side with scissors. Tape one end to a flat surface and tightly coil the loose end. Try to make your coils about half an inch in diameter and packed close together, but not overlapping. Take a second piece of tape and secure the other end of the coil. Now you have a rough model of a chromosome as it exists in a living cell. With the picture of a chromosome well in mind, let's explore a little of the everyday life of a chromosome.

"Each time a cell divides, a copy of the genetic library is made and passed to the daughter cell. The copying process takes place in the nucleus of the cell, with the chromosomes stretched out and indistinguishable under a microscope. To begin the duplication process, the base pairs begin to unhook at one end, thus allowing the two side chains to move apart—kind of like unzipping a zipper, but as the ends move apart, each strand attracts raw materials from the cell's fluids to construct new nucleotides and attach them to the proper order. This is where the A – T, and C – G base match becomes obviously important: The old chromosome half serves as a template to exactly duplicate the half that was zipped away.

"After the duplication is complete, the chromosomes coil tightly and become readily visible under a microscope as identical pairs. The wall of the nucleus dissolves, and the chromosomes line up, in pairs, at the midsection of the cell. Then each chromosome separates from its twin and each one slowly (in an hour or so) moves to opposite ends of the cell. A cell wall then forms at the midsection, creating two cells from the one. A new nucleus forms in each cell, encompassing the chromosomes which now unwind, disappear from view, and begin again the process of duplication. The word used to describe this whole process is mitosis.

"A similar, but slightly different process takes place when gametes are formed. (Gametes are the sex cells of an organism, meaning the sperm and eggs of animals and the pollen and ovules of plants). The process of gamete formation is called meiosis, and results in a reduction in the number of chromosomes by one-half. The gametes are said to be haploid (containing half the normal chromosome number) and when the pollen fuses with the ovule, or the sperm with the egg, the normal (diploid) number is restored.

"Meiosis begins, as in mitosis, with each chromosome duplicating itself. But this time, instead of lining up with all the other chromosomes at the center of the cell, each chromosome unzips and pairs up with its homologue (the chromosome bearing alleles, or "other version of the same book"). The chromosome pairs then line up and migrate as in mitosis, except that the end to which each homologue migrates is random, thereby creating a random mix of the genetic information contained in the two versions of each chromosome. The daughter cells from this division then divide again as in mitosis, creating four haploid gametes from the original diploid cell, each carrying slightly different information.

"To visualize this in another way, visualize the chromosomes in a cell as two suits from a deck of cards—thirteen diamond chromosomes and thirteen spade chromosomes. In this example, the diamonds come from the maternal parent and the spades come from the paternal parent. Homologues would be like "jacks" or "queens" in different suits.

"In mitosis, each set of cards duplicates itself, and all twenty-six pairs of cards line up and separate to opposite ends of the cell. Each daughter cell gets a full complement of black and red cards. In meiosis, each duplicated pair seeks its homologue, so each jack of diamonds would pair up with a jack of spades. The direction in which the member of each pair migrates is random, so when the migration is completed the two new cells contain an uneven mixture of diamonds and spades. The next division divides these two sets of cards (now numbering 52) in half, creating from the original twenty-six cards four stacks of thirteen cards each, each (likely) having a different proportion of black and red cards." (To review definitions of terms used in this chapter see Note 5-3.)

Note 5-3.

Genome—the "library" containing all the genetic information of an organism.

Chromosome—a huge molecule of deoxyribonucleic acid (DNA), a "book" in the library, covered in a protein sheath and containing the blueprints needed to keep an organism humming. Chromosomes come in pairs, one member from the male parent and one from the female parent. Humans have 23 chromosome pairs, or 46 total chromosomes.

Base—short for the nucleobases important to DNA structure. The bases adenine, thymine, cytosine and guanine, referred to simply as A, T, C and G, comprise the alphabet of the DNA code. When chromosomes are paired, A always pairs with T and C always pairs with G. These couplings are called base pairs.

RNA—Ribonucleic acid, a single strand of bases that match a sequence in a gene and carries the gene's instructions to a ribosome. The ribosome, a specialized RNA-protein, then assembles the amino acids called for in the instructions into a protein or peptide. RNA strings are assembled as needed and disassembled when the task is accomplished.

Nucleotide—a building block of DNA, composed of a sugar compound, a phosphate compound, and one of the four above bases.

Gene—a unit of heredity. A series of nucleotides that serve as a template for making a protein or a part of a protein (peptide).

Peptide—a string of amino acids that make up a protein, or a part of a protein.

Alleles—two versions of the same gene, one from the male parent and one from the female parent.

Homozygous—meaning the same, as when both alleles are dominate or recessive.

Heterozygous—different, as when one allele is dominate and one is recessive.

Mitosis—the division of a cell into two daughter cells.

Meiosis—the division of a specialized sex cell into four gametes.

Gamete—the hereditary-carrying sex cells of an organism (sperm and eggs of an animal, pollen and ovules for plants.)

Haploid—having one-half the normal complement of chromosomes, as in a gamete.

Diploid—having two sets (normal) of chromosomes.

Polyploid—having more than two sets of chromosomes.

Cytoplasm—the fluid inside a cell in which all cell activities occur.

Organelles and plasmids (see note 5-5)—"organs" that float in the cytoplasm, have their own DNA and perform important functions in the cell. They are passed to new generations through the female gamete only.

By now the reader should have some appreciation for the chaos that results when a conventional cross between varieties (or races) of the same species is made. Transferring just one trait (leaf rust resistance for example) from an inferior variety to a superior variety can take 10 or more generations to weed out all the undesirable traits inherited from the plant with the one desired gene. Plant breeders have been manipulating the genetic information contained within a species (called a germ-plasm pool) since the early 1900s. They have even made inter-species crosses when the species share a good deal of genetic information. The grain called triticale is a species of the new genus *Triticale* created by crossing wheat (genus *Triticum*) with rye (genus *Secale*). Like the cross between a horse and a donkey which produces a sterile mule, the wheat-rye cross is also sterile. Geneticists got around this problem by treating the tiny plant from this cross (containing 21 wheat chromosomes and 7 rye chromosomes, or one-half the normal number for each species) growing in a petri dish with a dose of colchicine. Colchicine used in this manner causes the chromosomes to produce a copy of themselves, thus doubling every gene in the genome and passing them on to daughter cells. In the case of triticale it restored fertility.

This procedure using colchicine is called "inducing polyploidy". Ploidy refers to the number of sets of chromosomes. The normal number is two sets (diploid), one from each parent. Many plants, however, have merged genomes with other plants over the course of evolution, creating natural polyploids. Common wheat is a hexaploid, having three distinct genomes, or six sets of chromosomes. Rye is a diploid (one genome, two sets of chromosomes). Creating triticale merged a diploid with a hexaploid, making it an octoploid.[20]

Inducing polyploidy is a technique that has been used by generations of plant breeders. In a related technique called anther culture, pollen is collected from the anther of a flower and floated in a special nutrient solution in a petri dish. The pollen is the male gamete and as such has only one-half of the plants normal complement of chromosomes. Despite this deficiency of chromosomes, some of the pollen will start to

---

[20] Most modern triticale varieties, however, are hexaploids, being crosses with durum (macaroni) wheat which has two genomes (labeled A and B) of seven each. Bread wheat has three genomes of seven each, A, B and D (66).

109

divide, growing first a blob of callus tissue, but eventually fragile stems, roots and leaves will begin to grow. Such a plant is called a "haploid" because it is growing with only one-half its normal complement of genes. At some point the breeder will treat the growing points with colchicine and restore the succeeding growth to a normal diploid (two sets) chromosome number. It is not quite normal, however, since all the genes came from the male gamete. It is more appropriately called a "double haploid". The advantage of this process is that the chromosome alleles are instantly identical (homozygous), meaning they are both either dominant or recessive. The offspring of such a plant will not segregate into dozens of phenotypes (different versions due to the shuffling of dominate and recessive genes). What the breeder sees is what he (or she) gets and if she likes what she sees she can move directly towards variety testing and release, cutting perhaps three or five years off the normal ten years it takes to produce a new variety.

The double haploid method is becoming more popular with plant breeders partly because moving genes across species with genetic engineering techniques is receiving so much opposition from the public.[21] And geneticists find they can identify traits in a genome they never knew were there, obviating the need to transfer the trait from other species. But wouldn't you know it: this method now ranks in some activists' minds as just another form of GE so should also be banned. Activists in Jackson County, Oregon, in 2014 succeeded in passing an ordinance prohibiting growing any plant in the county that had been genetically engineered. Their definition of genetically engineered includes "gene deletion, gene doubling, introducing a foreign gene, changing the position of a gene…and any other technology or technique that

---

[21] There is a double standard here. If a breeder moves a gene from another species using conventional breeding, even if assisted with radiation or chemicals, no one calls it genetic engineering.

results in an organism that contains genes from more than one species..." It prohibits a host of technologies developed in the past 50 years that have been used to enhance the world's food supply [8]. For instance, the new species *Triticale*, a cross between wheat and rye, could not have been created under these rules. And corn hybrids would be much more difficult to produce (see Note 5-4). If this sort of prohibition becomes widespread, feeding the world of 2050 will be an insurmountable problem.

The activists who wrote the Jackson County ordinance excluded "traditional selective breeding", but they are apparently unaware that in nature species do cross, genes do double (polyploidy), genomes do merge, genes are deleted or turned off, genes "jump" positions, and most everything a genetic engineer does has been done by nature sometime in the distant past. Modern bread wheat is a hexaploid, meaning it has six sets of chromosomes, seven each, comprising three genomes of 14 chromosomes each, for a total of 42 chromosomes. Geneticists have traced the origin of these genomes, labeled A, B and D. About 8000 years ago, farmers in the Middle East were growing a primitive wheat called emmer (known today in its improved form as Durum, or macaroni, wheat). Emmer has the A and B genomes consisting of 28 chromosomes. A species of goatgrass (*Aegilops tauschii*), a weed still found in farmers' fields today and is known to hybridize with wheat, probably infested their fields. Somehow goatgrass got together with emmer and inserted its 14 chromosomes (D genome) into emmer, resulting in what we now grow for bread wheat (*Triticum aestivum*) having 42 chromosomes [9]. Nature accomplished this feat without petri dishes or colchicine.

Note 5-4. To produce corn hybrids, breeders must first produce two varieties (lines) that are homozygous in their alleles. This can be done by inbreeding--that is, forcing the

---

plants to reproduce using their own pollen and not the pollen from neighboring plants. Making a good inbred line takes several plant generations, a lot of time and money, and then the breeder has to figure out which lines to cross to get a desirable hybrid. Using the double haploid method to produce an inbred is a great time saver: They are instantly homozygous.

Photos 4 & 5. Growing Hybrid Corn. (Top picture) Two rows of an inbred line serving as the pollen (male) source for four rows of an inbred line designated to be the female recipient. The female recipient has had the tassels removed to force cross-pollination. (Bottom picture.) After pollination, the male plants are destroyed, and the female plants are harvested when mature, resulting in hybrid seed for sale to farmers. (Photos by Author.)

Where did the A and B genomes come from? The A genome comes from einkhorn (*Triticum urartu*), an ancient wild wheat domesticated and grown in the Fertile Crescent some

10,000 years ago [10]. The B genome most likely came from another goatgrass species, (*Ageilops speltoides*) [11]. The convergence of these two genomes produced emmer (*Triticum turgidum subsp. dicoccoides*); also conducted in nature without the help of petri dishes or colchicine. Actually, this type of convergence is quite common in nature. Important crop plants that originated by this process include strawberry, oat, upland cotton, oilseed rape, blueberry and mustard [12].

In the early days of artificial gene manipulation, now called genetic engineering (GE), the methods available to insert new genes into a plant were not very precise. One technique was to coat a nylon "shotgun shell" filled with millions of microscopic tungsten or gold spheres coated with the desired DNA and shoot it down a .22 barrel. A perforated steel plate at the end of the barrel stopped the bullet, but inertia carried the spheres through the plate and into the target cells in a petri dish. Another method was electroporation, in which an electrical charge was used to create pores in a cell's wall allowing DNA to "leak" in. Some scientists used extremely fine needles to inject DNA directly into a cell. These methods are still used by some scientists today, but the imprecise nature of these insertions freak out some activists because where the gene ends up in the genome is random, and therefore the gene may, they insist, perform in unpredictable ways. They are correct in that different phenotypes or genotypes[22] may be a result, but the geneticist will likely have much less trouble finding the desired trait and eliminating undesirable ones than if he/she had made a conventional cross, especially a wide cross between two species. The fear that some poisonous or severely allergenic "frankenfood" will be released undetected is unreasonable. If the desired protein is produced by the transformed plant the transfer is successful. If it isn't

---

[22] Genotype refers to all the properties of a plant, observed and unobserved. Phenotype describes only the observed properties, such as color, height, response to environment, etc.

produced the tissue is discarded. In any event, a plant transformed in this manner goes through multiple levels of vetting before it is released to the public. Genes are quite specific. If they produce a particular protein in one plant or organism they will likely produce the same protein in a new setting. For example, mice are commonly used to study the function of human genes. By "knocking out" a gene sequence in a mouse that matches a human sequence being studied a scientist can infer the function of the gene in humans [34].

Methods of plant transformation are becoming more precise with each passing year. One method that has been used for the last 30 years or so employs a natural genetic engineer, the soil bacterium *Agrobacterium*. *Agrobacterium* species are ubiquitous in soil. One species, *A. tumefaciens*,[23] will find its way into a plant through a wound and cause a tumor (gall) to grow on the roots or stem. It does this by transferring a small part of its plasmid DNA (see Note 5-5) into the nucleus and hence the genome of a cell in the host plant. The new genetic instructions cause the host plant to produce proteins useful to the Agrobacterium, enabling it to build a gall using host plant resources.

Note 5-5. A plasmid is a small molecule of DNA, usually circular in shape, floating freely in the cell fluids (cytoplasm), common in bacteria but not usually found in plant or animal cells. It replicates independent of the chromosomal DNA that resides in the nucleus. This DNA is quite often a virus benignly absorbed at some

---

[23] The genus Agrobacterium is now considered to be synonymous with the genus Rhizobium, and A. tumefaciens is now officially R. radiobacter. Agriculturists will recognize Rhizobium as the genus associated with species that nodulate the roots of legumes, producing nitrogen for the legume. It appears the difference between pathogenicity and symbiosis depends on just three genes, and also what host is infected [35]. Some authors prefer to use Agrobacterium for those species that are pathogenic and Rhizobium for those species that are symbiotic [31,32,33].

point over the millennia of evolution and passed on to succeeding generations (conserved) because it serves some beneficial function, such as antibiotic resistance.

There are other repositories of DNA floating in the cytoplasm that are somewhat larger and encased in a lipid (fat) layer, thus resembling a small nucleus, and are called organelles(because they perform vital functions as do organs in an animal). They have been absorbed, conserved and passed to succeeding generations in the same manner as plasmids. One example is the chloroplast in plants, the repository of chlorophyll and thus the organelle responsible for capturing energy from sunlight, making all plant and animal life possible. Another vital organelle is the mitochondria, whose function is to release the energy bound in sugar, thus powering cell functions and allowing plants and animals to perform their everyday tasks.

Figuring out how *Agrobacterium* accomplishes this feat of DNA insertion took approximately 40 years and scores of researchers working in dozens of laboratories on three continents [13]. The final kinks were worked out in the late 1980's, paving the way for Monsanto and other companies to commercialize this amazing technology based on a natural process.

Agrobacterium, it was found, initiates infection by utilizing genes contained in a large plasmid, a bacteriophage (virus that attacks bacteria) initially labeled P58 but now referred to as the Ti plasmid. (Ti stands for "tumor inducing", but don't conflate that with human tumors. Plant tumors, or galls, have no relationship to animal tumors.) An *Agrobacterium* cell sidles up to a wounded plant cell, a specialized protein cleaves the Ti gene from the Ti plasmid, along with protective base pairs on each end, and pilots it into the host cell. This strand of DNA then "hijacks cellular processes" [13] to transport it through the thick cytoplasm and into the nucleus. Once there enzymes cut a chromosome and fuse the new DNA to the cut ends.

Once this process was understood, commercialization, led by Monsanto, soon followed. Scientists quickly learned how to use various proteins to precisely cut the Ti gene out of the Ti plasmid and insert DNA of choice. The rest of the *Agrobacterium* machinery is left untouched, and the bacterium blithely inserts the new DNA into plant tissue growing in a petri dish, unaware that it can no longer disrupt plant processes to build a gall. This process has become so precise that scientists can target a particular cite on a particular chromosome for this "cut and paste" process. They do this by combining, in the laboratory, a string of base pairs ("letters" in the DNA alphabet) that match a particular sequence on a chromosome. When these "letters" are attached to the modified Ti sequence to be inserted, it guides the new gene to the matching letter sequence in the genome. Upon arrival, special proteins "cut and paste" the new gene precisely where the scientist wants it in the genome. The technology that enables this procedure is transforming the genetic engineering process. Besides installing new genes, this process can delete genes, or turn genes off, or ramp their activity up or down like a dimmer switch on a light. (See Note 5-6)

Note 5-6. Three slightly different methods have been developed to precisely alter genomes—adding a gene, deleting or editing a gene, or altering the protein activity (production) of a gene. They go by the names "zinc finger proteins", "TALENS" and "CRISPER". CRISPER, also called CRISPER Cas9, is the most recent tool and is fast becoming the tool of choice for plant and animal modification. It is a remarkably precise tool. Cas9 is an enzyme that, when guided to a particular base pair sequence in the genome by a CRISPER "construct", will cut the chromosome, allowing a scientist to introduce a change at a precise location in a genome without introducing any unwanted collateral damage. Here is a brief explanation of how it works: (For a more detailed explanation, see John Parrington's excellent book [59].)

The genetic instructions on a chromosome is composed of three letter (base pair) "words" (codons) arranged in a "sentence" which constitutes the instructions for making a protein. To visualize this in a more familiar way, suppose the sentence read:

See the boy run

Attached to each end of this "gene" will be words that may or may not have influence on the gene, or may just be junk DNA. Let's attaché some nonsense to each end:

Dot dot dot see the boy run etc etc etc

To edit this "gene" the scientist makes a "construct" to guide the cutting tool (the Cas9 enzyme) to this specific gene. (A construct is a short strand of ribonucleic acid (RNA) with a nucleic acid ((base) sequence that matches a base sequence on the chromosome the scientist wants to target.) The construct in our example will read "dot dot dot". With the Cas9 enzyme attached, the construct is inserted into the cell, it enters the nucleus and seeks the "dot dot dot" sequence in the genome and sidles up to it. The enzyme then cuts the chromosome precisely between the "dot" and the "see". Then cell machinery, always ready to repair broken chromosomes, goes to work mending the cut, but will sometimes drop a letter or two in the process. So the repaired sequence will read "dot dot dot e the boy run etc etc etc". The sentence "e the boy run" no longer makes sense, so the gene has been disabled. If the gene caused apples to turn brown when cut and exposed to air, the cell can no longer make the protein (enzyme) that causes the browning.

If the objective is to insert a new gene preceding the "see

the boy run" sequence, the construct would carry along the new gene as well as the Cas9 enzyme. A cut would be made as in the preceding example, and the new gene inserted. The cell machinery then stitches both ends of the new gene and the chromosome can now give instructions for a new protein.

The precision and ease of this method is nothing short of amazing, Compared to zinc-finger-proteins (ZFNs) and TALENS, CRISPER[24] constructs are cheap and easy to make. ZFNs and TALENS constructs are made from proteins, cost about $5000 each and take a month or so to make. CRISPER constructs use RNA, take a couple days to make and cost about $30 (59, p.93). The CRISPER Cas9 method promises to democratize the genetic engineering process, bringing it back to the small labs with puny budgets where genetic engineering started decades ago. To bring a new GE crop to market presently costs the big agribusiness firms as much as 136 million dollars [64], shutting small firms out of the business and insuring that only crops with large profit potential, such as corn, wheat and cotton, will get research attention. CRISPER Cas9 could bring the cost of introducing a new gene down to a few tens of thousands of dollars. Minor crops can now get the attention they deserve, improving nutrition, disease and insect resistance, drought resistance, etc.

Because the CRISPER method is so precise, changes in genotype and phenotype are more predictable than with other GE methods, and vastly superior to traditional plant crosses that always require years of backcrossing to eliminate unwanted genes. Stephen Hall writes in the March,

---

[24]CRISPER and TALEN are acronyms. CRISPER stands for "Clustered Regularly Interspaced Short Palindromic Repeats" and Cas9 means "CRISPER associated endonuclease (enzyme) number 9". TALEN stands for "Transcription Activator-Like Effector Nuclease".

2016, issue of *Scientific American* [14] that practitioners regard CRISPER as "the least biologically disruptive form of plant breeding that humans have ever devised—including the 'natural' breeding techniques that have been practiced for thousands of years." I would especially emphasize the advantage over the "natural" (conventional) crossing of plants, particularly those crosses that involve two species or wild relatives of a species. Such crosses bring along all sorts of unwanted DNA, often poisonous or allergenic genes that must be eliminated by years of backcrossing to the desired parent. In the case of the new species Triticale, the cross between wheat and rye, this process took decades.

WHY THE CRITICS ARE WRONG

The critics of the "shotgun" approach of the early days of genetic engineering has been extended to Agrobacterium gene insertions and all other methods of plant transformation except those that involve an exchange of pollen, deemed the "conventional" method. *Agrobacterium,* they maintain, can insert it's genes into bacteria in the human gut, or even into human cells. *Agrobacterium* has had the chance to do that for millions of years, and no evidence yet exists that it has succeeded in making a permanent home in the gut or in human tissue. Why do I claim it has had millions of years to do this? *Agrobacterium* is ubiquitous in soils. Humans have ingested it through dirty food throughout their evolutionary journey. There is no reason to believe a snippet of an *Agrobacterium* plasmid, benignly transformed, is any more likely to take up virulent residence in human tissue[25] or human gut bacteria in the present era. Plants transformed using *Agrobacterium* have been in our food supply since 1996 without any ill-effects on humans or animals.

In fact, humans have been eating at least one plant natu-

---

[25]Some species of *Agrobacterium* have been known to cause opportunistic infections in humans with weakened immune systems [15].

rally transformed by *Agrobacterium* for millennia. Scientists working at the International Potato Center in Peru and Ghent University in Belgium discovered several transfer DNA (T-DNA) genes from *Agrobacterium* in 291 varieties of cultivated sweet potato. "One of the T-DNAs is apparently in all cultivated sweet potato clones, but not in closely related wild relatives, suggesting the T-DNA provided a trait or traits that were selected for during domestication." The scientists go on to say this discovery "may change the paradigm governing the 'unnatural' status of transgenic crops [38]." (I certainly hope so.) As I said before, nature has done everything genetic engineers have done, without laboratories, gene guns, colchicine, or petri dishes. Genetic engineers are really not doing anything new under the sun.

Some critics worry that antibiotic resistant genes attached to the plasmid snippet as a marker could be transferred to the human gut, because horizontal transfer of genetic material from one bacteria to another does occur this way. (Antibiotics are used to kill untransformed plant cells in a petri dish containing transformed cells, insuring that plants that grow from the petri dish callus will contain the desired gene.) Four reasons why this is not a legitimate worry. One, a functioning Agrobacterium genome is not being introduced to the gut, only a tiny snippet. Two, DNA that travels through the digestive tract is so chopped up that functional genes are unlikely to survive. Three, the antibiotics used are related to penicillin and resistant genes are already widespread in the environment and therefore relatively ineffective in treating infections. Four, geneticists are developing ways to eliminate or silence these genes before the plants are grown commercially (see Note 5-5).

Critics also worry that some unintended DNA can occasionally be transferred along with the transformed snippet and unintended consequences can result. Again, such fears are grossly exaggerated. Since it can't infect the plant and produce a gall, the *Agrobacterium* DNA will have nothing to do, and will be regarded as "junk" by the plant. Most plants already have a copious supply of inactive "junk" DNA acquired naturally. The possibility that some unexpected and undesirable protein would escape the vetting process is extremely unlikely.

An example of an unintended result and its resolution occurred in the early 1990s. Soybean seeds are low in the essential (for animals and humans) amino acid methionine, and Pioneer Hi-Bred Seeds attempted to fix the problem by adding a gene from Brazil nuts, which are high in methionine. Some people are allergic to Brazil nuts, so Pioneer had the transformed soybeans tested for the allergen, even though the beans were intended for animal consumption only. The test was positive, and the project was ended. No allergenic soybeans ever entered commercial food or feed markets [16].

Much of the fervor against genetically modified organisms (GMOs) is fueled by hatred for the Monsanto Company and its Roundup Ready crop seeds (GM crops that tolerate applications of glyphosate, the active ingredient in Roundup). It is baffling to me why there is so much militant antagonism toward a company that has provided technologies that benefit not only farmers, but consumers and the environment as well. Let me be more specific.

Roundup is an extremely effective herbicide (plant killer), yet is practically non-poisonous to animals and insects. It is particularly benign, as herbicides, go in interactions with the environment. Roundup kills by interfering with an enzyme essential to the production of amino acids by plant machinery, thereby preventing the assembly of plant proteins [17]. (See Note 5-7.) Only parts of a plant that are actively growing are affected. Bark of a tree or grapevine, for instance, can be sprayed without damaging leaves or roots. Plants that are fully dormant, such as evergreens in winter, can also be sprayed without damage.

Note 5-7. Glyphosate kills plants by interfering with an enzyme critical for the production of plant compounds essential for growth and maintenance. Glyphosate binds to the enzyme referred to as EPSPS (5-enolpyruvylshikemic acid-3-phosphate synthase) preventing it from catalyzing one of the seven steps required to produce the amino acids phenylalanine, tyrosine and tryptophan, precursors for many plant proteins and other compounds. The seven steps are referred to as the "shikimate pathway". This "pathway" does not exist in animals, so animals cannot produce these amino acids themselves and must obtain them from the plants they eat, making these amino acids "essential" for humans [72,73]. Partly because the shikimate pathway does not exist in animals, glyphosate is considered non-toxic to animals.

The shikimate pathway does exist in bacteria, and it is from a soil *Agrobacterium* species, strain *cp4*, that an EPSPS gene was found that would still function when glyphosate bonded to it. When inserted into a corn or soybean plant, the gene allows the shikimate pathway to proceed, making the plant resistant to an application of Roundup.

Could extra copies of the normal EPSPS gene make excess amounts of the enzyme, thus resisting a Roundup application? This, apparently, is one way weeds become resistant to glyphosate. Some highly resistant Palmer amaranth plants have up to 160 copies of the EPSPS gene, resulting in extra enzyme production that foils a Roundup application [70].

There are other ways to make Roundup-Ready (RR) crops. Older varieties of RR canola use two genes, the *cp4*EPSPS described above and another one from the soil bacterium *Ochrobactrum anthropi,* transgene goxv247. This gene governs the production of the enzyme glyphosate oxidoreductase (GOX) which can break glyphosate into aminomethylphosphonic acid (AMPA) and glyoxylate. Newer varieties of RR canola use only the *cp4EPSPS* gene [71].

After a Roundup application to varieties with the goxv247 gene, AMPA accumulates in the canola leaves, but is not toxic to the plants. Some other plants, e. g. RR soybean, have been found to convert some of the applied Roundup to AMPA, perhaps using the enzyme glycine oxidase, the enzyme some soil bacteria use to breakdown glyphosate [71].

Because the shikimate pathway exists in bacteria, some anti-GMO activists claim glyphosate can affect the gut bacteria of humans when ingested, causing all sorts of maladies from obesity, gluten intolerance, to autism. There is no credible science to support such claims. The human gut is estimated to harbor 100 trillion (100,000,000,000) microorganisms (Wikipedia, "Human Microbiota"). That the shikimate pathway could be altered in any significant portion of that population by the tiny amount of glyphosate present in some foods is highly unlikely. In addition, the bacterial population of the gut is in constant flux: any bacteria with a closed-down shikimate pathway will soon be eliminated in the natural course of events.

Roundup is considered non-poisonous to humans and other animals. Of course, anything can be lethal if a big enough dose is consumed. The toxicity of pesticides is measured by exposing test animals, usually rats, to high amounts through their feed, on their skin, or by inhaling fumes. Acute toxicity is expressed as the lethal dose that killed 50 per cent of the test animals (LD50). Here are the LD50s (rats, oral dose) for some pesticides and some familiar compounds [67, 68]:

(Small numbers are the most toxic)

	Milligrams per Kilogram of body weight	Theoretical LD50 dose for a 150 lb. person
Gasoline	50mg times .002913=ounces	.15
Caffeine	192	.56
Aspirin	1200	3.5
Malathion insecticide	1375	4.0
Household bleach	2000	5.8
Table salt	3000	8.7
Baking soda	4200	12.2
Glyphosate(Roundup)	5600	16.3
Vitamin C	11,900	34.7

And for some pesticides used by organic growers:

Rotenone [26]	132	.39
Bordeaux fungicide	300	.87
Pyrethrum insecticide	1500	4.4
Copper hydroxide	1000	2.9

Most Roundup formulations used on a farm contain one pound of glyphosate per quart, so a lethal dose by mouth would theoretically be one quart for a 150-pound person. Results relating to people who have attempted or have been successful at committing suicide by drinking Roundup are quite variable. Wikipedia reports on a study of 93 cases of acute poisoning by commercial formulations of Roundup that found drinking as little as 3-7 fluid ounces caused death in some cases, while a pint only caused mild symptoms in others [19]. The formulations contained an adjuvant (an additive that enhances wettability, permeability, etc.). Adjuvants can make commercial Roundup formulation slightly more toxic to animals [20,21].

The glyphosate molecule carries a positive charge. Soil mineral and organic particles are negatively charged. So when spray droplets fall on the soil, the negatively charged

---

[26]Rotonone is not approved for crops in the U.S. It could enter the U.S. as residue on organic produce from other countries [18].

soil particles grab the glyphosate and hold on, making it virtually unavailable to plant roots. It therefore resists leaching and removal by runoff unless soil is carried off site. Fields sprayed with Roundup one day can be seeded the next day without injury. I have done this many times in the last 40 years. There is no fear of residues harming the newly planted crop. Less than one per cent of the glyphosate in soil is absorbed by roots [22]. Roundup is the one herbicide that has made no-till farming possible on a large scale. Environmentalists should be singing its praises. No-till farming, enabled by Roundup, is a powerful conservation tool, saving billions of tons of soil every year worldwide. Roundup is now the most widely used herbicide in the world, and environmentalists should be thankful, because it replaces tons of more environmentally hazardous herbicides. Just ask any farmer who practices no-till.

The glyphosate molecule consists of carbon, hydrogen, oxygen, nitrogen, and phosphorus. It is an organic compound, which needs a bit of explaining if the reader has forgotten his/her high school chemistry. Compounds containing carbon are called "organic" because they can be produced by and dismantled by living things. Nearly all synthetically produced pesticides (herbicides, insecticides, fungicides, rodenticides, etc.) are organic compounds. It is an oxymoron that organic growers often apply inorganic pesticides based on metals such as copper or sulphur, while conventional growers apply pesticides that are technically organic.

Since glyphosate is an organic compound, some bacteria and other organisms in the soil see it as a food source and proceed to dismantle it. The rate at which this decomposition occurs is dependent on soil temperature and moisture conditions, and on the vigor of the soil biota. Soil studies by the EPA and others found the half-life of glyphosate to range from 3 to 130 days, and averaged 44 to 64 days [23,24,25]. A USDA researcher found that as much as 55 per cent of glyphosate applied to soil was given off as carbon dioxide within four weeks from a sandy loam soil [26]. The glyphosate molecule is attacked in soil by many species of bacteria, actniomycetes, fungi, and who knows what else [27], all seeking to use the nitrogen and phosphorus in the molecule as nutrients. The principal primary metabolite, containing the nitrogen and phosphorus, is aminomethylphosphonic acid (AMPA), which tends to accumulate in soil as it degrades somewhat slower than its parent, glyphosate. The other metabolites, composed of carbon, hydrogen and oxygen, disappear quite rapidly, being expelled as carbon dioxide or incorporated into biota body parts. Ultimately AMPA is broken apart and its nutrients, nitrogen and phosphorous, incorporated into the bodies of bacteria and other biota. When the biota die, the nutrients become available to plants, and the droplets of Roundup that wound up in the soil are benignly and fully recycled into the environment. This does not happen overnight, and a few molecules may stay attached to a soil particle for years and be picked up by sensitive instruments. But eventually, soil microorganisms will find every last molecule and recycling will be complete.

Some researchers claim glyphosate residues change the makeup of the soil biota. This may be true in the short term, as various species attack the new food source. Such phenomena occurs all the time as food sources wax and wane, or temperature and moisture fluctuate. USDA Scientists working at Washington State University investigated the effects of glyphosate on bacterial communities in a greenhouse experiment, applying a high rate (1.5 pounds glyphosate per acre) to various local soils and planting wheat, repeating the experiment for three growth cycles. Commenting on their results they wrote, "Glyphosate had little effect on soil bacterial community composition or diversity relative to farm site, management (no-till vs. CRP) or root proximity [39]."

AMPA can sometimes be detected in some food plants

that have been sprayed with Roundup. AMPA is considered non-toxic to plants, animals, and other living things and, like glyphosate, is benignly excreted if consumed in tiny amounts in food. Its behavior in the environment mimics that of glyphosate and, despite many internet claims to the contrary, is eventually completely and benignly recycled into plant and animal nutrients. Though glyphosate and AMPA may at times be detected in air, soil or water, their presence is temporary. Internet postings that claim Roundup is not biodegradable and remains in the soil indefinitely are outright lies.

Sugar beets are one target of the critics of Roundup Ready plants, with some food processors refusing to use beet sugar. This refusal is a prime example of how illiterate the general public (and even supposedly well-educated CEOs) are concerning science issues. Sugar does not contain DNA and sugar is not a protein, the plant product on which DNA works its magic. Sucrose (common table sugar) is a storage product of the plant, a compound consisting of one-half glucose and one-half fructose. Cane sucrose, beet sucrose, GM beet sucrose: They are all exactly the same compound. The protein and its DNA component ends up in the beet pulp.

The same is true for corn oil, corn sugar or corn starch. These products from a Roundup Ready GM corn kernel will be identical to a conventional corn kernel. Only the corn protein will contain the modified DNA. Food labeling laws do not take this fact into consideration, and so the consumer is, sadly, misled as to the presence of genetically modified DNA in many processed foods.

FOOD LABELING

In July of 2016, Congress passed and the President signed a food labeling law that supersedes state laws requiring a label on foods containing GMOs. The law requires certain foods that contain ingredients made from GMO crops to have a label—text, symbol or electronic code—that so informs consumers. Deemed unnecessary and harmful by GMO advocates, the government was nonetheless forced to act to prevent chaos in the marketplace by potentially 50 different regulatory actions by states. A Vermont law had already taken effect on July 1 that required labels and provided for penalties for noncompliance.

On the surface, the right to know if a food contains genetically engineered ingredients seems a reasonable demand. But if food processed from GMOs is identical to non-GMO food, as 20 plus years of research has proven, GMO labels will only promote fear that something is potentially harmful in the mind of the uninformed—more accurately, misinformed—consumer.

Labeling will entail extra costs way beyond the printing costs of new labels. To be sure that what the label claims is absolutely true, every handler, beginning with the farmer, will have to certify as to whether the grain or produce is GMO or non-GMO. Mistakes will be made. Some warehouseman receiving GMO and non-GMO soybeans, for instance, will mistakenly dump a farmer's load of GMO beans into the non-GMO bin, destroying the non-GMO status of the entire bin. That, at the least, would mean a loss of premiums due the warehouse company on that bin of soybeans. At the worst, if the mistake is not caught and the soybeans are sold as non-GMO and a company's product made from the beans is subsequently found to be falsely labeled, fines, lawsuits, and possible criminal judgments would ensue. Farmers, middlemen, and processors will need to buy insurance to mitigate such eventualities. All the extra costs associated with growing, warehousing and merchandising will be passed on to the consumers of both GMO and non-GMO foods. And the bureaucratic paperwork needed all along the food chain will be cumbersome and expensive to produce and organize.

"Some companies, fearing GMO labels will be a sort of scarlet letter and scare off consumers, are replacing ingredients altogether" [28]. Ben and Jerry's ice cream, for instance, decided several years ago to remove all GMO ingredients from their products. It took three years to find replacements for everything, and the new products cost an average 11 per cent more (28). Soybean oil, for example, is used in thousands of food products, and non-GMO soybeans require a two dollar or more premium per bushel to get farmers to grow them-- an approximate 30 per cent increase in price over genetically modified soybeans. And, as explained before, oils, starches and sugars from Roundup Ready crops are no differently, chemically, than those products from Roundup Ready crops. Only the proteins will be changed. Regulators, activists and consumers need to get their science straight.

The cost of all this, estimated to be $600 -$1000 per year per family, might be worth it if any real danger to health was involved. Eighty-eight percent of scientists say there is not (Pew Research Center poll, 2014). The USDA, the EPA, and the FDA say there is not. Agencies of the European government say there is not, even as their parliaments require labeling and ban the production of most, not all, GM crops.[27]

In August of 2011, the European Commission (the executive body of the European Union) published the results of a 10-year study of research projects concerning all aspects of GMOs. The 248 page compendium titled *A Decade of EU-Funded GMO Research* [30], cost the EU €200 million and involved 500 independent research groups. Their conclusions were summarized by Commissioner Maire Geoghegan-Quinn in a press release as follows: "The aim of this book is to contribute to a fully transparent debate on GMOs, based on balanced, science-based information. According to the findings of these projects, GMOs potentially provide opportunities to

---

[27]European bans are more political than scientific. Imports of GM feed grains, especially soybeans, are generally allowed because European farmers cannot produce enough. Imports of GM crops that compete with European farmers are generally denied.

reduce malnutrition, especially in lesser developed countries, as well as increase yields and assist towards the adaptation of agriculture to climate change."… **"there is, as of today, no scientific evidence associating GMOs with higher risks for the environment or for food and feed safety than conventional plants and organisms"** [29]. (My emphasis.)

SUPERWEEDS

There are problem weeds, but there are no "superweeds". "Superweeds" is a term bandied about by those in the anti-Monsanto-GMO-Roundup movement, hoping to seed people's minds with the notion that GMOs and Roundup somehow create weeds that require "powerful" herbicides to control. They don't realize, or perhaps just fail to mention, that the "powerful" herbicides required when Roundup fails are the ones farmers used before Roundup came on the scene. The problem is, Roundup did such a good job of replacing these "powerful" herbicides that farmers used it year after year on the same fields—a recipe bound to allow weed genotypes naturally resistant to Roundup to multiply and become dominate. Resistance of this type is not new—it has been occurring since the first herbicides were used after WWII.

As I walked my first fields of wheat In the spring of 1965, I noticed every square inch of soil surface between wheat plants was occupied by the weed henbit (*Lamium amplexicaule*), a low-growing weed not very competitive with wheat. But in such large numbers it would use copious amounts of moisture needed by the wheat plants. Henbit is resistant to 2,4-D, the herbicide that had been used on these fields for the preceding 15 years. With competing weeds controlled, henbit was now the dominate weed. I was alarmed by the extreme infestation, but I knew from my college studies that a relatively new herbicide, diuron, would kill henbit. Against the advice of my chemical supplier, I sprayed every acre with diuron plus 2,4-D, and had a weed-free crop.

Henbit was resistant to 2.4-D from the get-go, but it was

relegated to unimportance because of competition with other weeds and crop plants. With its competitors eliminated by 2,4-D, it had become dominate in my fields.

Acquired resistance is a little different. Mutations that impart resistance to an herbicide escape notice until repeated applications of the same herbicide allow a large population to build. This kind of resistance can be avoided by rotating to an herbicide with a different mode of action each time an application is made. Failure to recognize this management issue by farmers and dealers in the past means that worldwide, "weeds have evolved resistance to 21 of the known 25 herbicide sites of action and to 148 different herbicides."[37]. This does not mean the end of herbicide use is at hand: Resistance is a problem that can be handled through rotation of herbicides and crops, or, as a last resort, tillage.

Palmer amaranth (*Amaranthus palmeri*) is the weed in the news these days, most often getting the moniker "superweed". It is a difficult weed, but not because of Roundup and GMOs. A plant native to the deserts of the southwestern U.S. and northern Mexico, it thrives where moisture is plentiful—the irrigated fields of the plains or the rain-fed fields of the Corn Belt and southeast. Left untreated it will tower above corn plants and produce stalks thick enough to damage harvest machinery. It is especially troublesome in cotton and soybean fields, where it has become resistant not only to Roundup but also a class of herbicides called ALS inhibitors. Some fields also have plants resistant to atrazine, an herbicide used on corn since the 1960s [36].

Palmer amaranth is very good at building resistance because it is dioecious: That is, male and female flowers do not occur on the same plant, preventing inbreeding and forcing outcrossing. This means maximum mixing of the genes every generation, providing maximum opportunity for resistance to show itself. There are still herbicides that will kill this weed, and not all populations of Palmer Amaranth are resistant to Roundup. But farmers need to manage their rotations of crops and chemicals carefully to avoid further herbicide resistance. If all else fails, Palmer Amaranth will not become resistant to the cultivator and the hoe.

SCIENCE SUPPORTS THE SAFETY OF GMOs

Prestigious scientific organizations around the world have weighed in on the safety of GMO foods. For example the National Academy of Sciences (NAS) provides, (see its website), "science-based advice on critical issues affecting the nation." The work of the Academy is thorough, important, and of high quality. Congress and government agencies rely on the Academy's reports to formulate legislation and policy. For the past 30 years, it's conclusions regarding GMO technology "have been remarkably congruent: There are no unique risks from the use of molecular techniques of genetic engineering, which are extensions, or refinements of earlier, less precise, less predictable techniques"[41].

In May of 2016, the NAS released a 407 page report titled *Genetically Engineered Crops: Experiences and Prospects* [42]. The goal of the report was to "make available to the public, to researchers, and to policy makers a comprehensive review of the evidence that has been used in the debates about GE crops and information on relevant studies that are rarely referred to in the debates [p. ix]." In the Executive Summary, the adverse claims on human and animal health were summarized as follows: "Many reviews have indicated that foods from GE crops are as safe as foods from non-GE crops, but the committee reexamined the original studies of this subject. The design and analysis of many animal-feeding studies were not optimal, but the large number of experimental studies provided reasonable evidence that animals were not harmed by eating food derived from GE crops. Additionally, long-term data on livestock health before and after the introduction of GE crops showed no adverse effects associated with GE crops (see Note 5-8). The committee also examined epidemiological data on incidence of cancers and other human-health problems over time and found no substantiated evidence that foods from GE crops were less safe than foods from GE crops [p. xvii]." This conclusion is substantiated by comparing data on specific health problems (cancers, obesity, type II diabetes, chronic kidney disease, celiac disease, autism, and food allergies) in the U.S. and Canada with data from western Europe "where diets contain much lower amounts of food derived from GE crops" [p. 10]. Changes do occur over time in the incidence of these diseases, but the changes are similar in all data sets, before and after the introduction of GE food components.

On page 114 of the NAS report are sample statements from other prestigious organizations:

1."To date, no health effects attributed to genetic engineering have been documented in the human population." National Research Council (2004)

2."Indeed, the science is quite clear: crop improvement by the modern molecular techniques of biotechnology is safe." American Association for the Advancement of Science (2012)

3."Bioengineered foods have been consumed for close to 20 years, and during that time, no overt consequences on human health have been reported and /or substantiated in the peer-reviewed literature." Council on Science and Public Health of the American Medical Association House of Delegates (2112)

4."Genetically modified foods currently available on the international market have passed safety assessments and are not likely to present risks for human health. In addition, no effects on human health have been shown as a result of the consumption of such foods by the general population in the countries where they have been approved." World Health Organization (2014)

5."The main conclusion to be drawn from the efforts of more than 130 research projects, covering a period of more than 25 years of research, and involving more than 500 independent research groups is that biotechnology, and in particular GMOs, are not per se more risky than e. g. conventional plant breeding technologies." European Commission (2010a).

The conclusions of the European Commission, the executive body of the European Union, is especially significant, given the high distrust of GMOs by the European populace. It is also significant that the European Commission funded these 130 projects to the tune of €300 over the 25 years.

Note 5-8. Dr. Alison Van Eenennaam, University of California Extension Specialist, reviewed animal health data sets from 1983 to 1996 (before the introduction of GE feedstuffs in 1996), and compared them to data sets from 1997 to 2013. She published the results in *Archives of Animal Science*. Quoting from her abstract, "Numerous studies have consistently revealed that the performance and health of GE-fed animals are comparable with those fed isogenic (i. e., nearly identical) non-GE crop lines. United States agriculture produces over 9 billion food producing animals annually, and more than 95 percent of these animals consume feed containing GE ingredients...These field data sets, representing 100 billion animals following the introduction of GE crops did not reveal unfavorable or perturbed trends in livestock health and productivity. No study has revealed any differences in the nutritional profile of animal products derived from GE-fed animals [44]."

Support from scientists is not universal, but 100 percent agreement on a scientific subject is often elusive. In 2015 the Pew Research Center conducted a poll of members of the American Association for the Advancement of Science. On the question of safety of genetically modified food, 88 percent of the scientists surveyed said it was safe to eat. Alarmingly, from a scientific standpoint, only 37 percent of the general public thought GM foods were safe to eat. The seeds of doubt planted and nourished by the NGOs has prolific roots with the general public.

REGULATION—TOO MUCH OR TOO LITTLE?

In their book, *The Frankenfood Myth* [40], Henry Miller and Gregory Conko trace the regulation of genetically modified organisms from their inception in the 1970s to the beginning of century 21. It is their contention that regulation has become much too burdensome and expensive. Field testing required by the USDA, the EPA and the FDA costs millions of dollars and can take ten years to complete. These agencies focus on the **process** when they should be focusing on the **product.** In other words, the **process**, genetic engineering, is just another way of manipulating the genome, which breeders have been doing for over a hundred years, creating new varieties by irradiating seeds, treating seeds or tiny plants in petri diches with chemicals, crossing them with wild relatives or other species (such as the wheat-rye cross that produced triticale, a new species), all without government oversight. It is the **product,** they contend that should be regulated.

Allergens or other poisonous compounds can be the unexpected result of conventional breeding, (e. g., excessive psoralens in celery cited earlier in this chapter, page 5), but no government agency checks for them, nor should they. It is incumbent upon the breeder, or the company or university to vet their products for such unexpected outcomes, as Pioneer Seed Company did with their soybean-Brazil nut allergen (see pages 15-16). The crop now called canola was bred from rapeseed by Canadian scientists using conventional breeding methods. What exactly did they do? Rapeseed has been used in Asian countries for centuries as a cooking oil. It has not been used in that way in Western countries because it is high in euricic acid, a fatty acid that, when eaten, is detrimental to heart health. Canadian breeders succeeded in producing rapeseed varieties very low in euricic acid (2 percent vs. 50 percent in some rapeseed varieties), renamed them "canola", and a new industry was born. The government only had to weigh in on the **product,** low euricic acid content, not the **process** by which by which it was accomplished. Two percent is considered safe for human consumption in the U.S.; five percent in the EU. ("Canola" is an acronym for "Canadian-oil-low-acid".)

Miller and Conko blame the scientists involved in the birthing of genetic engineering and the companies that commercialized it for steering the regulation of this new technology in the wrong direction. "In 1975, scientists convened a historic conference at Asilomar Conference Center in Pacific Grove, California. Participants called on the National Institutes of Health (NIH) to oversee the use of the new research methods" (40, p. 10). Thus the controversy over genetic engineering was born. The Press flooded newspapers with stories of this new technology that was so dangerous the scientists were calling for government oversight. If you ask for government oversight, you are sure to get it.

At first, government regulation of GMOs was quite reasonable. The first GMO to be marketed was human insulin manufactured by genetically modified *E. coli* bacteria, which debuted in 1982. In 1986 the White House Office of Science and Technology (OSTP) recommended that oversight and regulation be limited to traits that pose some risk to the environment or could be toxic to people or animals, in other words, focus on the end product, not the process that produced it. OSTP reaffirmed that stance in 1992.

But by then the drumbeat for more regulation was coming from activist organizations who were spreading doubts about the new technology, and from scientists and even from involved industries which believed more transparency and regulation would reassure a doubting public. The Government's answer, through the USDA, the EPA, and the FDA, was to ramp up oversight of genetic engineering at all levels, and require onerous field testing that has lengthened the time it takes to get a new trait approved to ten or more years, increasing the total cost to as much as 136 million dollars (45). These costs have shut out all but the biggest companies, and limited research to the crops with the largest acreages—such as corn, cotton, soybeans, canola, sugar beets, and alfalfa. According to Miller (45), "'Biopharming', the once promising biotechnology area that uses genetic engineering techniques to induce crops such as corn, tomatoes, and tobacco to produce high concentrations of highvalue pharmaceuticals… is moribund because of the Agriculture Department's extraordinary regulatory burdens." And, "thanks to EPA's policies… the high hopes for genetically engineered 'biorational' microbial pesticides and microorganisms to clean up toxic wastes has evaporated."

It is hoped these governmental bodies will take a more benign approach to regulating "gene editing" using the CRISPER-Cas9 technique, as this method does not involve the introduction of foreign DNA. As I write this, the USDA is leaning towards the regulation of the **product,** not the **process,** where CRISPER is used to edit genes. However, activist organizations are lobbying hard to over-regulate this technique also. If we are going to see the promise of nutritional benefits, new and benign pesticidal properties, drought resistance, and a host of other plant improvements that promise to keep food plentiful and affordable over the next 30 years, we cannot keep tying the hands of scientists with unreasonable regulations.

GMO BENEFITS—CURRENT AND FUTURE

We have already discussed many of the benefits, and examined some of the risks of GMOs, real and imagined. Anti-GMO activists often argue that GM crops have not fulfilled the promise of greater yields. In some cases that is true. But the introduction of crops that tolerate herbicides and resist insect damage have been rapidly adopted by farmers. Why? Because they lower costs for farmers. Tillage is reduced, saving diesel, labor and wear and tear on equipment. Pesticide use is reduced, saving application costs and decreasing the pesticide load in the environment. And most of the time, farmers see increased yields.

For example, Roundup Ready (RR) sugar beets save Idaho and Eastern Oregon growers $22 million per year. They planted 178,000 acres of RR beets in 2014. Growers normally spend $66 per acre on herbicides and spend $42 applying them. Herbicide expenses for RR beets were $11 and required half as many trips across the field to apply them, reducing total herbicide expense from $108 per acre to $31. Better chemical weed control eliminated hand-weeding, saving another $60 per acre. RR seeds cost $100 more per acre, but yield is increased. Combining the increase in yield with the savings in weed control expense leaves an average net margin increase of $122 per acre [62].

Worldwide, "on average, GM technology adoption has reduced chemical use by 37 percent, increased crop yields by 22 percent and increased farmer profits by 68 percent." This is the conclusion of German researchers who analyzed all 147 studies of the agronomics and economic impacts of GM crops published in English between 1995 and 2014 [63]. The authors further conclude "the average agronomic and economic benefits of GM crops are large and significant... Yield and farmer profit gains are higher in developing countries than in developed countries." These conclusions are true even with the inclusion of "NGO reports and other publications without scientific peer review (that) bias the impact estimates downward."

Opponents of GMOs claim pesticide use has not decreased with adoption of genetically modified crops. They are misinterpreting pesticide statistics, and ignoring the testimony of farmers who plant GMO seeds. Overall herbicide use is increasing, but "herbicide increases (are) more rapid in non-GE crops" [74]. Roundup is now the most widely used herbicide in the world, replacing millions of pounds of herbicides that are less environmentally friendly and more destructive if misused. Environmentalists need to get over their hatred of Monsanto and embrace the fact that Roundup is the most environmentally friendly herbicide ever produced.

Roundup is generally applied at one pound of active ingredient per acre, often replacing herbicides that are applied at ounces or fractions of ounces per acre. This fact skews use statistics if a person only considers pounds applied. And one should not be fooled into thinking that because some herbicides are applied at very low rates that they are more environmentally friendly. Quoting from the National Academy of Sciences, "Researchers should be discouraged from publishing data that simply compares total kilograms of herbicide used per hectare per year because such data can mislead readers" [75]. For example, BASF chemical company patented a wheat gene, called CLEARFIELD, that will allow a wheat variety containing the gene to tolerate a BASF herbicide named Beyond. I can spray a field of CLEARFIELD wheat with four ounces of Beyond (containing 0.5 ounces active ingredient) and kill most grassy weeds. But I cannot plant barley in that field for nine months after that application because residual Beyond would injure my crop. If I wanted to plant sugar beets or canola I would need to wait 26 months. Now, if there was a Roundup Ready wheat variety (which there is not), I could apply Roundup, kill all the grassy and broadleaf weeds, and suffer no plant-back restrictions. Why is there not a Roundup Ready wheat variety? Because 50 percent of U.S. wheat is exported and anti-GMO activists have inculcated foreign customers with anti-GMO propaganda.

Insect resistance using genes from the soil bacterium *Bacillus thuringiensis* (commonly referred to as Bt) is another well-established GE technology. Bt is found naturally in soils and on plants worldwide. The toxins the various strains produce attack the larvae (worm or caterpillar stage) of many destructive insects. The larvae must ingest the toxin to be affected. The toxin attaches to the wall of the gut, breaks it down, and normal gut bacteria essentially consume the worm from the inside out, killing it in 24-48 hours. Bt is non-toxic to humans, all animals, birds and fish, and the adult form of all insects. We have all likely consumed this toxin as the bacteria are commonly found on leaf surfaces.

Organic growers rely heavily on Bt to control many insects, and it is also used by conventional growers who use integrated pest management (IPM) systems (insect and disease control programs that use natural controls as much as possible).

The gene that produces the Bt toxin has been introduced into the genomes of major crop plants such as corn, soybeans, cotton and canola. Larvae feeding on such plants ingest the toxin and suffer the same fate as occurs with surface applied Bt. Growers using these seeds have experienced decreased losses from insect infestations, especially cotton growers who, in many cases, have cut their pesticide use in half, and sometimes much more. Julie Murphree, writing in Progressive Farmer [56], relates the first time her father grew Bt cotton in Maricopa, Arizona. His "pesticide applications dropped from 15 or 18 in a given season to one. The impact was so positive, he never looked back."

Nowhere has the impact of Bt cotton been more dramatic than in India. Prior to 2002, India's cotton industry was "characterized by stagnation in cotton production, decelerating trend in cotton yield and reliant on significant cotton imports" [65]. Then, in 2002 a revolution started with the introduction of the first hybrid varieties containing Monsanto's Bt gene by Mahyco Monsanto Biotech.[28] Resource –poor farmers, subsisting on an average of less than 4 acres, soon saw their lives improve. A study of 533 farmers growing Bt cotton found their yields increased 24 percent and their profits rose 50 percent between 2002 and 2008 because of less insect damage and less pesticides purchased [57]. India is now the world's biggest producer of cotton, a net exporter, and growing 25 percent of the world's cotton. In 2002, there were 5.5 million small landholders growing cotton. In 2014, that number had grown to 8 million, with 95 percent (7.7 million) growing Bt cotton [65].[29]

Chinese scientists conducted a 16-year landscape-level study of 36 sites in six provinces in northern China growing large acreages of Bt cotton. They found "a marked increase in abundance of three types of generalist arthropod predators (ladybirds, lacewings, and spiders) and a decreased abundance of aphid pests associated with widespread adoption of Bt cotton and reduced insecticide sprays in this crop. We also found evidence that the predators might provide additional biocontrol services spilling over from BT cotton fields onto neighboring crops" [58].

The National Academy of Sciences reports that **"in some cases, widespread planting of these crops decreased the abundance of specific pests in the landscape and thereby contributed to reduced damage even to crops that did not have the Bt trait, and planting Bt crops has tend-**

---

[28] Mahyco Monsanto Biotech (MMB) is a 50-50 joint venture. Mahyco is a major seed producer in India. MMB has licensed the Bt genes to 28 other seed producing companies in India. See the company website.

[29]The claim by critics that Bt cotton has increased the number of farmer suicides in India is false. Suicide among farmers from 1997 to 2007 remained steady at approximately 20,000 per year, while the total number of suicides in the same period rose 20 percent (from 100,000 per year to 120,000) [57].

ed to result in higher insect biodiversity on farms than planting similar varieties without the Bt trait that were treated with synthetic insecticides" [42, p. xvii], (my emphasis). This brings up a point that is never recognized by organic growers: The disease and insect controls used by conventional farmers can lower the population of damaging insects and the inoculum of fungal diseases in the environment around organic crops. A case in point is the elimination of stinking smut described previously in Chapter 1. Without seed treatments that combat the family of smut diseases they would again plague farmer's fields.

Organic farmers claim the synthetic insecticides conventional farmers use destroy beneficial insects and thereby compromise organic pest control. Yet I have several times witnessed a rapid natural buildup of ladybugs in my wheat fields in response to an aphid infestation, even though neighbors were spraying their fields. With a little patience to let the ladybugs work, I was able to avoid spraying. It appears to me that there are always enough unsprayed areas to allow beneficial insects to rapidly multiply if a good food source is available.

The first generation of genetically engineered crops have mainly benefitted farmers through weed and insect control. The next generation promises to benefit consumers through better nutrition and less food waste. The example of Golden Rice has already been discussed. Potatoes that resist bruising, resist browning when cut, and reduce by 50 percent the unhealthy chemical acrylamide when fried have been developed by the Simplot Company. These potatoes, called Innate, were produced by moving genes from wild potatoes using genetic engineering techniques. These genes could have been moved by conventional breeding techniques, but moving the genes with GE methods avoided bringing along unwanted, perhaps poisonous, traits that would have taken years to eliminate. USDA clearance for commercialization was granted in March, 2014.

But because these genes were moved using GE methods, McDonald's, which sells 3.4 billion pounds of french fries per year, is refusing to use them. So also has Frito-Lay, the biggest potato chip maker [52]. These are examples of company CEOs making marketing decisions based on customer perceptions rather than scientific evidence. Most companies do not have the courage to buck irrational customer perceptions, even when they know the customers are wrong. **If we continue to allow scientific illiteracy to make the rules, sustainability and food security in 2050 will be unattainable for much of the world.**

It is the high temperatures of french fry and chip making that turn asparagine (an amino acid required for life, but humans can make their own) in the potatoes to acrylamide, a carcinogen,[30] and both companies could serve a more healthful food if they used Innate potatoes. So, until they are more widely accepted Simplot will sell these potatoes mainly in the fresh market.

Besides being healthier because of the reduced acrylamide, the anti-bruising properties will save potato farmers (and their consuming customers) billions of dollars by reducing the incidence of bruised, blackened potatoes that are thrown away. "Company studies show a 15 percent increase in useable spuds when Innate is packed" [51]. And sliced potatoes will resist browning because the gene controlling an enzyme that goes into action when a cut is detected has been turned off. This is a great advantage to the food service industry which can now furnish customers with pre-cut, fresh potatoes

---

[30] Acrylamide is produced in many starchy foods when they are heated above 248 degrees Fahrenheit. The chemical has also been found in black olives, prunes, dried pears and coffee. It is classified as a group 2A carcinogen by the International Agency for Research on Cancer (IARC). "Cigarette smoking is a major acrylamide source... According to the American Cancer Society it is not clear, as of 2016, whether acrylamide consumption increases people's risk of developing cancer." [Wikipedia, "Acrylamide".]

that stay white sans preservatives. Simplot has also received approval by the USDA and the FDA to commercialize second generation innate potatoes that will, besides the aforementioned traits, have resistance to late blight, the fungus-like disease that caused the great potato famine in Ireland in 1845. Presently controlled with costly sprays applied weekly when the pathogen is present, this new resistance is expected to reduce pesticide sprayings in half, a significant benefit to the farmer and the environment. Because of the anti-pest component, EPA must also approve commercialization, which should be forthcoming in 2017.[31]

The enzyme responsible for the potato browning, polyphenol oxidase, also causes apples to turn brown when bruised or sliced. Contact of the apple or potato flesh with air sets the enzyme in motion, causing a chemical reaction with oxygen in the air that turns the white flesh brown. Some of the vitamin C and antioxidants are oxidized (burned up) in this reaction. It is estimated that 40 percent of apples worldwide are thrown away because of this chemical reaction that gives the appearance of rot but does not significantly lower the quality of the apple. The development of non-browning apples, described below, is a significant bonus for consumers and growers.

A Canadian biotechnology company, Okanagan Specialty Fruits, has succeeded in turning off the production pf polyphenol oxidase in apples. Founded by British Columbia apple grower Neal Carter in 1996, Okanagan Specialty Fruits scientists found the genes responsible for the enzyme's production and succeeded, using genetic engineering techniques, in dampening the gene activity responsible for the enzyme to near zero. After growing the apples in test orchards for several years in the USA and Canada, the company applied for unregulated access to the marketplace in both countries under the brand name "Arctic Apple". In early 2015, permis-

[31]Approval was given, March, 2017 [69].

sion was granted in both countries for Golden Delicious and Granny Smith varieties containing the "Arctic" modification; permission to commercialize other varieties is expected to soon follow.

No foreign DNA was introduced to produce "Arctic" apples, but that has not silenced the critics. The critics say this enzyme is activated when insects or diseases attack apples, and turning it off will cause more pesticides to be used. Polyphenol oxidases, called PPOs, are produced by many plants, apparently as one of many defenses plants have developed to resist insects and diseases. This one works by destroying the nutritive value of the tissue surrounding an insect bite or infection site [53]. Research with tomato plants engineered to produce 10 times the normal amount of PPOs exhibited 15-fold less lesions than control plants when infected with the pathogen *Pseudomonassyringae* PV. tomato [54]. The facts to be noted here are (1), both control and engineered plants had lesions and would likely need a pesticide treatment, and (2), the prospect of engineering plants to produce more PPOs in hopes of controlling pests could suffer unknown side-effects (e.g., increased psoralen production in celery described on page 100).

The tradeoff here is a slight reduction in pest resistance to gain browning resistance that will result in less apples wasted. Food service companies will no longer need to "spray or dip apples with ascorbic acid, citric acid, calcium salts or some combination of the above" to prevent browning [55], a plus for consumers and food service companies.

There are many other examples of how genetic engineering is improving nutrition and expanding the ability of plants to be productive in unfavorable environments, such as drought or salty soils. Soon we will have crops that have more omega-3 fatty acids (the heart-healthy fat in fish oil), pink pineapples with cancer-fighting lycopene, and canola that uses 50 percent less nitrogen fertilizer [58].

Researchers are working on ways to increase the efficiency of photosynthesis in plants. Some desert plants use a special trick to utilize water more efficiently. Called crassulacean acid metabolism, or CAM, these plants open their stomata (breathing pores in the leaf) only at night when temperatures are cooler, the reverse of most plants which must open them during the day to take in carbon dioxide to photosynthesize sugars. CAM plants take in the carbon dioxide at night and store it in a pool of malic acid. During daylight the carbon dioxide is released to photosynthesize sugars without opening the stomata and losing precious water. CAM plants can survive on as little as one-fifth as much water as "normal" plants. Does this mean we could someday grow food crops where only cactus now grows? Possibly.

In 2015, 444 million acres worldwide (11.3 percent of arable land, 28 countries) were planted to GE crops [42, p.45-46]. One-third of worldwide corn acreage and 80 percent of soybean acreage planted was genetically modified. These two crops accounted for 80 percent (356 million acres) of GE worldwide acres. Crops making up the rest of the acreage include apples (Arctic), canola, cotton, sugar beet, papaya, potato, squash, eggplant, alfalfa, and poplar trees.

Genetic engineers in many countries are working to solve disease and nutritional deficiencies, and to enhance production potential for local crops. Crops in various stages of development around the world include dry beans, eucalyptus, rice, wheat, sorghum, cassava, banana, citrus, chickpea, cowpea, camelina, groundnut, mustard, pigeon pea, safflower, and a blight resistant American chestnut [42, p.46].

Growing more food with less inputs and using less land is a goal researchers must meet in order to adequately feed, clothe and house the expected population of 9-10 billion people by 2050 in a sustainable manner, while preserving the environment and wildlife space. Genetic engineering of plants and animals is a crucially important technology needed to accomplish these goals. It is a powerful technology holding great promise for the common good. Regulation is justified, but it needs to be aimed at the **product**, not the **process.**

CHAPTER 5 REFERENCES

1. Humphrery, J. H., West, K.P. Jr., and Sommer, A. "Vitamin A Deficiency and Attributable Mortality in Under-Five-Year-Olds." WHO Bulletin. Vol. 70, No. 2, pp. 225-232. 1992.

2. Wheat Life. December 2012, p.42.

3. Ronald, P. and Adamchak, R. Tomorrow's Table—Organic Farming, Genetics, and the Future of Food. Oxford University Press, 198 Madison Avenue, New York, New York. 2008.

4. Oreskes, Naomi and Conway, Eric M. Merchants of Doubt. Bloomsbury Press. 2010.

5. Engdahl, F. William. Seeds of Destruction. 2007. Center for Research on Globalization (CRG). http://www.globalresearch.ca

6. DeWitt, J.L. "Bridging the Gap". Wheat Life. Vol. 33, No. 2, Feb., 1990, pp.1,8.

7. "Gene Expression." Wikipedia. April 14, 2016. https://en.wikipedia.org/w/index.php?title=Gene_expression&oldid=715195801

8. Jackson County, Oregon, Resolution 635, "The Genetically Engineered Ordinance". Filed August 8, 2012.

9. Brydon, Edward. "Bread Wheat's Large and Complex Genome is Revealed". Nov. 17, 2012. www.cshl.edu/news-a-features/bread-wheats-large-and-complex-genome-is-revealed.html.

10."Einkhorn Wheat". Wikipedia. Jan. 10, 2016 https://en.wikipedia.org/w/index.php?title=Einkorn_

wheat&oldid+699058937.

11. Hong-Qing Ling, et al. "Draft Genome of the Wheat A-genome Progenitor Triticum Urartu". Nature, Vol. 496, issue 7443, April 2013, pp. 87-90.

12. Meru, Geoffrey. "Polyploidy". Chapter from Plant Breeding. Available on the internet through Creative Commons Attribution-Noncommercial-Share Alike 3.0. Accessed July 2016.

13. Nester, Eugene. "Agrobacterium: The Natural Genetic Engineer 100 Years Later". University of Washington Department of Microbiology, Seattle, WA 98195. 2008. http://www.apsnet.org/publications/apsnetfeatures/Pages/Agrobacterium.aspx

14. Scientific American, March 2016

15. Hulse, Michelle; Johnson, Stuart; Ferrieri, Patricia. "Agrobacterium Infections in Humans: Experience at One Hospital and Review". Clinical Infectious Diseases, Vol. 16,(1) 1993. http://cid.oxfordjournals.org/content/16/1/112.short

16. Nordlee, Julie A., et.al. "Identification of a Brazil-Nut Allergen in Transgenic Soybeans". The New England Journal of Medicine. Vol. 334, No. 11, Mar. 14, 1996, pp. 688-692.

17. Schurtte, J. "Environmental Fate of Glyphosate." Environmental Monitoring and Pest Management. Dept. Of Pesticide Regulation, Sacramento, Ca. 1998.

18. Fernandez-Salvador, Lindsay. Internet search: Mother Earth News Blogs, "Use and Status of Rotenone in Organic Growing". May 1, 2014.

19. Talbot, A. R., et al. "Acute Poisoning With Glyphosate-

Surfactant Herbicide 'Roundup', a Review of 93 Cases." Human and Experimental Toxicology. Vol. 10, No. 1, pp.1-8. 1991.

20.BfR (Bundesinstitut fur Risikobewertung). "Glyphosate: no more poisonous than previously assumed, although a critical view should be taken of certain co-formulants." Press release, March, 2014.

21.Polyethoxylated Tallow Amine. Wikipedia, Oct. 5, 2015. https://en.wikipedia.org/w/index.php?title=Polyethoxylated_tallow_amine&oldid=684206322

22.Ghassemi, M., et al. "Environmental Fates and Impacts of Major Forest Use Pesticides". P. A-149-168. U.S. Office of Pesticides and Toxic Substances, Washington, D.C. 1981. (As cited by ref. 18).

23.U.S. EPA Pesticide Fact Handbook. Vol. 2, pp. 301-302. Noyes Data Corporation. Park Ridge, New Jersey. 1990. (As cited by ref. 17.)

24.U.S.D.A Forest Service. "Pesticide Background Statements". Agricultural Handbook No. 633, Vol.1, Herbicides, part 2. 1984. (As cited by ref. 17.)

25.Kollman, W., and R. Segawa. "Interim Report of the Pesticide Chemistry Database." Environmental Hazards Assessment Program. Dept. of Pesticide Regulation, Sacramento, Ca. 1995. (As cited by ref. 17.)

26.Rueppel,M. L., et al. "Metabolism and Degeneration of Glyphosate in Soil and Water". Journal of Agriculture and Food Chemistry, 1977, Vol. 25, No. 3 pp. 517-528. (As cited by ref. 18).

27.Duke, S. O. "Glyphosate Degradation in Glyphosate-Resistant and Susceptible Crops and Weeds". Journal of Agriculture and Food Chemistry, 2011, Vol 59, pp. 5835-5841.

28.Gasparro, Annie; Bunge, Jacob. "GMO Labeling Law Roils Food Companies". Wall Street Journal, March 21, 2016, pp. B1, B2.

29.Geoghegan-Quinn, Maire. European Commission Compendium of Results of EU-funded research on Genetically Modified Crops. Press release August 6, 2011.

30.European Commission. A Decade of EU-Funded GMO Research, 2001-2010. Directorate-General for Research and Innovation, Biotechnology, Agriculture, Food. August, 2011. https://ec.europa.eu/research/biosociety/pdf/a_decade_of_eu-funded_gmo_research.pdf

31.Young, J. M., et al. "A revision of Rhizobium Frank 1889, with emended description of the genus, and the Inclusion of all species of Agrobacterium Conn 1942 and Allorhizobium undicola de Lajudie et al. 1998 as new combinations: Rhizhobium radiobacter, R. rhizogenes, R. rubi, R. undicola and R. vitis." International Journal of Systematic and Evolutionery Microbiology. Vol. 51, issue 1. Published online, 01/01/2001.

32."Agrobacterium tumefaciens". Wikipedia. April 8 2016.

33. Gancii, Miranda. "Rhizobium rhizogenes=Agrbacterium rhizogenes". Pathogen profile. Requirement for PP 728 Soilborne Plant Pathogens, fall 2012. Dept. of Plant Pathology, North Carolina State University.

34."Knockout Mouse". Wikipedia. March 20, 2016.

35.Velazquez, Encarna, et al. "The Coexistence of Symbiosis and Pathogenicity-Determining Genes in Rhizobium rhizogenes

Strains Enables Them to Induce Nodules and Tumors or Hairy Roots". Molecular Plant-Microbe Interactions. Vol. 18, No. 12, Dec. 2005, pp. 1325-1332.

36.Legleiter, Travis; Johnson,Bill. "Palmer Amaranth Biology, Identification, and Management." Purdue University Extension. Nov, 2013.

37.Lyon, Drew; Burke, Ian. "Herbicide-Resistant Weeds Coming to a Field Near You?" Wheat Life, January, 2014, p. 51.

38.Kyndt, Tina; et al. "The Genome of Cultivated Sweet Potato Contains Agrobacterium T-DNAs with Expressed Genes: An Example of a Naturally Transgenic Food Crop." Proceedings of the National Academy of Sciences, Vol 112, No. 18, May 5, 2015. http://www.pnas.org/content/112/18/5844.abstract.

39.Schlatter, Daniel C.: et al. "Effect of Glyphosate on Soil Bacterial Communities in Long-Term No-Till and CRP." Washington State University, 2016 Field Day Abstracts, p 74

40.Miller, Henry I, and Conko, Gregory. The Frankenfood Myth. Prager Publishers, 88 Post Road West, Westport, CT 06881. 2004.

41.Miller, Henry I. "National Academy of Sciences' 'GMO' Report Does Science No Favors". Forbes/Opinion/#GMO, May 24, 2016.

42.National Academies of Sciences, Engineering, and Medicine. 2016. Genetically Engineered Crops: Experiences and Prospects. Washington, DC: The National Academies Press. doi: 10.17226/23395.

43.Directorate-General for Research and Innovation. European Commission. A decade of EU-Funded GMO research, 2001-2010. (This report was preceded by a 15-year study of GMOs by the European Commission.)

44.Van Eenennaam, Alison. "Prevalence and Impacts of Genetically Engineered Feedstuffs on Livestock Populations." American Society of Animal Science, Vol 92, pp. 4255-4278. 2014.

45.Millar, Henry I. "Regulators put the Brakes On Biotech." Wall Street Journal, Jan. 14, 2015.

46.Nakazawa, M, et al. "Spontaneous neoplastic lesions in aged Sprague-Dawley Rats". Experimental Animals, Vol. 50, No.2, pp. 99-103. 2001.

47.Seralini, Gilles-Eric, et al. "Long-term Toxicity of a Roundup Herbicide and a Roundup-tolerant Genetically Modifies Maize". Published in Food and Chemical Toxology, September 2012. Retracted in November, 2013. Republished in Environmental Sciences Europe in June, 2014.

48.Entine, Jon. "Zombie Retracted Seralini GMO Maize Rat Study Republished To Hostile Scientist Reactions". Forbes. June 24, 2014.

49.Carroll, Rory. "Zambians Starve as Food Aid Lies Rejected." The Guardian, Oct. 16, 2002.

50."Zambia Refuses GM 'Poison'". BBC News on line. Sept 3, 2002.

51.O'Connell, John. "Simplot Plans GMO-only Seed Potato Farms." Capital Press, July, 2016, p. 7.

52."Will anybody use genetically engineered potatoes?" Agri-Times Northwest, Feb. 6, 2015, p. 11

53.Peter, Constabel C., and Ryan, Clarence A. "A Survey of Wound and Methyl Jasmonate-Induced Leaf Polyphenol Oxidase in Crop Plants." Phytochemistry, Vol. 47, No. 4, pp. 507-511. Feb. 1998.

54.Li, L., and Steffens, J. C. "Overexpression of Polyphenol Oxidase in Transgenic Tomato Plants Results in Enhanced Bacterial Disease Resistance." Planta, Vol. 212, No. 2, pp.239-247. June 2002.

55.Watson, Elaine. "Arctic Apples Creator Neal Carter: We Really Think This Will Be a Game Changer." Feb. 17, 2015. http://www.foodnavigator-usa.com search "Arctic Apples".

56.Murphree, Julie. "A Passion for Storytelling." The Progressive Farmer, Sept. 2016, p. 42.

57.Gruere, G., Mehta-Bhatt, P. and Sengupta, D. "Bt Cotton and Farmer Suicides in India". Discussion Paper 00808. International Food Policy Research Institute, 2008.

58.Yanhui Lu, et.al. "Widesoread Adoption of Bt Cotton and Insectiside Decrease Promotes Biocontrol Services." Nature, June 13, 2012. http://dx.doi.org/10.1038/nature11153

59.Parrington, John. Redesigning Life. Oxford University Press, Great Clarendon Street, Oxford, ox2 6DP, United Kingdom. 2016

60.Rogers, Christian, and Oldroyd, E. D. "Synthetic biology approaches to engineering the nitrogen symbiosis in cereals." Journal of Experimental Botany, Vol. 65, No. 8, pp.1939-1946. 2014.

61.Mus, Florence, et al. "Symbiotic Nitrogen Fixation and the Challenges to Its Extension to Nonlegumes." Applied and Environmental Microbiology, Vol. 82, No. 13, pp.3698-3710. July 2016.

62.Ellis, Sean. "GM sugar beets Save Idaho, Oregon Growers Millions." Capital Press, Jan. 23, 2015, p. 17.

63.Klumper, Wilhelm, and Qaim, Matin. "A Meta-Analysis of the Impacts of Genetically Modified Crops." PLOS ONE, Nov. 3, 2014. http://dx.doi.org/10.1371/journal.pone.0111629

64.McDougall, Phillips. "The cost and time involved in the discovery, development and authorization of s new plant biotechnology derived trait." A Consultancy Study for Crop Life International. 2011.

65.Choudhary, Bhagirath and Gaur, Kadambini. "Biotech Cotton in India, 2002 to 2014." International Service for the Acquisition of Agri-Biotech Applications. ISAAA: Ithaca, NY. 2015.

66.Acquaah, George. Principles of Plant Genetics and Breeding. Second Edition, 2012, p. 461. John Wiley & sons, Ltd.

67.Kard, Brad; Shelton, Kevin; Luper, Charles. "Toxicity of Pesticides." Oklahoma Cooperative Extension Service Pesticide Applicator Certification Series. EPP-7457. Undated.

68.Warner, John. "Toxicities of some Commonly Used Pesticides Compared to a Few Household Chemicals." shalompest. homestead.com/common_pesticide_toxicities.pdf. Undated.

69.Roller, Kieth. "U.S. approves 3 types of blight-resistant GMO potatoes." The Associated Press, March 5, 2017.

70.Duke, Stephen O. "Biotechnology: Herbicide-Resistant Crops." In: Neal Van Alfen, editor-in-chief. Encyclopedia of Agriculture and Food Systems, Vol. 2, San Diego: Elsevier; 2014, pp. 94-116.

71.Correa, Elza Alves, et al. "Glyphosate-Resistant and Conventional Canola (Brassica napus L.) Responses to Glyphosate and Aminomethylphosphonic Acid (AMPA) Treatment." Journal of Agricultural and Food Chemistry, vol. 64, no. 18, pp. 3508-3513. 2016.

72.Wikipedia. "Shikimate pathway." Aug. 5, 2017.

73.Funke, Todd, et al. "Molecular Basis for the Herbicide Resistance of Roundup Ready Crops." Proceedings of the National Academy of Sciences. Vol. 103, no. 35, pp. 13010-13015. Aug., 2006.

74.Kniss, Andrew R. "Long-Term Trends in the Intensity and Relative Toxicity of Herbicide Use." www.nature.com/nature-communications. DOI: 10.1038/ncomms14865.

75.National Academies of Sciences, Engineering, and Medicine. "Genetically Engineered Crops: Experiences and Prospects." The National Academies Press, 2016. Cited in: Kniss [74].

CHAPTER 6.

PESTICIDES: IS OUR FOOD SAFE?

"All things are poison and nothing is without poison: only the dose makes a thing not a poison."—Paracelsus, father of toxicology.

The selecting of plants by hunter-gatherers to grow in concentrated patches near their dwellings provided convenience for people and for pests. As reliance on a good harvest to provide food became a priority, so did the importance of protecting the harvest from the ravages of diseases and insects. The Sumerians, the ancient peoples of the Fertile Crescent who are credited with inventing cities, writing, the wheel, the plow, and civilization itself, recorded, on clay tablets, the first use of pesticides 4500 years ago [1,2,3]. They used sulphur compounds to control mites and insects. Sulphur compounds have been used as crop protectants ever since; still a mainstay for organic farmers, and used by conventional farmers also.

Arsenic compounds also have a long history of use as herbicides, insecticides and fungicides. The Chinese, who used sulphur approximately 3000 years ago to control fungi, were using arsenic sulfides by A.D. 900. Paris green (copper acetoarsenite) was used extensively in the U.S. and other countries beginning about 1850 to control a wide range of insects, including potato beetles, coddling moths (apple worms) and mosquitos. By 1900 lead arsenate was the insecticide of choice, and its use continued until replaced by DDT and other carbon-based insecticides after WWII [4,5].

Washington State banned the use of lead arsenate in 1948. Use continued in other states until the mid-1960s, and in Europe until the mid-1970s. It was not officially banned in the U.S until 1988, but by then all registered uses had ceased. The legacy of lead arsenate is that some fruit orchards cannot be used for any other purpose because of the high levels of residual arsenic and lead in the upper few inches of soil. Residential or playground use means too much exposure for children. Vegetables growing in such soils can take up toxic amounts of these metals [4].

In 1919, experiments concluded that washing produce failed to remove all the lead arsenate residue, but effective substitute insecticides were not available [4]. So, for 100 years or more consumers of healthy fruits and vegetables were also consuming small amounts of toxic, carcinogenic metals. The general public today frets about poisonous chemicals in their food: Their exposure is miniscule compared to past generations. As I related in Chapter One, I ate my share of lead and arsenic from my Mother's garden and from canned goods purchased at the grocery store. Looking back, our food is much safer today than it was in my childhood.

So pesticides have been a part of agriculture for thousands of years, but safety has always taken a back seat before the modern era. Since Rachel Carsen's book, *Silent Spring*, published in 1962, and the establishment of the EPA in 1970 at the urging of President Richard Nixon, public safety has been a priority, for both applicators and consumers.

Absolute safety can never be absolutely proven, but it can be assessed and inferred by experiments with test animals, usually laboratory rats. As explained in Chapter Five, the dose that kills 50 percent of the test animals over a given time period (LD50) is the standard assessment of toxicity. And it should be pointed out again that all farmers, organic and conventional, use pesticides. Further, just because an insecticide is made from chrysanthemum flowers, (pyrethrum), or the roots of tropical legumes (rotenone), or the leaves of tobacco plants (nicotine), and is natural does not mean it is less toxic to or better tolerated by humans than synthetic insecticides.

After toxicity is established, a no–observed-adverse-effect-level (NOAEL) is determined by lowering the dose given test animals until no adverse effects are observed. Then that dose is reduced by a factor of 100 to allow for differences in response that may occur between humans and test animals and for differences between humans. In other words, the dose (per kilogram of body weight) that is allowed to enter a human's diet is 100 times less than the dose that was safe for test animals. This dose is referred to as the Reference Dose (RfD), the maximum daily dose that gives demonstrative assurance that no short-term or long-term adverse health effects will result from registered use of the product over the lifetime of an individual. For chemicals children may encounter, the RfD is lowered by another factor of 10, making the RfD 1000 times lower than the NOAEL.

The next step is to assess how people may be exposed—through food, inhalation, work or other activities that may lead to direct contact with residues. All sources of exposure are then added up to determine the ADI (Average Daily Intake). If the ADI exceeds the Rfd, some uses of the chemical must be denied.

Besides testing for safety to humans, data must be submitted and approved on the safety of metabolites (breakdown products), safety to the environment, residue chemistry, and hazards to domestic animals, wildlife, aquatic organisms, non-target insects, toxicity to target and non-target plants, and much more. Only about one prospective new pesticide out of 160,000 chemicals tested will survive to commercialization. The whole process takes eleven or more years, and costs the developer an average of 286 million dollars [60].

Pesticide critics say data submitted by the company requesting approval cannot be trusted. But government provides rules for running experiments, called Good Laboratory

Practices (GLP). Experimenters must keep copious notes on what they do and what they find, and these notes and the lab or field experiments being conducted are subject to governmental inspection at any time. Fines for falsifying or withholding data can be severe, monetarily as well as public relations-wise [61].

Experiments conducted by academics who do not follow GLP standards is often rejected by regulators. Such experiments are the source of much of the anti-pesticide data cited by activists and published on the internet. For examples of such experiments, see Note 5-1 in Chapter 5.

Testing for carcinogenetic risk of a pesticide goes way beyond the establishment of the RfD. The EPA *Guidelines for Carcinogen Risk Assessment* is 122 pages long [5]. Carcinogenic risk assessment examines all available data on a particular chemical, organized into four areas:

1. Hazard. Can the chemical present a carcinogenic hazard to humans, and, if so, under what circumstance?

2. Dose Response. At what exposure level might effects occur?

3. Exposure. What are the conditions of human exposure?

4. Risk. What is the character of the risk? How well do data support conclusions about the nature and extent of the risk from various exposures?

The EPA considers epidemiologic studies (animal feeding trials that result in tumors of various types) to be of primary importance in assessing risk. Also very important is the mode of action of a particular chemical. Any of the attributes of a potential pesticide listed below could promote tumor formation:

1. Does exposure to the chemical cause mutations?

2. Does the chemical promote cell division (mitogenesis)?

3. Does the chemical inhibit normal cell death (promote cell immortality)?

4. Does the chemical promote cell death and/or promote reparative scarring?

5. Does the chemical depress the immune system?

The unpredictable nature of cancer and the lack of certainty in its many causes means no chemical, natural or synthetic, can be fully exonerated regarding tumor initiation. The EPA, however, strives to "treat uncertainty in a predictable way that is scientifically defensible, consistent with the agency's statutory mission, and responsive to the needs of the decision makers" [5]. The guidelines further state that "estimates (of risk), while uncertain, are more likely to overstate than understate hazard and/or risk." We consumers should have extreme confidence that our food, both conventional and organic, is safe vis-a-vis registered pesticide use.

Dr. BRUCE AMES AND THE AMES TEST

Anyone concerned about pesticide residues in food should familiarize themselves with the work of Dr. Bruce Ames, Professor Emeritus, biochemistry and molecular biology at the University of California, Berkeley. He is still an active researcher at age 88 focusing on cancer and aging. He has authored over 550 scientific publications, and is among the few hundred most-cited scientists in all fields [6].

In the early 1970s, Dr. Ames was convinced man-made chemicals in the environment were causing cancer and set out to prove it. He developed a quick test that would indicate if a chemical was a mutagen. Chemicals that are mutagens can be suspected of being carcinogenic. Using the bacteria *Salmonella typhimurium*, which requires the amino acid histidine for growth, but cannot synthesize it, he developed a biological assay by growing the bacteria on a petri dish with a medium containing a small amount of histidine and the chemical to be examined. A control dish without the test chemical is incubated at the same time.

When the histidine is used up, a few bacteria in the control dish will have mutated so as to make their own histidine and will produce colonies[32] of mutated cells. If the dish containing the test chemical shows more colonies of mutated bacteria than the control, then the chemical is assumed mutagenic, and the extent of mutated colonies is a rough measure of the potency of the mutagen. The probable carcinogenicity can then be confirmed or rejected with animal testing. The Ames test is one of the first tests a prospective new chemical is put through, and is one of eight required by the EPA. It has been shown to correctly predict carcinogenicity of chemicals 70 percent of the time. It is a quick, convenient and cheap way to estimate the carcinogenic potential of a compound [7].

Dr. Ames first used his test in the early 1970s to test some common synthetic chemicals, some of which were found to be carcinogenic and were subsequently banned. A flame retardant used in children's sleepwear, called Tris, was one of the most famous chemicals banned. Others were some formulations used in hair dye and the food additive AF-2 [8].

The testing and ultimate banning of these synthetic chemicals made Dr. Ames a hero of the environmental movement. Then he began testing both natural and synthetic pesticides, and concluded that the presence of synthetic pesticides in food was no more dangerous than the thousands of compounds plants make to protect themselves. His research "led him to denounce what he saw as environmentalists' idyllic and romantic view of a past world that never existed "[9]. The environmental community then considered him a traitor. Here is an abstract from one of his papers:

"The toxicological significance of exposure to synthetic chemicals is examined in the context of exposures to naturally occurring chemicals. We calculate that 99.99% (by weight) of the pesticides in the American diet are chemicals that plants produce to defend themselves. Only 52 natural pesticides have been tested in high-dose animal cancer tests, and

---

[32]Colonies in a petri dish arise from a single cell, and appear as isolated round bumps on the growth medium (augur).

about half (27) are rodent carcinogens; these 27 are shown to be present in many common foods. We conclude that natural and synthetic chemicals are equally likely to be positive in animal cancer tests. We also conclude that at the low doses of most human exposures the comparative hazards of synthetic pesticide residues are insignificant" [10]. By 2001, the number of natural pesticides tested had risen to 71, with 37 (52%) proving to be rodent carcinogens at high doses [32].

In another paper, Dr. Ames and colleague Dr. Gold claim "More than 1000 chemicals have been described in coffee: 28 have been tested and 19 are rodent carcinogens" [11]. Yet, in recent years, coffee has been lauded by many researchers for its beneficial effects. Dr. Ames argues that overzealous environmental regulation of toxic compounds, estimated to cost $140 billion per year (in 1997), takes research money away from the real causes of cancer—smoking, dietary imbalances due to insufficient intake of fruits and vegetables, chronic infections, and hormonal factors "influenced primarily by lifestyle"[11].

Opponents of pesticides argue that humans evolved with plant-produced pesticides and therefore our bodies are able to handle them. That argument lacks logical support. The foods we eat today were unknown to early humans. New world crops—potatoes, tomatoes (both produce low levels of toxic compounds),[33] corn, sunflowers, squash—were unknown to Europeans before the 1500s, and could not have entered the diets of native Americans before settlement of the Americas some 20,000 years ago.

Coffee, which originated in Ethiopia, has no history of use before A.D. 1000. By the early 1500s it was well known in the Middle East, and had spread to the rest of Europe within 100 years [12]. Humans certainly did not evolve consuming its host of carcinogenic compounds. Other foods containing

---

[33]"Potatoes contain solanine and chaconine, which are fat-soluble, neurotoxic, natural pesticides that can be detected in the blood of all potato-eaters" [32].

natural pesticides that have been shown to cause cancer in rats and mice include "anise, apples, bananas, basil, broccoli, brussel sprouts, cabbage,[34] cantaloupe, carrots, cauliflower, celery, cinnamon, cloves, cocoa, grapefruit juice, honeydew melon, horseradish, kale, mushrooms, mustard, nutmeg, orange juice, parsley, parsnips, peaches, pineapples, radishes, tarragon, and turnips" [13].

Could you find a list of more healthful foods? We are constantly told by nutrition experts to eat more fruits and vegetables to provide fiber and vitamins, to protect against heart disease, diabetes, and cancer. Dr. Ames says, "The quarter of the population eating the fewest fruits and vegetables has double the cancer rate for most types of cancer than the quarter eating the most" [11]. How can this be, that foods containing natural carcinogens that cause cancer in rats (in high doses) can also protect humans against cancer when eaten in a normal diet? Perhaps the answer lies in the next subject.

HORMESIS:

Paracelsus, a Swiss-German philosopher in the early 1500s, is credited with being the founder of toxicology for his studies of toxic substances used in small doses to treat medical conditions. He is the originator of the phrase, "The dose makes the poison" [18]. When small quantities of a substance have an effect opposite of a large dose, the substance is said to be "hormetic".

Loosely defined, hormesis is, "what doesn't kill you makes you stronger". When a person vigorously exercises, for instance, body functions and cells are put under stress. When

---

[34] *Brassica oleracea*, a mustard plant growing wild in the Mediterranean, is the progenitor of the family of cruciferous plants we all consider among the healthiest of vegetables--cabbage, cauliflower, brussel sprouts, broccoli, kale, kohlrabi, collard greens. Domestication and the resulting variations of Brassica oleracea began several thousand years ago when "the peoples of the Mediterranean began cultivating wild cabbage. Through artificial selection for various phenotypic traits, the emergence of variations of the plant with drastic differences in looks took only a few thousand years" [14].

allowed to rest and recover, they are stronger for the next exercise session. If an exercise session is too vigorous, bodily damage is done and recovery may not be complete.

We are all familiar with the beneficial effect of low doses of medicines, and also realize that taking more than the prescription allows can damage our organs, or even kill us. Pharmaceutical compounds all exhibit hormetic effects.

We've been told over and over that antioxidants in fruits and vegetables are important for protection from cancer and other diseases. But "in controlled trials in animals and humans, antioxidants, such as vitamins C, E and A, have failed to prevent or ameliorate disease. How then do fruits and vegetables promote health?" [15].

One reason, of course, is that fruits and vegetables are important nutritional sources of vitamins and minerals. But it is a paradox that foods known to contain natural carcinogenic chemicals when concentrated and fed to rodents can be proven to also protect against cancer in humans. This is the essence of hormesis: A salutatory, even protective, effect at low levels and poisonous effects at high levels. Several vitamins and minerals fit this category. A deficiency of vitamin A causes blindness and even death, while an excess of 10 times the RDA (Recommended Daily Dose) over several months can cause toxic effects, such as loss of hair, skin dryness and peeling, headaches and bone and joint pain. Higher doses can even cause coma and death. Toxic effects of high doses of vitamins E, D, B6 and Niacin are also well known [16].

The body needs small amounts of several minerals, but the kidneys must excrete any excess, and if they are overwhelmed serious health complications can result, even death. Too little or too much magnesium or potassium can cause heart arrhythmias, sometimes resulting in heart failure. Selenium is essential for prostate health, but too much encourages cancer [17].

Many researchers have come to the conclusion that the

hormesis that happens when we exercise also happens when we eat our fruits and vegetables. Body processes are put under mild stress when plant compounds the plant produced to protect itself are encountered. The body revs up its defense mechanisms—liver and kidney detox functions, free radical scavenging, DNA repair, etc.—and dismantles and excretes chemicals the body can't use and could be harmful if left lying around in the cell. Consuming a generous amount of fruits and vegetables daily keeps these protective functions in good working order, the same as regular exercise keeps muscles in good shape [15].

There is also reason to believe some synthetic chemicals act in hormetic ways in the human body the same as natural chemicals. DDT, which can produce tumors in rats at high doses, can be protective against tumor production at low doses [21, 22]. TCDD, the terrible toxin found in Agent Orange, and also found in trace amounts sometimes in cooked meat, fish, and dairy products [23], was found to have anticancer effect at low doses in a long-term (2-year) study by Kociba, et al [24]. Their study also formed the basis of the EPA decision declaring TCDD a carcinogen [23], but research done by Cole, et al [27], suggests "the long-term accumulation of negative, weak, and inconsistent findings suggests that TCDD will eventually be recognized as not carcinogenic for humans". Acrylamide, a group 2A carcinogen we met in the discussion of Innate potatoes in Chapter 5, was found by Mucci, et al, [25,26] to decrease risk of colorectal, kidney and bladder cancers with increasing dosage.

Hayes [23], who reviewed the above papers, concludes that "Evidence for nutritional hormesis arising from essential nutrients (vitamins and minerals), dietary pesticides (natural and synthetic), dioxin and other herbicides, and acrylamide… is an operational definition of Paracelsus' dictum that the efficacy of toxic chemicals depends on dosage which in no way negates the historic misuse and dangers of many of these things. Nutritional hormesis could very well be applicable as a pro-health intervention by extending human healthspan."

Dr. Ames and others are convinced that the natural anti-toxin defenses animals (including humans) possess are of a general nature and protect against both synthetic compounds and plant–produced toxins. As a species, we are well-buffered against the miniscule amounts of synthetic pesticides we consume daily as opposed to the amount of natural plant toxins (1500mg of natural pesticides per day vs. .09mg of synthetic pesticides [28]). Quoting from Ames et.al [19], these defenses include:

1. "The continuous shedding of cells exposed to toxins: The surface layers of the mouth, esophagus, stomach, intestine, colon, skin, and lung are discarded every few days."

2. "The induction of a wide variety of general de-toxifying mechanisms, such as antioxidant defenses," enzymes that detoxify carcinogenic agents, and resistance to cell damage because of prior low-dose exposure to an oxidant such as hydrogen peroxide or the herbicide paraquat.[35]

3. Active excretion of xenobiotic (foreign) molecules (natural or synthetic) out of liver and intestinal cells.

4. DNA repair in response to adducts (attachment of natural or synthetic molecules to the DNA strand) that could result in cancer.

Dr. Ames, et al, summarizes their paper thusly: "Synthetic pesticides have markedly lowered the cost of plant food, thus increasing consumption. Eating more fruits and vegetables and less fat may be the best way to lower risks of cancer and heart disease, other than giving up smoking."

---

[35] The current practice of feeding young children small amounts of peanuts to condition them against peanut allergy is an example of the "prior low-dose" defense.

HORMETIC EFFECTS IN FARMERS' FIELDS

Hormetic effects of herbicides applied at sub-lethal doses has been commonly observed, beginning with 2,4-D in the middle of the 20th century. Belz and Duke [20] reviewed a number of peer-reviewed reports of hormetic effects and summarized them in their paper. They list the beneficial effects from sub-lethal applications of 16 different herbicides. Effects ranged from increased dry weight of shoots or roots to increased yield or protein content or increased disease resistance. Low-dosage glyphosate has been shown to increase the yield of chickpeas and barley, increase the growth of corn, soybeans, Eucalyptus and pine trees, and have various hormetic effects on 15 other plants [62]. Experimental results are variable, however, and very sensitive to environmental conditions and the stage of growth when the application is made, making it difficult to make sensible recommendations to farmers. Egyptian researchers report that glyphosate can hormetically increase the growth and yield of Faba beans [30]. Several different herbicides hormeticaly increase the sugar content of sugar cane when applied as a ripening aid [31].

"Drift related hormesis by 2,4,D has been reported to enhance tomato yields considerably, to the benefit of the farmer" [20]. Belz and Duke conclude that yield enhancement may also be relevant for drift associated with glyphosate applications, as drift rates equate to stimulatory doses reported for crops.

PESTICIDES IN THE NEWS: THE REST OF THE STORY

Roundup. We reviewed glyphosate (the active ingredient in Roundup) quite extensively in Chapter 5, but the allegations that it causes cancer need to be addressed. In March of 2015, the International Agency for Research on Cancer (IARC, the research arm of the United Nations World Health Organization) designated glyphosate as category 2A carcinogen (probably carcinogenic to humans). For comparison, other things classified as 2A include working as a barber or hair stylist, working the night shift, indoor emissions from burning wood, very hot beverages (over 149°F) and acrylamide, the compound created from the amino acid asparagine when some foods are cooked.

The designation of 2A was met with much glee by the anti-Monsanto press and NGOs, and by disbelief and anger by pesticide experts worldwide. Monsanto was understandably furious, and quickly funded a study by Intertek Scientific & Regulatory Consultancy, which employed 16 independent scientists to do a review. The study was published in the *Journal of Critical Reviews in Toxicology,* Vol. 46, Sept., 2016. The reviewers examined evidence excluded by IARC and concluded glyphosate is unlikely to pose a cancer risk to humans. Not a surprise to cynical critics of Industry-funded research.

More difficult to ignore is the opinion rendered by the German Federal Institute for Risk Assessment (BfR). They state The IARC conclusion was based on only a few studies that were poorly understood [33]. The IARC based its risk assumption on three epidemiological studies from the USA, Canada and Sweden on farm workers. The Canadian and Swedish studies were too small to be conclusive, and the American Health Study of 57,311 pesticide applicators reported 32 cases of multiple myeloma among 54,315 applicators that had ever used glyphosate. This was not enough cases to be statistically significant, even at a low (95%) confidence level. The study therefore provides "no convincing evidence...for a link between multiple myeloma risk and glyphosate use" [34].

Further damaging the IARC position on glyphosate is expert opinion from the U.N.'s Food and Agriculture Organization and World Health Organization (IARC's sponsor) who say glyphosate is "unlikely to pose a carcinogenic risk to humans" through food [35]. In addition, the US EPA issued a 227 page report on glyphosate in Sep. 2016 that concludes: "The available data at this time do not support a carcinogenic process for glyphosate", [36, p. 140]. Add to that a similar conclusion reached by the European Food Safety Authority (EFSA), charged with setting maximum chemical residue levels in the European Union. They conclude "glyphosate is unlikely to pose a carcinogenic hazard to humans and the evidence does not support (i.e., IARC) classification with regard to its carcinogenic potential..." [37, abstract].

Photo 6. Concerned about Roundup drift? This field was sprayed with Roundup preparatory to planting. One nozzle on a 90-foot boom was plugged. Note there is no discernable damage to the plants under the plugged nozzle from drift coming from nozzles 20 inches on either side. (Photo by Author.)

The IARC action, which disregarded dozens of studies that countered their conclusion, smacks of a politically driven, reckless and irresponsible committee that disregards the paranoia their decisions can cause in a scientifically illiterate population. Thousands of lawsuits were soon filed against Monsanto claiming Roundup caused their cancer, no matter what kind, while the IARC only found limited evidence for multiple myeloma among pesticide handlers. It has also sparked a wave of erroneous blogs about Roundup, such as the charge that Roundup is applied to all wheat as a pre-harvest desiccant. Totally false. It is legal to use Roundup in that manner to kill weeds that may still be alive and troublesome after the wheat is ripe, but a ripe plant absorbs zero Roundup. And very few farmers ever need to use Roundup in that way (less than three percent of U.S. wheat acres [63]).

Agent Orange. Monsanto seems to catch all the blame for the evils of Agent Orange. The anger towards Monsanto by the environmental movement and the press is totally unfair. Monsanto was one of seven (one website says 9) wartime government contractors who manufactured the product to the specifications of the US military. The other six manufactures were Dow Chemical Co., Hercules Inc., Diamond Shamrock Corporation, Uniroyal Inc., Thompson Chemical Company and Thompson-Hayward Chemical Company [38]. These companies were not the original formulators of the two herbicides, 2,4-D and 2,4,5-T, that were mixed 50-50 to make Agent Orange, so named because of the orange band painted on the drums containing the mix.

According to a 1967 herbicide book, AgChem Products, Inc.—a paint formulator in Pennsylvania that got into the agricultural pesticide business--is credited with originating 2,4-D in 1942 and 2,4,5-T in 1944 [39]. Wikipedia [45] implies they were developed in response to government efforts to produce biological warfare agents during WWII. The company manufactured these herbicides in Ambler, Pennsylvania, until 1979 when the company was sold to Henkel [40,41]. Henkel is a German chemical company, the maker of leading brands Dial soap, Purex, and Loctite. Not a manufacturer of pesticides according to their website.

2,4,5-T contaminated with the dioxin TCDD[36] was the poisonous culprit in Agent Orange. 2,4-D was the innocent partner, and hundreds of studies over the past 60 years have proven its safety. 2,4,5-T can be manufactured with safe (some people will argue there is no safe level) levels of TCDD when manufactured at low temperatures. High-temperature manufacture was used by makers of 2,4,5-T for the Department of Defense because it's a cheaper process, and cheaper is how you win government contracts.

In 1952, years before Agent Orange was formulated according to Department of Defense specifications, "army officials had been informed by Monsanto Chemical Co., later a major manufacturer of Agent Orange, that 2,4,5-T was contaminated with a toxic substance" [42]. Dow Chemical, according to internal memos revealed in court, knew their product was contaminated with dioxin as early as 1964. In another memo in 1965, Dow warned other manufacturers of the need to resolve the problem, and took steps to lower TCDD content in their product, but other manufacturers did not [43]. As a result, the court settlement of 1984, in which the manufacturers settled claims against them regarding Agent Orange, let Dow pay a lesser share because they had taken steps to remove dioxin [44].

Dow did the morally right thing here, but that doesn't make the rest of the manufacturers "bad guys". In 1988, 13 years after the war ended, an Air Force officer and scientist involved in "Operation Ranch Hand", James Clary, "dropped a bombshell" in a letter to then Senator Tom Daschle: "Military scientists had known that herbicides shipped to Vietnam were contaminated with dioxin and had 'the potential for damage' to human health. 'However, because the material was to be used on the enemy, none of us were overly concerned…We never considered a scenario in which our own personnel would become contaminated with the herbicide [43].'"

_____

[36] Dioxins are ubiquitous in the environment whenever anything is burned--from high-temperature waste incineration to wood stoves to burned toast. Seventy-six different chlorinated dioxins are known, 17 of which are regulated in manufacturing processes and the environment by the EPA. TCDD (2,3,7,8-tetrachlorodibenzo-p-dioxin) is by far the most poisonous [46].

I am using space to detail the involvement of Monsanto with Agent Orange and the association of 2,4-D with the mixed herbicide because now that crops are being genetically engineered to tolerate 2,4-D, the environmental spokespersons waste no opportunity to point out, unfairly in my view, that 2,4-D was a component of Agent orange, and the inventor of Roundup and Roundup Ready seeds (Monsanto) also manufactured Agent Orange. Their argument is misleading: 2,4-D has been safely used by farmers around the world since WW II. Monsanto was not the progenitor of Agent Orange, the U.S. military owns that distinction.

Farmers who are encountering weeds resistant to Roundup need this 2,4-D tolerant technology to be able to continue a no-till farming strategy that is so important in controlling erosion and maintaining productive soils. I know many people will counter that weeds will also become resistant to 2,4-D. Perhaps they will, but farmers and chemical companies have learned from the Roundup experience, and strategies to prevent weed resistance are being more universally applied: Rotation of herbicides, rotation of crops, and tillage when necessary. Also, resistance to two or more herbicides in a single weed genome is a more difficult project for a weed species to accomplish.

Neonicotinides. The August 19, 2013 cover of Time magazine is an extreme example of media bad news hyperbole. "A World without Bees—the Price We Will Pay if We Don't Figure Out what's Killing the Honeybee". The feature story starts with," You can thank the *Apis Mellifera*, better known as the Western honeybee, for 1 in every 3 mouthfuls of food [47]." That is the first of several exaggerations in the article. The truth is, grain crops, including soybeans, provide most of the world's calories, and they don't require a pollinator. It is true that diets would be boring without the plants that benefit from honeybee pollination—squashes and melons, fruits such as apples and blueberries, and some nuts (especially almonds). These crops wouldn't disappear if the honeybees and other pollinators became extinct, but yields would go way down and they would be expensive luxury foods. After all, squashes and tomatoes, both New World crops, didn't see a honeybee until the Europeans brought them to the Americas in the 1600s.

So what's killing the bees? Pesticides, according to environmentalists, especially the class of pesticides called neonicotinides or neonics. These insecticides are chemically similar to nicotine and are neuro-active (brain-affecting). One of them, imidacloprid, is the most widely used insecticide in the world [48]. They are more toxic to insects than to birds or mammals, unlike the organophosphates and carbamate insecticides they replace. They are systemic when applied to seeds or leaves, meaning they spread through the plants circulation system to all parts of the plant. As a result, they are especially effective against sucking insects, such as aphids. When used as a seed treatment, soil insects such as wireworms (larval stage of click beetles) are killed when they consume the seed.

Surviving seeds will spread the chemical to the growing plant parts, and when the plant is small the chemical concentration will be an effective insecticide against sucking insects. As the plant matures, the chemical becomes increasingly diluted in plant tissues. By the time flowers are produced and bees are feeding on the nectar and pollen, the chemical is too dilute to harm the bees. The experience of beekeepers in Canada proves this point. Canadian farmers grow 19 million acres of canola yearly. Canola doesn't need bees to pollinate, but beekeepers love to place their hives close to canola fields because bees working canola flowers produce lots of honey. Most canola seed is treated with neonics, but Canadian beekeepers "say their hives are generally thriving" [49]. A large scale field experiment by researchers in Canada in which bee

174

hives were exposed to fields of canola found that, "colonies were vigorous during and after the exposure period, and we found no effects of exposure to clothianidin seed-treated canola on any endpoint measures" [50].

Colony collapse disorder (CCD) has been in the news since 2006 when beekeepers first began reporting excessive hive collapse of 30 percent or more during the winter and spring. Beekeepers expect to lose 10 percent of their hives each year, but several years of excessive losses followed the 2006 collapse. The affected hives often have a queen and plenty of food, maybe a few nurse bees, but no worker bees and no clues to their disappearance. Colony collapse is not a new phenomenon; it comes and goes and is as old as beekeeping, but has gone by other names [51,52]. But the severity of the losses the past decade in the United States and Europe has been cause for concern.

Even with yearly losses of 20-30 percent, beekeepers have been able to rebuild hive numbers each year (though at increased expense), and, worldwide, hive numbers have never lost their upward momentum. The threat of extinction is an environmentalist fabrication. Just another excuse to blame pesticides and GMOs. The writer of the *Time* article accuses farmers of "dousing their fields with pesticides "and "soaking" seeds with systemics before they are planted. Seeds are not "soaked". They are covered with a light patina of fungicide (to prevent attacks by soil-borne pathogens), and often also with an insecticide to protect against soil-inhabiting insect larva as well as sucking insects as the plant grows. A tiny amount of pesticide applied to the seed can obviate the need for pesticide sprays later in the growth cycle, a savings for the farmer and the environment. And fields are never "doused". Five to ten gallons of water per acre containing a few ounces of pesticide is not "dousing".

So what is killing the bees? According to research the last 10 years, a combination of many different things that can affect colony health. Beekeepers must constantly fight a host of parasites and pathogens, with the worst being a tiny mite that sucks the hemolymph (bee blood) from a bees body, compromising the immune system and vectoring "more than a dozen viruses into the bee colony"[52]. Called the *varroa destructor* mite, it has plagued U.S. beekeepers since its introduction in the late 1980s. It is a worldwide problem with the exception of Australia which has so far avoided its importation. Beekeepers must carefully use insecticides and fungicides in their hives to control this mite and other parasites and pathogens that can destroy a hive.

Two studies done by Chensheng Lu of Harvard University [58,59] portend to blame neonics for CCD, and are cited by environmental groups as proof the insecticides should be banned. However, the studies have been regarded by other scientists as not typical of "real world" exposure, and are therefore meaningless. Lu fed bees different rates of two neonic pesticides in sugar water for a total of 13 weeks. No symptoms of bee distress were observed during the 13-week treatment period, and bees were alive 12 weeks following treatment. However, 23 weeks post-post treatment, 94 percent of the treated hives were empty of bees—symptomatic of CCD [58]. This study was highly criticized because of (a) small number of hives (4 treatments of 4 hives each), (b) atypical exposure time (13 weeks vs. 2 weeks in the "real world"), and (c) dosages five to ten times higher than those typically encounteredl in the "real world".

Several studies of the role of neonics in colony collapse disorder have exonerated this class of insecticides as a major cause of CCD. Australia, which has no varroa mites, uses neonic pesticides on many crops where bees forage, but beekeepers have little problem with CCD [47]. In Washington State, researchers from the State University collected samples of stored pollen (beebread) from 149 apiaries in rural and urban areas across the state in 2014. Neonic residues were detectable in 50 percent of apiaries in agricultural landscapes and five percent of apiaries in urban or non-agricultural rural landscapes. The amounts of neonics detected "were substantially smaller than levels shown in other studies to not have effects on honeybee colonies" [53]. "The calculated risk quotient based on a Dietary No Observable Effect Concentration (NOAEC) suggested low potential for negative effects on bee behavior or colony health" [54]. And a 2010 study by the USDA Agricultural Research Service "looked at 170 pesticides or their residues in honeybees, beeswax, and pollen. The data showed no consistent pattern of pesticide residues that differed between healthy and CCD-affected colonies. The most commonly found pesticide in the study was coumaphos, which is used by beekeepers to treat honey bees for Varroa mites" [55]. Coumaphos is an organophosphate insecticide that is neuro-toxic like the neonics, and the effects of the two pesticides are additive [56], which could be a factor in CCD [57].

CONCLUSIONS

Pesticide paranoia promulgated by the NGOs and distributed by a gullible and hyperbolic press is irresponsible when one considers the many hoops a pesticide must jump through and the wide margin of safety (100-1000 times the **No Observable Adverse Effect Level,** or NOAEL), built into the allowable ADI (Allowable Daily Intake). These government programs cost our economy an estimated $140 billion per year, and would be worth it if they significantly reduced cancer and other disease, which, according to the research of Dr. Ames and others, they do not. Our daily intake of carcinogenic substances produced naturally by plants exceeds the daily dose of synthetic carcinogens by 16,667:1 (1500mg vs. .09mg). We eat natural pesticides every day in parts per thousand or parts per million: Synthetic pesticides, when consumed, are eaten in parts per billion or trillion.

The Food and Drug administration conducts a yearly food basket survey to determine pesticide residues on food. Most foods show no residues at all, and when they do the amount rarely is above the one percent level of the ADI, usually no more that .01 percent of the ADI and often less than .01 percent [29]. The fact that pesticide residues can be detected does not mean they pose a health problem. The author of the above paper [29] concludes: "Chronic dietary exposure to pesticides in the diet...continue to be at levels far below those of health concern. Consumers should be encouraged to eat fruits, vegetables, and grains and should not fear levels of pesticide residues found in such foods."

Research strongly suggests that low doses of otherwise carcinogenic chemicals, natural and synthetic, likely rev up the body defenses against cancer in a process called hormesis. Hormesis has also been shown to be an active process in the plant kingdom, with very low doses of otherwise plant-killing herbicides stimulating growth in target plants.

Pesticides have been used by farmers to protect their food supply for centuries. Without them, food would be much more expensive, and much more land would be needed to insure an adequate food supply, resulting in less habitat for wildlife. And fungus diseases of grains and other crops that can produce aflatoxins and fumosisins (very carcinogenic), ergot (very poisonous) and other poisonous mycotoxins, as well as allergens (e, g., smuts), would be a common problem in foods based on grains and/or nuts. Organic farming methods offer no significant protection from these diseases, and their occurrence would likely become more common if synthetic protective products that reduce the natural fungus spore load in the environment were banned. For a sustainable agriculture that produces a safe, abundant food supply for a growing world population while preserving wildlife habitat, synthetic crop protection chemicals (pesticides) are indispensable.

CHAPTER 6 REFERENCES

1.Unsworth, John. "History of Pesticide Use". May 10, 2010. http://agrochemicals.iupac.org/index.php?option=com_sobi2&sobi2Task=sobi2...

2.Wooley, C. Leonard. The Sumerians. Barnes & Noble, Inc. 1995.

3.Redman, Charles L. "Mesopotamia and the First Cities". Great Civilizations. Fog City press, 814 Montgomery Street, San Francisco, CA, 94133. 2003

4.Peryea, Francis J. "Historical Use of Lead Arsenate Insecticides, Resulting Soil Contamination and Implications for Soil Remediation." Washington State University Tree Fruit and Extension Center. August, 1998.

5.Guidelines for Carcinogen Risk Assessment. EPA/630/P-03/001F. March, 2005.

6.Wikipedia. Bruce Ames. Dec., 2016.

7.Wikipedia. Ames Test. Dec., 2016.

8."Bruce Ames, Testing for Carcinogens." Science Policy Ad. Search Bing: Tris-BP, bruce ames. May 22, 2015.

9.Prono, Luca. "Bruce Ames: American Biochemist and Geneticist". Jan 16, 2014. Search: Britannica.

10.Ames, Bruce; Profet, M.; Gold, L. S. "Dietary Pesticides (99.99% all Natural)". Proceedings of the National Academy of Sciences. Vol. 87, No. 19, Oct. 1, 1990, pp. 7777-7781.

11.Ames, Bruce; Gold, L. S. "Environmental Pollution, Pesticides, and the Prevention of Cancer: Misconceptions." The Federation of American Societies for Experimental Biology Journal, vol. 11, no. 13, pp. 1041-1052

12.Wikipedia. "History of Coffee." Dec., 2016.

13.Commentary, The Scientist, July 10, 1989.

14.Wikipedia. "Brassica oleracea." Dec., 2016.

15.Mattson, mark. "What Doesn't Kill You…" Scientific American, July, 2015, pp.41-45.

16.The Merck Manual of Medical Information, Second Edition, 2003, pp. 890-914.

17.National Cancer Institute "Selenium and Vitamin E Cancer Prevention Trial (SELECT)": Questions and Answers. July 7, 2015.

18.Wikipedia. "Paracelsus."

19.Ames, Bruce N.; Profet, Margie: Gold, Lois Swirsky. "Nature's Chemicals and Synthetic Chemicals: Comparative Toxicology". Proceedings of the National Academy of Sciences, vol. 87, pp. 7782-7786,. Oct., 1990.

20.Beltz, Regina; Duke, Stephen. "Herbicides and Plant Hormesis." Pest Management Science, vol. 70, no. 5, pp.698-707. May 2014.

21.Kushida, M, et al. "Low Dose DDT Inhibition of Hepatocarcinogenisis inhibited by Diethylni-trosamine in Male Rats: Pssible Mechanisms." Toxicology and Applied Pharmacology. Vol 208, pp.285-294. 2005.

22.Sukata, T, et al. "Detailed low-dose study of 1,1-bis(p-chlorophenyl)-2,2,2-trichloroethane carcinogenesis suggests the possibility of a hormetic effect." International Journal of Cancer. Vol. 99, pp.112-118. 2002.

23.Hayes, Daniel P. "Nutritional Hormesis an Aging." Dose-Response:an international Journal. Vol. 8, no. 1, pp.10-15. 2010. University of Massachusetsetts.

24.KOciba, R. J., et al. "Results of a two-year chronic toxicity and oncogenicity study of 2,3,7,8-tetrachlorodibenzo-dioxin in rats." Toxicology and Applied Pharmacology. Vol 46, pp. 279-303. 1978.

25.Mucci, L. A., et al. "Dietary acrylamide and cancer of the large bowel, kidney, and bladder: absence of an association in a population-based study in Sweden." British Journal of Cancer. Vol. 88, pp. 84-89. 2003a.

26.Mucci, L. A., et al. "Reply: dietary acrylamide and cancer risk: additional data on coffee." British Journal of Cancer. Vol. 89, pp.756-775. 2003b.

27.Cole, P, et al. "Dioxin and cancer: a critical review." Regulatory Toxicology and Pharmacology. Vol. 38, pp. 378-388. 2003.

28.Brody, Jane E. "SCIENTIST AT WORK: Bruce N. Ames: Strong Views on Origins of Cancer." The New York Times, Science Section, July 5, 1994.

29.Winter, Carl K. "Chronic exposure to pesticide residues in the United States." Springer Open International Journal of Food Contamination. July 10, 2015. DOI: 10.1186/s40550-015-0018-y.

30.El-Shahawy, T. A. and Faida A. A. Sharara. "Hormesis Influence of Glyphosate in Between Increasing Growth, Yield and Controlling Weeds in Faba Bean." Botany Dept., National Research Centre, Dokki, Cairo, Egypt. Journal of American Science. Vol. 7, no. 2, pp.139-144. 2011.

31.McDonald, Lisa; Morgan, Terry; Jackson, Phil. "The Effect of Ripeners on the CCS of 47 Sugarcane Varieties in the Burdekin." Proceedings of the Australian Society of Sugar Cane Technology. Vol. 23, pp.102-108. 2001.

32.Gold, Lois Swirsky, et al. "Pesticide Residues in Food and Cancer Risk: A Critical Analysis." Chapter 38 in Handbook of Pesticide Toxicology, Second Edition, R. Krieger, ed., pp.799-843. Academic Press, San Diego, Ca. 2001.

33.Tribe, David. "German agency says IARC glyphosate decision based on poor evidence." Genetic Literacy Project. March 24, 2015.

34.Sorahan, T. "Multiple myeloma and glyphosate use: a re-analysis of US Agricultural Health Study (AHS) data." International Journal of Environmental Research and Public Health. Vol. 28, no. 2, Jan. 28, 2015, pp. 1548-59.

35.Reuters, as reported in No-Till Farmer, July 2016, p. 9.

36.Glyphosate Issue Paper: "Evaluation of Carcinogenic Potential." EPA's Office of Pesticide Programs, Sept 12, 2016.

37."Peer review of the pesticide risk assessment of the active substance glyphosate." European Food Safety Authority Journal, vol. 13, no. 11. November, 2015.

38.Dow Chemical Co. ehttp://www.dow.com/en-us/about-dow/issues-and-challenges/agent-orang August 23, 2012.

39. Thomson, W.T. Agricultural Chemicals Book II—Herbicides, 1967 Revision. Thomson Publications, Davis, California.

40. Dioxin Registry report for Amchem Products, Incorporated, Ambler, Pennsylvania. www.osti.gov/scitech/biblio/5812199 Jan. 1, 1991.

41. Amchem Products, Inc. records. http://hdl.library.upenn.edu/1017/d/pacscl/HSP_WVHS06 1925-1986.

42. Schuck, Peter H. Agent Orange On Trial: Mass Toxic Disasters in the Courts. Page 17. Harvard University Press.

43. Brown, Drew. "Makers of Agent Orange followed formula dictated by U.S. government." McClatchy News, July 22, 2013. mcclatchydc.com/news/nation-world/article24781345.html

44. "Waiting For an Army to Die?" Agent Orange Record, 2010. agentorangerecord.com/information/the_quest_for_additional_relief

45. Wikipedia. "Agent Orange."

46. Sears, Meg. "Dioxins in Herbicides—A Primer." The Coalition for a Healthy Ottawa. http://www.flora.org/healthyottawa/2,4-d-dioxin-herbicide-pesticide.htm Jan. 9, 2014.

47. Walsh, Bryan. "The Plight of the Honeybee." Time, Aug. 19, 2013.

48. Wikipedia. "Neonicotinoid."

49. Entine, Jon. "Bee Deaths Reversal: As Evidence Points Away from Neonics As Driver, Pressure Builds to Rethink Ban." Forbes. Feb. 5, 2014.

50.Cutler, G. Christopher, et al, "A large –scale field study examining effects of exposure to clothianidin seed-treated canola on honey bee colony health, development, and overwintering success." PubMed 25374790. Oct. 30, 2014. https://doi.org/10.7717/peerj.652

51.Wikipedia. "Colony Collapse Disorder."

52."Beepocalypse Myth Handbook: Dissecting claims of pollinator collapse." Genetic Literacy Project, Jon Entine, editor. July 28, 2016. https://www.geneticliteracyproject.org/2016/28/beepocalypse-myth-handbook-dissecting-claims-of-pollinator-collapse/

53.Wheat, Dan. "Neonics pose low risk for honeybees, WSU says." Capital Press, Aug. 19, 2016.

54.Lawrence, T. J., et al. "Survey and Risk Assessment of Apis mellifera (Hymenoptera: Apidae) Exposure to Neonicotinoid Pesticides in Urban, Rural, and Agricultural Settings." Journal of Economic Entomology, online, Jan. 19, 2016. http://dx.doi.org/10.1093/jee/tov397

55."ARS Honey Bee Health and Colony Collapse Disorder." USDA ARS Office of Communications. Oct. 20, 2016. https://www.ars.usda.gov/oc/br/ccd/index

56.Morelle, Rebeca. March 27, 2013. http://www.bbc.co.uk/news/science-environment-21958547

57.Wikipedia. "Coumaphos."

58.LU, Chensheng, et al. "In situ replication of honey bee colony collapse disorder." Bulletin of Insectology 65 (1): 99-106, 2012. ISSN 1721-8861.

59.LU, Chensheng, et al. "Sub-lethal exposure to neonicoti-noids impaired honey bees winterization before proceeding to colony collapse disorder." Bulletin of Insectology 67 (1): 125-130, 2014. ISSN 1721-8861.

60.Mc Dougall, Phillips. "The cost of New Agrochemical Product Discovery, Development and Registration in 1995, 2000, 2005-8 and 2010 to 2014." A Consultancy Study for CropLife International, CropLife America and the European Crop Protection Association. March, 2016.

61.(Web Search) EPA Good Laboratory Practices Standards Compliance Monitoring Program. Accessed May, 2017.

62.Brito, BFS Ivana, et al. "Hormetic Effects of Glyphosate on Plants." Society of Chemical Industry. Published online Jan. 17, 2017, wileyonlinelibrary.com DOI 10.1002/ps.4523.

63.The National Wheat Foundation. "How do Wheat Grow-ers Use Glyphosate?" df. October, 2017, pp. 38-40.

CHAPTER 7.

SEEDS OF DESTRUCTION?
THE WAR AGAINST BIG AG

*"And he gave it for his opinion, that whoso-
ever could make two ears of corn or two blades of
grass grow upon a spot of ground where only one
grew before, would deserve better of mankind and
do more essential service to his country, than the
whole race of politicians together."*
—Jonathan Swift, *Gulliver's Travels.*

In 2007, William Engdahl, an engineer and economist writing under the auspices of the Centre for Research on Globalization, published *Seeds of Destruction. The Hidden Agenda
of Genetic Manipulation* [1]. As in other books he has written about oil, global warming, and politics, conspiracy is his
theme. He accuses the decades-long effort by foundations
and governments to alleviate hunger and starvation in developing countries to be nothing more than a long-running
conspiracy to allow America's big grain exporters and big
agricultural chemical companies to control world agriculture. The Green Revolution and Food for Peace programs
were a part of this 60-year-plus conspiracy. So was Ronald
Reagan's efforts to make the U. S. the center for research
on genetically modified organisms. All these were merely
programs to promote the domination of world agriculture by
America's corporate giants.

To maintain a conspiracy for three generations would be
a remarkable feat. Only a mind that sees cynicism in every
decision by government and industry to promote agricultural
efficiency, crop yields, nutritional quality and sufficiency for

the world's poorest and hungriest people, could write such a book. I concede that corporate activities in government or in the marketplace are not always completely honest or in the best interest of the environment. It is the job of government regulators to see that corporations do not harm the environment, employ monopolies in the marketplace, or otherwise cause harm to customers. The people who write and enforce these regulations are not infallible: That regulations sometimes fail to protect is inevitable.

The fact that businesses will lobby government to pursue policies favorable to them is as old as business itself. Companies do not pursue new technologies for altruistic or generous motives. They pursue them because they see a potential profit. Companies seek to produce products that people and businesses want: Technologies that will improve productivity of workers and, in the case of Big Ag, productivity of the land or animal resource. If they can make money for the farmer, the company will make money. Saying that begets "control" over agriculture by big agricultural supply corporations (Big Ag) is like saying the grocery store gets control over its customers by increasing the food choices available. No one is forcing any farmer to adopt any new technology.

Norman Borlaug is credited with "fathering" the Green Revolution that saved India from a future of mass starvation and turned it into a self-sufficient, sometimes wheat exporting country. For his extraordinary accomplishments, supported by the Rockefeller Foundation, Norman Borlaug received the Nobel Peace Prize in 1970. India awarded him their second highest civilian honor, The Paduma Vibhushan. President Carter awarded him the Presidential Medal of Freedom in 1977. He is credited with saving a billion lives from starvation worldwide. According to Engdahl, the Green Revolution was all part of the Rockefeller Foundation's conspiracy to control world agriculture. If showing third world farmers how to produce enough calories to keep a billion extra people fed is controlling, then control can't be all bad.

Engdahl also makes much of the fact that companies won't allow farmers to save seed that has been patented. This, he alleges, makes the world farmers dependent on the seed companies for the means of their production, thereby making control of agriculture by the big corporations complete. One thing should be made very clear here: No one can prevent a First or Third World farmer from saving seed varieties he has always planted if that is what he/she wants to plant. Farmers in the First and Third worlds buy the patented, improved seeds because they make them money, even if they can't save the seed for planting the next year. Let's be real. Companies can't spend millions of dollars developing a variety only to get paid one time. No one expects pharmaceutical companies to do that. Or software companies. Why should seed companies be expected to do that?

Corn growers haven't been able to save seed from their fields since the introduction of hybrids in the 1930s. Doing so would result in plants that segregate into many different phenotypic characteristics, and likely would not yield well. To forgo hybrids and plant an open-pollinated variety (not a hybrid), as much of the Third World still does, is to harvest approximately 50 bushels per acre instead of 150-200.

Farmers in developing countries know a good technology when they see one. In the biography of Norman Borlaug, *Facing Starvation*, Borlaug relates a story of an uncontrolled release of his first semi-dwarf wheat crosses that would eventually feed billions of people. Borlaug had come to Mexico in 1944 to survey the state of Mexico's agriculture for the Rockefeller Foundation. He was appalled by the poverty of the farmers, who had been growing the same crops on the same fields until there were no nutrients left, and their wheat crops were plagued almost yearly by ruinous rust diseases. Their government was indifferent to their plight, and they did not trust meddling politicians and academics such as Borlaug.

Supported by the Rockefeller Foundation, Borlaug planted his first plots at a rundown, abandoned experimental farm near Obregon, Mexico, in 1945, pulling his seeder with a rope because no farmer would lend him a tractor. It took years for Borlaug to gain the trust and respect of Obregon's farmers. The first time he held a field day to showcase his breeding efforts to area farmers, no one came. Later, in 1960, Borlaug's rust-resistant wheat varieties had saved Mexico's farmers millions of pesos, and they revered him. Not only had he given Mexico new varieties, he had taught a cadre of young *agronomos* to carry on the breeding work themselves.

This field day in 1960 was a special one, because the first crosses displaying semi-dwarf (short straw) characteristics were on display, plants from which the Green Revolution would emerge. Farmers came from far and wide to these field days now. Flatbed trucks and trailers were used to transport the attendees around the thousands of plots, stopping regularly so that the *agronomo* in charge could lecture the farmers. The farmers were told to stay on the trucks, but when they stopped at the plots displaying the short wheats, no one waited for the lecture. They jumped off the trucks and began grabbing wheat heads and stuffing them in their pockets. Alarmed agronomos tried to push them back, and fistfights broke out. When the melee was over and the trucks moved on, 20 percent of the new, short-strawed plants left in the pockets of the farmers. The *agronomo* in charge was upset: he didn't even get to give his lecture. The farmers, who now knew about fertilizers and were often over-fertilizing their tall crops and watching them fall over (lodge), knew a good thing when they saw it. The next summer, Borlaug toured the wheat-growing area and saw small patches of his shorty wheat growing everywhere [2, pp.236-239].

In the present century, poverty-stricken Indian farmers reacted similarly to Monsanto's Bt cotton (cotton that resists the boll-weevil). When the Indian government finally approved the sale of cotton seeds genetically modified with Monsanto's Bt gene, resource-poor small landholders rapidly adopted the technology, and within a few years they took India from a net importer of cotton to a net exporter. India is now the world's largest cotton producer, producing 25 percent of the world's supply [3].

Saving seed from one's own field is not always the best practice. In my Father's day, every farmer saved seed. Dad began growing Jenkin's Club wheat early in his farming career, a variety that could be seeded in the spring or fall.[37] He was still growing it when I started college and began to learn about newer varieties. To keep the variety pure, every few years a small area of bundles would be set aside during harvest, and Grandad would go through the bundles, cutting out the off-type heads of grain. Those bundles would be threshed separate from the rest of the field, and the grain seeded that fall.

It was now the mid-fifties, I was in college, learning to be an agronomist. Walking Dad's fields, I became aware that they were teeming with dozens of off-types. I asked Dad why he had grown Jenkin's Club for so many years. "Because, when we were custom threshing around the county, Jenkin's Club was always the one that yielded the most." It was a good variety in its day, but much better varieties were now available, and I convinced him to stop saving seed and purchase the best variety of the day.

I also saved wheat seed most of my farming career, but every few years I would buy a small amount of Foundation seed from the Crop Improvement Association and increase it to plant my fields.[38] It no longer makes sense for most grain farmers to save their own seed unless they have very high

---

[37] Called a facultative wheat, a wheat that has some winter-hardiness but does not require vernalization (a period of cold temperatures required to initiate the growth stage leading to a head of grain). True fall wheats undergo vernalization during the winter months.

volume needs and can economically justify a cleaning and treating operation of their own. I have not saved seed for over 10 years, and most farmers in my area have not done so in 30-40 years.

Another reason for a wheat farmer to not save his own seed is the plethora of varieties now available, and every year brings new possible varieties that may better fit a particular farm. Fifteen years ago I had a choice of maybe three varieties that would fit my conditions. This past fall my supplier had 24 varieties to choose from. Why so many? Until a few years ago, the only varieties available came from the breeding programs maintained by the Land Grant Universities.[39] When it became possible to patent varieties, private breeders got into the act. At first it was small companies, who merged into bigger companies, who sold out to Ag Giants such as Syngenta and Monsanto. For several years now, I have grown seeds from these companies, not because I have to, but because their varieties fit my growing conditions and offer the greatest yield potential. I cannot save the seed, but I don't want to. Their prices are competitive with seeds I could save, and I have the flexibility to change varieties up until the day I put the seed in the ground.

Sometimes a variety from one of the University breeding programs is the best fit, and I grow that. But to be competitive with Big Ag, the University varieties are also often patent protected and earn royalties in order to keep their programs adequately funded. This understandably upsets many farm-

---

[38] The standard practice to insure the purity of a variety begins with the breeder or his/her representative picking, from a field or plot, heads (or pods) that most represent the phenotype of that variety. These are planted and the resulting production called "breeders seed". The increase from planting breeders seed is called "foundation seed", the next generation is "registered seed', and the final generation before the process starts all over again is "certified seed".

[39] At least one in each state. Authorized by the Morrill Acts of 1862 and 1890. Federal land was granted to the states to establish institutions that would focus on the teaching of practical agriculture, science, military science and engineering.

ers who have supported these programs for years with assessments deducted from their proceeds when their crop is sold. And these programs are also supported with general funds from State or Federal governments. Research work done with public funds should be public property, so the argument goes. Therefore royalties and prohibitions on saving seed should not be allowed on University-produced varieties. On the other hand, these public programs must be well-funded if they are to compete with the resources available to Big Ag. In my estimation, it is in the grower's best interest to keep University programs solvent if only to serve as a quality check on Big Ag.

If First World farmers are reluctant to give up the opportunity to save seed without recourse, it is easy to understand Third World farmer's complaints about patented seeds. But once they experience the benefits such seeds can bring, as is the case with India's cotton farmers, buying new seed each year is not that big a burden. Third World governments need to promote superior seeds with education and subsidies. Saving seed from one's own field as my Dad did for 30 years is not taking advantage of the best current technology, and is not a wise economic practice.

The critics of Big Ag focus most of their wrath on Monsanto. It is the company, they say, that "gave us saccharin, aspartame, Agent Orange, PCBs, Roundup and Roundup-Ready seeds", all deplorable products according to their litany. I have defended Monsanto several times in this book, and the reader may think I have some special connection to the company: I do not. I have benefitted from their products, and from their stock while I owned it in the 90s. My son worked as a field representative for Monsanto for a few years before joining me in our farming partnership, but that is now 30 years in the past. I defend Monsanto because (a) their major product, Roundup, and their seeds work for me, and (b) I feel they are unfairly treated by environmentalists and the media.

I would do the same for Bayer, BASF, Dow and other companies that are spending millions to make better products and seeds for farmers to use. But these other companies don't seem to attract the same kind of negative publicity, despite the fact that they have produced some deplorable products in the past.

Dow also produced Agent Orange, and was the principal manufacturer of napalm. BASF and Bayer produced the chlorine gas and other terrible chemical warfare agents used by Gemany in WWI. In WWII, BASF, Bayer, Hoechst and other German chemical firms joined together in a company called IG Farben, which produced all the explosives for the German military, looted the chemical industries of the occupied countries, used slave labor from the concentration camps, and provided the chemicals for the gas chambers [4]. After the war, 24 IG Farben executives were charged with war crimes and tried by the Nuremberg Tribunal. Thirteen received prison sentences. Bayer executive Fritz ter Meer received the longest sentence, but was out of prison in 1952. By 1956 he was chairman of the supervisory board of Bayer.

IG Farben was dismantled after the war, but its principle component companies, BASF and Bayer live on. BASF is the largest chemical company in the world and Bayer is one of the largest chemical and pharmaceutical companies. Both are "BIG AG" powerhouses in pesticide development and manufacture, and both are active in developing genetically modified crops.

Bayer produces Glufosinate, an herbicide that, like Roundup, is not selective, and can only be applied to crops genetically engineered to tolerate it. It is sold under the tradename Liberty, and crops tolerant to it are called Liberty-Link crops. Crops engineered to tolerate Liberty include corn, cotton, soybeans, and canola. Its mode of action is different than Roundup, and will kill most weeds that have developed Roundup resistance.

In no way do I condone all the past actions of these companies. But to condemn the production of PCBs (polychlorinated biphenyls) and Agent Orange and let slide the horrible wartime sins of BASF and Bayer is a double standard I don't understand. The double standard extends to Monsanto's aspartame vs sucralose. Aspartame is composed of two amino acids—phenylalanine and aspartate—held together by a bond provided by a small amount of methanol. Both of these amino acids are required by the human body. Human cells can make aspartate, but phenylalanine must be obtained from the foods we eat. Aspartame is, therefore, a source of these two amino acids. So why is there so much anti-aspartame litany from the anti-Monsanto activists?

Phenylketonuria is a hereditary disease that affects 1 in 15,000 people worldwide. People with this disease lack a liver enzyme that converts excess phenylalanine in the blood to another necessary (but not "essential")[40] amino acid, tyrosine. Excess tyrosine is then eliminated in the stool. Since phenylketonurics can't convert excess phenylalanine to tyrosine, they must monitor their intake of foods high in phenylalanine: An excess can injure the brain [5]. Another strike against aspartame is the slight amount of methanol produced when it is metabolized in the body. Neither of these factors is justification for the anti-litany. The amino acids are metabolized as if they came from any other protein source, and the small amount of methanol is not harmful, even though it degrades further into formaldehyde. "A person would have to drink 600 cans of diet soda to get as much of either substance as is contained in one orange" [7]. The LD50 for aspartame is 10,000mg/kg, or nearly 2 pounds for a 150 pound person [6]. Since aspartame is 150 times sweeter than sucrose (table

---

[40]There are 20 amino acids required (necessary) to make all the proteins needed by living cells. Most can be made by cell machinery from foods we eat. Those that cannot must be obtained from proteins we eat, and are termed "essential" components of a diet.

sugar), it is diluted 150-200 times to make the table sweeteners Equal or NutraSweet. That means a person would have to consume approximately 100 pounds of Equal or NutraSweet at one meal to commit suicide, an impossible task.

Sucralose, on the other hand, is made from sugar so it is safe (???). Sugar molecules are stripped of three of their eight hydroxyl (OH) groups, and these are replaced with three chlorine atoms. Sucralose (Splenda) is a chlorinated sugar. Some authors compare it to DDT, a chlorinated hydrocarbon, but that is a bit of a stretch. The LD50 for sucralose is the same or higher than that for aspartame [10]. DDT is fat-loving and not readily dissolvable in water. Sucralose is easily dissolvable in water. It can, apparently, accumulate in the environment, having been detected in sewage wastewater, and is only slowly broken down by microorganisms [9]. Most of the sucralose consumed passes through the body unchanged because our systems don't recognize it as a usable item. About 20 percent is absorbed into the blood and then mostly removed by the kidneys [9]. Four to seven percent is unaccounted for five days after a single dose, and is presumably bio-accumulated in human fat or organ tissue [8]. Of that transiting the colon, some bacteria in the gut might break it down, and that could cause the owner some digestive distress.

That other artificial sweetener, saccharin, for which Monsanto gets the blame, is derived from coal tar. It has a long and somewhat notorious history. In 1907, Teddy Roosevelt's director of the bureau of chemistry for the Food and Drug Administration, Harvey Wiley, insisted on banning it as "injurious to health". But Roosevelt was a user, and called Wiley "an idiot". It was the end of Wiley's career [11]. In 1977, the FDA made another attempt to ban saccharin after studies showed it caused cancer in rats. But opposition from diabetics and dieters caused Congress to override the FDA decision, so it remains in the marketplace because of an Act of

Congress [11].

Monsanto did not invent saccharin. Its intense sweetness was discovered serendipitously in 1879 by Constantin Fahlberg of John Hopkins University. He obtained patents in several countries and began producing it in a German factory in 1886, soon becoming a wealthy man [11]. In 1901, John Francis Queeny founded Monsanto Co. in St. Louis, Missouri, to manufacture saccharin. Within a few years he added other food additives, such as vanillin and caffeine. In the 1920s, the company expanded into industrial chemicals, which eventually included the notorious PCB family.

There is ample evidence of the toxicity and environmental harm caused by PCBs in their many industrial uses. I do not defend them, nor do I defend the companies who made them and used them. The long defense of these chemicals by Monsanto, Westinghouse and other companies in the face of mounting evidence of environmental harm and human toxicity is justifiably criticized as corporate arrogance. But that is the past. The present Monsanto is a life sciences company, having spun off its chemical business (with the exception of Roundup) into a separate company, Solutia, in 1997.

Monsanto also gets most of the bad press over so called "Terminator Genes". These are genes inserted into a plant's genome that then causes the seed it produces to be sterile. The purpose is two-fold: (a) To protect a company's patented seed from being illegally used to grow a crop without paying the royalties due the patent owner, and (b) to prevent gene flow to wild relatives or a neighbor's crop through pollen drift. Seeds developing from such pollen drift would be sterile, so could not escape into the wild or infiltrate a GMO-free seed source. The USDA was active in developing this technology in partnership with Delta & Pine Land Corporation, and a joint patent was granted to these entities in 1996. Delta was granted the exclusive right to license the new technology to other parties [12]. The technology was incorporated into a cotton variety by Delta & Land, but never released due to fierce opposition from activists. Delta & Land was purchased by Monsanto in 2007.

Industry calls this technology "Genetic Use Restriction Technology" or "GURT". A patent for this technology was first filed by DuPont and granted in 1994. Today there are over 40 granted or submitted patents related to GURT, and they are mostly held by universities and Big Ag companies such as Bayer, Monsanto, BASF, Syngenta and their subsidiaries [12]. The first patents are due to expire in 2018, having never been put to use.

GURT came under heavy criticism worldwide because it was deemed unethical to sell a farmer seeds that could never be saved. "Seed saving is estimated to account for between 15% and 20% of the world's food supply, practiced by 100 million farmers in Latin America, 300 million in Africa and one billion in Asia" [11]. As a result of this criticism no company has yet commercialized this technology. A sister technology dubbed "traitor genes" by activists would protect proprietary traits by requiring a chemical initiator to be applied to the crop in order for the gene to be expressed, say a proprietary gene for resistance to a disease. The farmer could save the seed, but he/she would not benefit from the gene unless the chemical was purchased and applied. This technology has also not been commercialized.

So it is a dilemma for Third World farmers. The best technologies Big Ag has to offer won't be available to them if the developers can't make a profit. They will be dependent on whatever new technologies altruistic NGOs, such as the Bill and Melinda Gates Foundation, and government research can deliver. In the 1950s, 60s and 70s, it was the Rockefeller Foundation's supporting role that enabled the Green Revolution. Saving seed was not an issue then, and the new seeds were quickly adopted, along with the fertilizers and pesticides that brought them to their full potential. Farmers were willing to purchase those inputs because they now had seeds that could take advantage of them.

Governments and activist NGOs should just step back and let the farmers decide if they want to invest in seeds they cannot save in order to improve their yields and income. India's cotton farmers rapidly adopted hybrid cotton seeds that had been genetically engineered to resist insects when the Government got out of the way, even when they knew they could not save the seed. No one forced them to adopt: They adopted because it made them money. Why not let African farmers do the same? **Big Ag can only offer farmers choices: They cannot control farmers anywhere in the world. It is the NGOs that insist they know best what technologies farmers should use that are seeking to control farmer's choices, and in doing so are putting the world's future food supply in jeopardy.**

A sample of NGO trash talk concerning GMOs in Nigeria follows, quoted from a GMWATCH blog, Jan. 31, 2017: "one million Internally Displaced Persons (IDPs) from the Northeast are to be assisted with improved seeds and agricultural inputs in the process of rebuilding destroyed communities (i.e. destroyed by Boko Haram) during this year's cropping season. However, what was kept silent and unknown to the poor Nigerian farmers is that their natural crops were destroyed by hired mercenaries called Boko Haram by the same billionaire sponsors, so that they would be replaced with GMO and hybrid seeds from Monsanto and Cargill... the situation is dire and is an international emergency. It reveals that Bill Gates and Monsanto, in collaboration with the World Food Program and the World Bank, are implicated in the carnage created by Boko Haram [13]."

Bill Gates and Monsanto hired Boko Haram to kill and destroy indiscriminately so they could control Nigerian farmers with new seeds??? This is the kind of warped conspiracy thinking that led some people to blame the U.S. government

198

for the attack on the World Trade Center on September 11, 2001. Unfortunately, such "alternate facts" pervade the internet; all who read anti-GMO blogs should beware of pervasive and bizarre falsehoods such as this one.

The seeds that farmers now grow will not be lost to future generations. Seed banks all over the world are preserving seed varieties and accessions (crosses never commercialized) by the millions. If I wanted to grow my Fathers old Jenkin's Club variety, I could request a sample from Washington State University's seed bank and increase it. Internet stories that encourage gardeners to grow heirloom seeds to keep varieties alive are unnecessary. Universities and seed companies keep every variant of a variety, wild or commercialized, in climate-controlled long-term storage. And stories that ancient wheats or other grains were revived from Egyptian tombs are fairy tales: The crops have always been grown someplace in the world.

The activists that see conspiracies in everything Big Ag does are a drag on progress. The new technologies being developed by Big Ag, Universities, Foundations and private entities, be it seeds with unique traits, or new methods of controlling pests, or new machinery applications, or any other technology that increases efficiency of food production while preserving sustainability, should be encouraged. By 2050 it is estimated we will need 70 percent more food than we now produce to adequately feed the expected population of 9-10 billion people.

The shortsighted vision of GMO opponents in this regard is demonstrated in another current blog from GMWATCH. On February 1, 2017, they reported on an upcoming experiment by British researchers at the Rothamstead Research Station who have inserted a gene from a distant relative of wheat and other grains, *Brachypodium distachyon,* also known as the weedy grass Purple False Brome. The gene causes the wheat plant to have significantly broader leaves, resulting in more area exposed to sunlight, thus increasing photosynthetic workspace. In the greenhouse these modified plants have increased yield 40 percent. The researchers will plant the modified plant outdoors in spring 2017 to see if the yield enhancement will be maintained [14].

Thirty anti-GMO organizations have lodged objections to the experiment. GMWATCH quotes agrimoney.com, "The forecast for world wheat surplus just keeps getting bigger and bigger, and wheat prices are set to fall to 15-year lows." GMWATCH then comments, "It is therefore mind-boggling as to why the genetic engineers at Rothamsted Research think it's a good idea to genetically engineer wheat to use sunlight more efficiently and give higher yields" [14]. The anti GMO activists apparently have no clue that it takes 10-15 years lead time to develop a new agronomic trait. Shortages of wheat will occur again, and if we follow the low-input, low-yield vision of the anti-technologists, hunger could once again dominate the news.

The wild, false charges that activist NGOs spread on the internet and the media concerning emerging technologies and the entities developing them needs to stop. **No company is going to gain control over independent farmers anywhere in the world—only governments can do that.** Governments need to be beneficent regulators, and support their farmers with production subsidies and/or loans, and give them a crop insurance safety net. The Green Revolution was successful in India only because Borlaug was able to convince the Indian government to subsidize farmer's purchase and use of fertilizers and pesticides that enabled the new seeds to reach their full potential.

To feed the world of the future in a sustainable way, new technologies must be allowed to be developed and applied to the land. Low-input, low-yield, organic only practices will not sustainably feed the world, and will not universally protect the soil resource from erosion and productivity decline.

High-input, high-yield practices, combined with no-till, can feed an increasing population, protect the soil resource, and preserve wildlife and recreational resources. The technology choices we make now will determine what kind of world we have 20 years in the future.

CHAPTER 7 REFERENCES

1. Engdahl, William F. Seeds of Destruction. The Hidden Agenda of Genetic Manipulation. Global Research, Center for Research on Globalization. 2007

2.Bickel, Lennard. Facing Starvation. Readers Digest Press. 1974.

3.See reference 65, chapter 5.

4."Bayer: A History." GM Watch, Feb.1, 2009.

5."Phenylketonuria." The Merck Manual, Second Home Edition, 2003, p. 1618.

6."Aspartame." Chemicalland21.com. Search Bing "LD50 Aspartame." Accessed May 5, 2015.

7.Selim, Jocelyn. "Hitting the Sweet Spot." Discover magazine, August, 2005, p18-19.

8. Federal Register, Vol. 63, No. 64, Friday, April 3, 1998, p.16429.

9."Sucralose." Wikipedia. Jan. 24, 2017.

10.Goldsmith, L. A. "Acute and subchronic toxicity of sucralose." Food Chemical Toxicology. 2000; 38 Supplement 2:S53-69. http://www.ncbi.nlm.nih.gov/pubmed/10882818

11."Saccharin." Wikipedia. Nov. 28, 2016.

12. Lombardo, Luca. "Genetic use restriction technologies: a review." Plant Biotechnology Journal. Vol. 12, issue 8, Oct. 2014, pp. 995-1005.

13.Nissl, Slavko. "Monsanto GMO seeds in Nigeria, breaking the agricultural cycle, complicity of UN World Food Program." Global Research, January 29, 2017.

14."UK GM wheat trial gets go-ahead." GMWATCH.com, February 1, 2017.

CHAPTER 8.

MEAT,EGGS,MILK:
HOW SHOULD THEY BE RAISED?

"My Favorite animal is steak."—Fran Lebowitz

Some pundits of current times want to solve all of agriculture's problems by bringing livestock back to the farm. Others say meat production is an inefficient way to produce food, and farmland should only be used to grow human food, not animal food. Except for niche markets, neither is going to happen. When income rises in developing countries, demand for animal products goes up. No amount of moral or ethical persuasion will keep people who have spent most of their lives unable to afford meat to abstain once income will allow its purchase. The world will need to produce more meat in the future, not less.

A fact ignored or misunderstood by most pundits is that approximately one-half of the feed energy that goes into producing a steak comes from pasture or rangeland not suited for cash crops. The first 600 pounds that goes on a feedlot steer comes from grassland. Critics of beef production love to point out that it takes seven pounds of grain to put a pound of meat on a steer, versus two pounds to make a pound of chicken or three-four pounds to make a pound of pork. But when you consider that the first 600 pounds of gain by a beef animal is from range grasses--a feed source only a ruminant can utilize-- and average that with the last 600 pounds that comes from grain, a pound of beef only takes three-and-one-half pounds of grain per finished pound of beef.

As for those who advocate bringing livestock back to the farm, the land resources necessary to give every pig, chicken and dairy cow free range pasture is just not available if we are going to adequately feed even today's population and still save room for wildlife. And most farmers are not going back to the days when they were tied to the farm 24-7 because animals had to be cared for.

I remember those days. I was often visiting my best friend when his Dad would come in after milking the cows in the evening, following the evening meal. He would pour the milk into the separator {a hand-cranked centrifuge) to separate the cream portion of the milk so it could be sold to the local creamery, from which they made butter and other products. The "creamless" milk, called "skim milk" was then fed to the farm's pigs. This was part of the "chores" required morning and evening, every day of the week. And I remember going to visit another neighbor with Dad on a harvest evening, and feeling sorry for the farmer having to milk cows after a grueling day on the combine. My Dad didn't have to do that because he had no livestock.

Dairies nowadays are generally big enough or automated enough that work can be divided up among several people. At big or small diaries, cows line up for a turn on the milking carousel. When the gate opens to let one enter, she is treated to an automated udder cleaning and massage, then an automatic milking apparatus is attached which extracts the milk while the carousel turns and the cow munches on a snack of grain. The grain is apportioned by computer just for her according to her particular nutritional needs. When the carousel arrives at the exit, she leaves to join the herd to relax and munch on hay. Some will get back in line to be milked again because the experience was so enjoyable, but the computer is watching, and an alternate gate opens at the carousel entrance, sending her back to the herd. Does she miss a nice green pasture? Most dairymen will tell you the cows prefer a yard with straw bedding, hay to munch on, and a roof for protection from the elements.

Debate over raising animals in confined spaces has been raging for years now. As with conventional crop production, meat production has become a specialized agricultural occupation, with a constant drive to be more efficient than the next fellow. By moving cattle, hogs and chickens into concentrated facilities where the workforce can specialize in feeding and caring for the animals full time, facilities can be tailored to make the job of feeding and caring as efficient as possible. This trend to specialization and efficiency has resulted in cattle feedlots with 30,000 or more cattle, dairies with up to 50,000 cows, egg laying factories with multiple houses containing 10,000 caged hens each, and hog confinement systems where thousands of the pigs spend their lives on slatted floors built to facilitate manure collection.

While my farmer instincts are to be ever more efficient in whatever I do, animals, sentient beings, pull at the heartstrings. When five chickens are put in an 18" by 20" cage at birth, living their whole lives never feeling anything but wire with their feet, or lacking space to spread their wings; when gestating sows are put in cages too small to turn around in for weeks at a time; when young calves destined for the veal market are also put in cages too small to turn around in, I begin to feel efficiency has gone too far.

On the other hand, I realize the market forces that produced these practices. Consumers vote with their dollars, and so the competition for the consumer's dollar has driven companies to seek every possible way to cut costs and deliver meat, milk and eggs at a cheaper price than the competition. It has gotten to the point that many companies don't let the farmer own the chickens-- only the building and processing facilities. The company delivers new chickens to the farmer on a regular basis, and the old ones are retrieved for slaughter. The farmer is then left with some expensive, empty buildings if the egg buyer abandons their contract. The term "industrial" truly applies here.

PETA (People for the Ethical Treatment of Animals) has campaigned for years against AFOs and especially CAFOs (Animal Feeding Operations and Concentrated Animal Feeding Operations) and have been successful in several state legislatures in getting more room for caged hens, restrictions on the amount of time sows can be in gestation cages, and getting larger crates for veal calves. Required changes in one state, especially if that state is California, tend to extend to neighboring states, or even to all states, because meat and eggs are shipped across state lines.

CAFOS are defined by the USDA Natural Resources Conservation Service as AFOs housing more than 1000 animal units. An animal unit is defined as "an animal equivalent of 1000 pounds live weight and equates to 1000 head of beef cattle, 700 dairy cows, 2500 swine weighing more than 55 pounds, 125000 broiler chickens, or 82,000 laying hens" [5].

So what is life like for animals in these CAFOs? Are PETA descriptions the norm or the exaggeration? For facilities I have visited, such descriptions are hyperbolic. Enter a chicken house with 10,000 egg-laying hens and the noise from their constant chatter can be uncomfortably loud. The hens do not seem to be under stress; on the other hand, they have been in a cage all their lives and know no other existence. Is that inhumane for an animal with such a small brain? I don't profess to know. I do know such facilities were built to make egg collecting and basic animal care as labor-saving and efficient as possible. Feed and water can be delivered by augers and pipes. Eggs fall through the cracks in the cage, roll down a slope onto a conveyor belt that delivers them to cleaning and sorting machinery. Feces are collected in a similar manner. Anything that restricts these efficiencies will raise egg prices.

Visit a pig gestation facility and the sows in their crates

grunt contentedly, not seeming distressed at their predicament. Pigs are not noted for their desire to exercise. At any rate, temporary confinement of pregnant sows is necessary until her litter is born and has grown enough to run out of the way when mother lays down. She seldom looks at what might be under her when her short, 400 pound frame descends to the ground. When I was in high school, we were taught to build farrowing pens with shelves one foot off the floor on all sides of the pen. The little piglets could run under the shelves when mama decided to lay down, sparing a smashing end to life (most of the time). At any rate, pregnant sows need private pens: They tend to fight when penned with other sows.

As for pigs raised on slatted floors--which facilitate efficient gathering of feces—I think it makes little difference to them what kind of surface is under them as long as it's comfortable to lie on between meals. As I said before, pigs are not noted for their desire to exercise. They are noted for their desire to eat. And confinement facilitates climate control, which is important for pigs as they have no sweat glands. Otherwise, pigs in hot weather need a mud hole to wallow in to keep cool.

Michael Pollan in his book *Omnivore's Dilemma* [1] devotes 20 pages to describing his experience with cattle raising and feedlots. He buys a steer, number 534, from a cow-calf operation in South Dakota where it has spent its first six months of life on green pastures with its mother. For the next two months, calf 534, after being weaned from its mother, spends its days being "backgrounded"--a term used to describe time spent converting its diet from a low-energy, 100 per cent grass diet to a high-energy diet consisting of about 75 percent corn, a protein supplement, some molasses, and a roughage source (hay, straw, beet pulp, etc.). The calf also learns to eat from a trough.

Pollan says this backgrounding diet is unnatural and unhealthy, but that isn't necessarily so. Cattle love grain. If a cow breaks into the granary, she will eat until she makes herself very sick, perhaps fatally. Cattle let loose in a harvested corn field will seek the unthrashed cobs that lie on the ground first, and if they eat too many, digestive trauma results.

To put cattle on a diet high in grain takes some time, because the bacteria and fungi in the rumen (the compartment of the cow's stomach where fermentation of grasses takes place) must adjust gradually to the new food. Some bacterial and fungal species diminish, others increase, not unlike what happens in the human gut when we drastically change our diets. This process is helped along by a feed additive from Elanco called Rumensin. Rumensin inhibits the growth of fiber-fermenting bacteria, thereby favoring an increase in activity by starch-fermenting bacteria needed to digest grain [2].

After backgrounding, Pollan's steer is sent to a custom feeding operation called Poky Feeders in Garden City, Kansas, where he is one of 37,000 steers being boarded for $1.60 per day each. "Custom feeding" means the feedlot owners don't own the steers; they are owned by the various cow-calf operations that sent them there. The feedlot provides a specialized service for cattle owners who don't want to do the "finishing" step before slaughter.

After steer number 534 had been at Poky's for a couple months, Pollan paid him a visit. Amazingly, among the thousands of pens, each with 100 or so animals, feedlot managers told him where to look, and soon Pollan was face to face with Number 534. He describes the encounter, "I don't know enough about the emotional life of a steer to say with confidence that 534 was miserable, bored, or indifferent, but I would not say he looked happy. He's clearly eating well, though, my steer had put on a couple hundred pounds since we last met..." [1, p.80]. If 534 could talk, he would probably say he was happy. He's a herd animal and he has 90 pen mates to keep him company, adequate space to move around or lie down, and plenty of delicious food.

Steer number 534 was apparently gaining about 3.3 pounds

per day, costing Pollan 48 cents per pound of gain. In 2006, a 700 pound feeder steer would have cost Pollan about $800. After five months in the feedlot, steer 534 would probably weigh about 1200 pounds, and sell for about $1,100 [3]. Five months of room and board for number 534 would cost $240. Adding that to the $800 purchase price brings the total cost to ready him for the slaughter house to $1,040. Pollan would then make $60 on his investment. So much for a lesson on feedlot economics. It should be noted, however, that market volatility can turn the net gain into a net loss for the owner of the steer.

Because of privacy laws, getting an accurate count of how many AFOs there are in the U.S. is impossible. It depends on what agency is doing the guessing and how an AFO is defined. The EPA defines an AFO as any facility where (a) "animals have been, are, or will be stabled or confined and fed or maintained for a total of 45 days or more in any 12-month period, and (b) crops, vegetation, forage growth, or post-harvest residues are not sustained in the normal growing season over any portion of the lot or facility" [4]. The USDA census of agriculture tallies farms with animals differently, counting any hobby farm with one animal as an "animal feeding operation". They thereby come up with more "operations" than there are farms, due to the fact that many farms keep more than one kind of animal. The USDA Natural Resources Conservation Service tally is probably the most accurate as that agency works with farmers to solve manure containment problems. Their count is "approximately 450,000 AFOs" in the U. S. [5]. As to how many AFOs are CAFOs, the Union of Concerned Scientists puts the number of CAFOs at 9,900 [6].

Pollution from animal feces is a concern with CAFO operations. Any AFO, no matter what size, is considered a CAFO by the EPA if it discharges manure or wastewater into a ditch, stream or other waterway.

Environmentalists love to say that livestock on pastures are fertilizing the grass as they feed, thus solving the manure dis-posal problem. But, as it was pointed out in Chapter 3 (Note 3-2), manure dropped on the ground in a pasture loses 40-60 percent of its nitrogen content. Pastures never given supple-mental nitrogen will soon consist of small round patches of very green, healthy grass surrounded by broad areas of ane-mic-looking, unproductive grass.

Manure is a problem no matter what method of raising and finishing livestock is used. Animal feeding operations at least have the opportunity to save most of the nitrogen and return it properly to the land by collecting it in tanks or covered la-goons and then hauling it to fields and injecting it into the root zone. As explained also in Chapter 3, this becomes prohibi-tively expensive if the collected manure has to be hauled more than a few miles. So this option is only feasible for smaller AFOs that can utilize the manure on their own crops or crops of nearby neighbors. Large operations, if they are not already doing it, will have to treat their manure as a city treats its sew-age. Some cover their lagoons, capturing the methane pro-duced by digestive bacteria and burning it to power their fa-cilities. Solids can be bagged and transported longer distances for use as soil amendments.

Grass fed beef is the darling of the media these days, in-cluding farm magazines. It is said to be healthier, more ome-ga-3 fats, more natural, better for the environment, etc., all arguable points. But growing good tasting, tender grass-fed beef is not easy to do. To make tender, tasty meat the steer needs to gain at least 2 pounds per day for 3-4 months, and 3-4 pounds per day is better. It takes high quality, very nutritious grass to do that, which means using the best, most produc-tive soils combined with meticulous management; soils and management skills that might earn better returns if applied to cash crops. Grass-fed beef must sell at a premium to keep the farmer in business. Therefore it becomes another elite food product not affordable by many people.

HORMONES AND ANTIBIOTICS:
WHY ARE THEY USED? ARE THEY SAFE?

Sustainability in food production involves, among other things, using production resources as efficiently as possible. Confining animals in small spaces conserves land resources. Using hormones that result in more gain or more milk per pound of feed consumed conserves land resources. Hormones and confinement also conserve labor resources. However, confinement does increase the probability of disease, hence the increase in both prophylactic and curative use of antibiotics. So let's examine the science and safety of these production enhancers.

BOVINE SOMATOTROPIN (BST)

BST is a hormone produced in a cow's pituitary glands and is important in regulation of milk production. A cow's milk output normally reaches a maximum about 70 days after giving birth to a calf [7], after which output slowly decreases until milking stops 40-50 days before expected birthing of her next calf [8]. This "dry period" is necessary to maximize milk output after birthing.

Milk output decreases after reaching the maximum because milk-producing mammary cells slowly die off, and do not regrow until the next calf is born. Giving a cow extra BST slows this process and keeps the cow producing at maximum level longer. This discovery was made in 1937, but supplementation with extra BST was not widely used because the only source was bovine carcasses [7]. In the late 1970s, the biotech company Genentech succeeded in cloning the BST gene and patented it. Collaborating with Monsanto, the gene was inserted in the *E. coli* bacteria, which were then grown in bioreactors. The BST, now called rBST (recombinant BST), was then purified into an injectable hormone.

After over 10 years of studies, investigations and public input to determine its safety and ethics, the FDA approved the commercialization of the hormone, and Monsanto began selling it in 1994 under the name Posilac. Lilly, American Cyanamid and Upjohn also applied to commercialize rBST, but Monsanto, being the first, gets the blame for another modification of nature. Monsanto sold its Posilac division to Eli Lilly in 2008.

In a review after 20 years of use, Collier and Bauman [9] found no human health issues with use of rBST. BST is present in milk from both treated and untreated cows. As with other proteins, it is completely dismantled in the digestive tract of humans. Even if directly injected it has no effect on humans. The safety of rBST has been endorsed by "the American Medical Association, The American Academy of Pediatrics, The National Institutes of Health, the Congressional Office of Technology Assessment, The Endocrine Society Clinical Review, the American Council on Science and Health, a joint expert committee of the World Health Organization, regulatory agencies in more than 30 countries, the American Dietetic Association, the inspector General of the U. S. Department of Health and Human Services, and the Council for Agricultural Science and Technology" [10]. But, as is with the case of most other GMOs, the European Union bans its use.

More than 1500 studies worldwide have established that "biweekly injections of rBST into dairy cows will increase milk production 10 to 15 percent and increase feed efficiency of feed utilization 5 to 15 percent" [10]. This lowers costs for farmers and consumers, conserves soil resources, reduces the amount of greenhouse gasses produced in dairy operations, and reduces the amount of feces that must be disposed of. Feeding more people with less earth resources. Isn't that the foundation of sustainability? "When conventional, conventional with rBST, and organic dairy operations are compared, 8 percent fewer cows are needed in an rBST-supplemented population, whereas organic production systems require a 25 percent increase to meet production targets. This is due to a lower milk yield per cow due to the pasture-based system which is attributed with a greater maintenance energy expenditure associated with grazing behavior" [7].

Opponents argue that cows treated with rBST are more prone to infections of the udder (mastitis) leading to excessive use of antibiotics that can end up in the milk. Cows that give more milk do tend to have more mastitis infections, but every tanker load of milk arriving at the processing point is tested for the presence of antibiotics, and if tolerances are exceeded,[41] the milk is dumped.

Another argument against use of rBST is that it increases the level of another hormone, IGF-1 (Insulin-like Growth Factor-1), a natural component of milk and a natural component of human blood. The concern is that excess IGF-1 can promote cancer growth. But a 2008 study of conventional, organic labeled, and rBST-free labeled milk published in the *Journal of the Dietetic Association* [11] found no meaningful difference in content of IGF-1, BST, or antibiotics in the three milk types. The authors conclude, "It is important for food and nutrition professionals to know that conventional, rBST-free, and organic milk are compositionally similar so they can serve as a key resource to consumers who are making milk purchase (and consumption) decisions in a market place where there are **misleading milk label claims**" (my emphasis).

Despite the science that supports the safety and effectiveness of BST, opponents of anything "unnatural" being used in food production—or, in this case something natural used in an "unnatural way"—have successfully convinced the public to question its safety. Therefore, today only about 17 percent of dairies use BST (see Wikipedia—Bovine Somatotropin).

---

[41]The FDA establishes a safe tolerance for a drug in milk before it is approved for use in dairy cows. Tolerances vary. Ampicillin has a tolerance of 10ppb (parts per billion). Ciprofloxin has a zero tolerance. Bactricin has tolerance of 500ppb, and tetracycline 300ppb [28].

BEEF ON STEROIDS

Hormones that promote growth of beef cattle have been approved for use in the U. S. since the 1950s. Other meat-exporting countries, such as Canada, Australia, New Zealand, South Africa, Mexico, Chile and Japan, also allow the use of growth-promoting hormones. The European Union bans them, however, and bans imports from countries that use them unless the meat is certified as grown without hormones. This ban has been the source of a trade dispute between the U. S. and the European Union for decades [12].

It is estimated that 90 percent of U. S. cattle in feedlots, and nearly 100 percent in large feedlots, are given a hormone treatment. "Cattle producers use hormones because they allow animals to grow larger more quickly on less feed and fewer other inputs, thus reducing production costs, but also because they produce a leaner carcass more in line with consumer preferences for diets with reduced fat and cholesterol" [12]. Compounds used include natural ones--estradiol, progesterone and testosterone—and synthetic versions of natural hormones. All products require approval for safety and effectiveness by the FDA. Some products can be added to feed, but generally a slow-release pellet is implanted in the animals' ear.

Using steroids to promote beef cattle growth is not without its critics. Critics fear residues in meat can disrupt human hormone balance and contaminate the environment through animal feces. But the residues in meat are tiny. A six-ounce serving of beef from a treated steer will contain less than 4 nanograms (one nanogram is one billionth of a gram), while a non-pregnant woman produces about 480,000 nanograms of estrogen daily [13], and a man produces 4-7 million nanograms of testosterone daily [14]. "A person would need to eat 3,000,000 hamburgers made with beef from implanted cattle to get as much estrogen as the average adult woman produces every day, or 50,000 hamburgers to get as much estrogen as the average adult man produces every day" [15].

Hormone treatment generally results in a 20 percent increase in growth rate on 15 percent less feed per pound of gain. This means significant savings for feedlot operators, most of which is passed on to consumers. It also results in less demands on the environment, a positive for sustainability.

ANTIBIOTICs and IONOPHORES

Antibiotics have been used as an animal growth stimulant since the 1950s, but criticism of the practice has gained steam in recent years as antibiotic-resistant "superbugs" become more of a problem in human health. Proof that use in animal feeding operations is exacerbating the problem is elusive. Antibiotics fed to animals do end up in the feces, but if the feces are contained in a lagoon or applied to a field, dispersal of significant amounts of these compounds or resultant resistant bacteria beyond the confines of the feedlot or field is minimal. Most of the antibiotics and resistant bacteria found in the waters of the U. S. come from sewage effluent [27]. People excrete antibiotics and resistant bacteria also.

Antibiotics and bacteria with resistant genes in manure or bio solids (from sewage treatment facilities or feedlot lagoons) applied to land will eventually be degraded, with half-lives for most antibiotics reported to be from a few days to 300 days [25]. No lasting effect on the soil community from these antibiotics has been observed, nor has any toxicity to plants been observed [27]. Some resistant genes could be transferred to soil bacteria, but genes with no beneficial use to an organism will eventually be mutated away. And, as explained in a later paragraph, these resistant genes could exist naturally in the soil already.

Critics claim that 80 percent of antibiotics sold in the U.S. are used in AFOs. This is an exaggeration. The more accurate figure is 50 percent. The remaining 30 percent are products such as ionophores and peptides not used to treat humans and are not true antibiotics [31]. Ionophores are compounds that affect the transfer of ions across cell walls, and do not generally result in cell death, but do affect cell vigor. An example is Rumensin, which is used to alter the bacterial species in the rumen of a cow. Peptides are short protein chains with antibacterial properties.

Growth-promoting use of antibiotics that are medically important to humans was outlawed by the FDA as of Jan. 3, 2017. Such antibiotics can only be prescribed by a veterinarian for temporary use to treat sick animals or contain the spread of disease to other animals. Products not important to human health can still be used as growth promoters. Often added to feed in very small amounts--50 to 100 milligrams per ton [16]--, the exact way in which these feed additives promote weight gain is unknown. Many veterinarians and researchers believe that "their use functions in maintaining gut health by suppressing bacteria causing subclinical disease. Subclinical infections may not be readily apparent but can affect an animal's ability to efficiently utilize nutrients to reach its optimal production potential. This was most evident when withdrawal of antibiotic growth promoters from pigs (In Demark) resulted in the outbreak of intestinal disease in weanling pigs, leading to...increases in mortality" [17].

The Animal Health Institute sites several reports that show no difference between the existence of resistant strains in organic or conventional poultry and milk production [18]. One study states, "We found a high prevalence of resistance to tetracycline, sulfanomides, and streptomycin in all commercial flocks, although these drugs were not used in most cases. These results were supported by data from the experimental flocks which demonstrated that even in controlled settings with clean pens and fresh bedding, there was high prevalence of resistance to antimicrobials not commonly used in broiler chicken husbandry. These data are similar to data in previously published studies that illustrated that usage patterns may not correlate with resistance prevalence" [19].

The data described in the above paragraph supports the argument that "It has been widely shown that ARGs (antibiotic resistant genes) are a natural phenomenon, and that we have been living with ARGs in the environment (and within our microbiome), since the dawn of our species" [27]. D'Costa, et al, extracted "a highly diverse collection of genes encoding resistance" from 30,000-year-old permafrost sediments [26]. This is not surprising when one realizes the soil is not a benign "everyone gets along" place. It is a dog eat dog world. One bacterial strain develops an antibiotic to clear space in which to grow: Another strain develops resistance to hold its territory. The soil is a battleground where anything goes[42]—gluttony, overcrowding, cannibalism[43], chemical "bombs"—and thousands of years later we humans harvest these results of bacterial warfare and declare the soil a harmonious and inventive place.

Antibiotic resistant genes have also been discovered in the colon of a 1000-year old naturally mummified female from South America. "Putative antibiotic-resistant genes including beta-lactamases, penicillin-binding proteins, resistance to fosfomycin, chloramphenicol, aminoglycosides, macrolides, sulfa, quinolones, tetracycline, and vancomycin, and multi-drug transporters were…identified" (29).

So, it appears mutated genes for resistance can occur in a bacterial population before exposure to a particular synthetically-made antibiotic, the same as mutated genes exist in weed populations that impart resistance to a pesticide before exposure to the pesticide. Only when the same pesticide

---

[42]I am indebted to Dr. Kate Reardon, Research Microbiologist, UDSA Agricultural Research Service, Columbia Basin Research Center, Adams, Oregon, for the symbolism expressed here.

[43] Bacterial cannibalism is being investigated as a possible human antibiotic [30]

is used repeatedly does a resistant weed population become noticeable. The same mechanism occurs in bacteria vis-a-vis antibiotics, and the data suggests resistance can show itself even if no antibiotics were ever given to animals. This is likely why some of the worst resistant bacteria, such as MRSA, show up first in hospitals, where infected people concentrate and lots of antibiotics and other antibacterial substances are used. "The drugs kill off susceptible bacteria yet allow the resistant bugs, suddenly devoid of competition, to thrive—making it easier for them to contaminate medical equipment, staff and other patients." [32]. The Centers for Disease Control lists 18 bacteria that comprise the antibiotic threat, only two of which might come from animals through food--Salmonella and Campylobacter [20].

Even though a link between antibiotic use in animals and antibiotic resistance in humans is not proven, the problem of antibiotic resistance is a serious one, and all possible steps must be taken to reduce its spread. Ideally, manure from AFOs should be treated in such a way that antibiotics are removed or destroyed before environmental release. Municipal sewage treatment plants should do the same. Technologies exist to accomplish this: They should be employed. Where cost is a significant burden, government subsidies should be made available. Payback in the form of reduced health expenditures by individuals and government would be significant.

EUROPEAN BANS ON HORMONES, ANTIBIOTICS AND GMOs: A LEGACY OF MAD COW DISEASE?

In 1986, mad cow disease was discovered in Britain. Technically called bovine spongiform encephalopathy (BSE), the disease causes a spongy degeneration of the brain and spinal cord. It has a long incubation period, and usually shows up in cattle older than four years. It is caused by a prion, a misfolded protein. In the next 12 years, Britain would slaughter

4.4 million animals in an attempt to wipe out the disease [21].

For 10 years, the authorities assured the public that the disease could not be transmitted to humans. Then, in 1995, three people died from a new version of Creutzfeldt-Jakob disease (vCJD). In March of 1996, The British health Secretary "announces to the British House of Commons that mad cow disease is 'the most likely explanation at present for 10 cases of CJD in people aged under 42.' This is the first time the British government admits BSE could be transmitted to humans in a variant form of CJD [22]."

The announcement was devastating to the British beef industry. The European Union and other countries immediately banned imports of British beef, and some bans lasted for up to 16 years [21]. Eventually BSE would be diagnosed in cattle from 30 countries including Canada, the United States, Japan, and Saudi Arabia. A total of 229 cases of vCJD in humans would be diagnosed worldwide, with most occurring in Europe, especially Britain (176 deaths) and France (27 deaths). Three people would die in the U.S [21].

Outside of Europe, outbreaks were quite quickly eliminated. The cause was eventually blamed on feeding bone meal and meat scraps, especially brains and spinal cords, from infected animals as a protein supplement. This was never much of an issue in the U.S. because protein supplements generally come from plant sources (soybeans and cottonseed), whereas in Europe meat sources are cheaper than plant sources.

The long denial by government sources in Europe that BSE could be transferred to humans undermined the confidence in government agencies to protect the food supply, and likely contributes to this day to the adversarial public opinion of hormones and antibiotics use in meat production and the consumption of GMO crops, despite expensive European Union studies confirming their safety.

CONCLUSIONS

McDonald's is pledging to source 85 percent of its beef from sustainable sources by 2020. This is a massive amount of beef—McDonald's is one of the largest buyers of beef globally, and what it does can move the market [22]. First, McDonald's will have to define what sustainability in beef production is, and I expect that definition will be watered down by what is possible so that marketing goals can be met. To their credit, they have joined with Tyson Foods, The Samuel Roberts Nobel Foundation, Beef Marketing Group, and Golden State Foods in a "two-year pilot research project that will seek methods to improve sustainability across the entire beef value chain…"[24].

"The U.S. beef herd numbered around 140 million head in 1970. Today (2017) that number is around 90 million, yet we produce roughly the same tonnage of beef. As for dairy production, the U.S. herd of around 9 million head today produces 60 percent more milk that 16 million did in 1950." (Frank Mitloehner, air quality and sustainability specialist at the University of California, Davis, as quoted in [23].) Similar gains have been made in poultry and hog production. If we were to move production back to the small farms as many pundits propose, most of these efficiency gains would be lost.

Perhaps we don't need the very large AFOs to efficiently produce meat and eggs, but that's where we are, and finding ways to efficiently and productively handle manure and animal comfort and health should be our goal, not breakup into tiny production units.

Sustainability in food production is a laudable and necessary goal, and the efficiencies gained over the last 50 years are necessary components of that goal. It is time to recognize that the responsible use of hormones and antibiotics is one of the pillars of those efficiency gains, and embrace them rather than rail against them.

CHAPTER 8 REFERENCES

1.Pollan, Michael. See reference 1, Chapter 4.

2.Hutjens, Mike. "Use of Rumensin in Dairy Diets." Extension Dairy Specialist, University of Illinois, Urbana. Aug. 21, 2012.

3.Brooks, Kathleen, Extension Livestock Marketing Specialist, University of Nebraska, Lincoln. "Annual and Seasonal Price Patterns for Cattle." Cornhusker Economics. Aug. 19, 2015.

4.U. S. Environmental Protection Agency. "Animal Feeding Operations (AFOs). Jan. 17, 2017.

5.USDA Natural Resources Conservation Service. "Animal Feeding Operations." Undated. Accessed May, 2017. nrcs.usda.gov/wps/portal/nrcs/main/national/plantsanimals/livestock/afo

6.Gurlan-Sherman, Doug. "CAFOs Uncovered: The Untold Story of Confined Animal Feeding Operations." Union of Concerned Scientists. April, 2008.

7."Bovine Somatotropin." Wikipedia. Feb. 7 2017.

8."Dry Period in Dairy Cattle." Lactation Resource Library, University of Illinois. Undated. Accessed May, 2017.

9.Collier, R. J. and Bauman, D.E. "Update on Human Health Concerns of Recombinant Bovine Somatotropin Use in Dairy Cows." Journal of Animal Science. Vol. 92, No. 4, pp. 1800-1807. Nov. 24, 2014.

10.Tucker, Allan H. "Safety of Bovine Somatotropin (BST)." Michigan State University Extension. April 30, 2010.

11.Vicini, John, et al. "Survey of Retail Milk Composition as Affected by Label Claims Regarding Farm-Management Practices." Journal of the Dietetic Association. Vol. 108, issue 7, pp. 1198-1203. July, 2008.

12.Johnson, Renee. "The U.S.-EU Beef Hormone Dispute." Congressional Research Service, Jan. 14, 2015.

13.Fact Sheet: Feedlot Finishing Cattle. National Cattlemen's Beef Association. Undated. Accessed May, 2017. https://assets.documentcloud.org/documents/838329/feedlot-finishing-fact-sheet.pdf

14.Bing search: How much testosterone does a man produce daily? May, 2017.

15.Furber, Debbie. Quoting Dr. Reynold Bergen, science director for Canada's Beef Cattle Research Council. "Straight Talk on Cattle Steroids." Canadian Cattleman. Dec. 9, 2014.

16.Croglia, Adam. "AHI Open Letter to Scientific American." Animal Health Institute, News and Publications. Feb. 2, 2017.

17."The Antibiotic Ban in Denmark: A Case Study on Politically Driven Bans." The Animal Health Institute, Issues and Advocacy, Antibiotics, Denmark Ban. Undated. Accessed May, 2017.

18."Organic Agriculture: Is it Safer?" The Animal Health Institute, Issues and Advocacy, Antibiotics. Undated, accessed May, 2017

19.Smith, J. L., et al. "Impact of Antimicrobial Usage on Antimicrobial Resistance in Commensal Escherichia coli Strains Colonizing Chickens." Applied and Environmental Microbiology. Vol. 73, No. 5, March 2007, pp.1404-1414.

20."Antibiotic Resistance Threats in the United States." U.S Dept. of Health and Human Services, Centers for Disease Control. 2013, pp. 49-93.

21."Bovine Spongiform Encephalopathy." Wikipedia. Last modified Feb. 23, 2017.

22.Kowitt, Beth. "McDonald's is Exploring a New Menu Item: Sustainable Beef." Fortune, Feb. 27, 2017.

23.Maday, John. "Sustainability Takes Root in Beef Industry." Drovers Cattle Network. Nov. 30, 2016.

24."National Colalition Launches Pilot Research Project to Improve Sustainability in US beef Industry." The Samuel Roberts Nobel Foundation livestock news release, Feb. 24, 2017.

25.Tasho, R.P., and Cho, Jae Yong. "Veterinary antibiotics in animal waste, its distribution in soil and uptake by plants: A review." Science of the Total Environment. April 20, 2016. https://www.researchgate.net/publication/301760542_Veterinary_antibiotics_in_animal_waste_its_distribution_in_soil_and_uptake_by_plants_A_review

26.D'Costa, Vanessa M., et al. "Antibiotic resistance is ancient." Nature. Vol. 477, issue 7365, pp.457-461. Sept 22, 2011.

27.Singer, Andrew C., et al. "Review of Antimicrobial Resistance in the Environment and its Relevance to Environmental Regulators." Frontiers in Microbiology, 2016; 7: 1728.

28.Eaton, Elizabeth S. "Scientists study an out-there approach to fight infections." Science News, June 24, 2017, p. 23.

29.Santiago-Rodriguez, Tasha M, et al. "Gut Microbiome of an 11th Century A. D. Pre-Columbian Andean Mummy." Plos One, Sept 30, 2015. https://doi.org/10.1371/journal.pone.0138135

30."Milk Drug Residue Sampling Survey." Food and Drug Administration, Department of Health and Human Services. March, 2015.

31."Antibiotic Use in Livestock." Wikipedia, Feb. 4, 2017.

32.Moyer, Melinda Wenner. "How Drug-Resistant Bacteria Travel from the Farm to Your Table." Scientific American, December 2016, pp. 70-79.

CHAPTER 9.

TECHNOLOGY AND THE FUTURE OF FARMING

"Feeding the world will be one of the greatest challenges of the 21st Century. It will be impossible without using scientific advancements and biotechnology."—Mike Pompeo, politician

PRECISION FARMING

When I was in high school (early 50s), my agricultural textbook predicted farmers of the future would have tractors that drive themselves following radio signals from wires buried in the ground. Tractors do drive themselves these days, but not quite like the textbook author envisioned. Following GPS signals, tractors have been steering themselves around fields for a couple of decades now. Ever wonder how a farmer gets those perfectly straight rows? He/she turns on the auto-steer at the start of a pass across the field, only turning it off at the end of the row in order to turn back and make another pass. Or, if a map of the field has been downloaded to the computer along with work instructions, tractors coming on the market now can till or seed a field without a driver in the cab. Or a farmer might drive one tractor and control a "tag-along" tractor that may not even have a seat for a driver. Think self-driving cars are a new invention? Down on the farm, tractors have been driving themselves for over a decade.

Following GPS signals, the computer in the tractor cab keeps track of where the machine has been and where it needs to go next. No more skips or laps when spraying or fertilizing. This feature alone is estimated to save the average farmer ten percent on chemicals and fertilizers—a dollar saving and an environmental saving. Smart sprayers can keep track of what's been sprayed, and turn nozzles off if the spray boom travels over an area that has already been sprayed. Fertilizer and seeding machines can do the same thing, and automatically change seed or fertilizer rates following instructions from a map loaded into the computer.

There are sensors that can be attached to a fertilizing machine used to apply nutrients to a growing crop that will sense the health and vigor of the plants as it passes by and automatically adjust the rate of application according to rules programed into the controlling computer, thus avoiding over-fertilizing some areas of a field and under-fertilizing other portions [1]. The gain in fertilizer use efficiency of such a program is obvious.

Crop protection chemicals no longer need to be mixed into water in the sprayer tank. The chemicals can each have their own small tank, and be injected into the hose feeding the sprayer boom. This solves the problem of having left over mix in the spray tank that creates disposal problems. And also, the spray mix can be changed "on the go" by the tractor driver or according to a pre-loaded map. The same can be done with fertilizer mixes. And a corn farmer can change seed varieties or seed rates "on the go" to match seeds to varying soil types across a field.

Computers in combines can give instant yield readings as it threshes grain, recording the data and producing a map showing how production varies over a field. These maps can then become the basis for changes in fertilizer or seeding rates described previously. If the operator chooses, the data collected can be sent in real time to a cloud-based program that compares it to results sent in by other farmers. Several "Big Ag" companies, such as Dow chemical, Monsanto and John Deere, use this data to make recommendations on seed and fertilizer that will best fit a participating farmer's field based on his/her unique soil and growing conditions. Farmers who have used this "prescriptive planting" technology say it increases their yields five to ten percent. But suppliers of this technology predict it could be a major component of raising the U. S. average corn yield from 160 bushels to 200 bushels per acre if most corn growers will participate in the program and share all the factors affecting their yields with other farmers [2]. Worldwide, such data sharing among subsistence farmers could produce significant production and soil-saving improvements, and lift millions from abject poverty, providing governments will provide financial help where needed.

Precision farming is not without its detractors. Those who say precision farming is just another way for "Big Ag" to control food production are only displaying their Luddite biases. Farmers who have been applying new technologies to save soil and produce food more efficiently for the last 100 years are perfectly capable of deciding which new technologies are beneficial and which are not, and who is trying to take advantage of them and who is not.

Combined with no-till, precision farming technologies are increasing yields and conserving inputs of energy, labor, seed, fertilizer and crop protectants—a big plus for sustainability in food production and significant dollar savings for farmers and consumers. These technologies could provide sustainability and food security worldwide. All that is needed is their universal application.

DRONES AND ROBOTS

Ever since tractors replaced horses, tractors have grown bigger and more powerful. My dad did his farming with 20-horsepower (hp) tractors, equivalent to the power rating of a modern riding lawnmower. I began farming in 1965 with 60hp tractors and never owned one with more than 120hp. Today, 500hp tractors are common, costing the buyer $500,000 and weighing 25 tons or more. Some manufactures are now marketing tractors producing nearly 700hp and weighing 30-plus tons.

Is there a limit on how big tractors can get? Jason Hoult, product manager for AGCO Corporation, believes the practical limit is near 700hp. In order to keep the wheels from spinning when a load is applied, a tractor needs to weigh about 100 pounds per horsepower, or 35-tons for a 700hp tractor. Tractors bigger than that will be too heavy and too big to transport in one piece, and tillage machinery big enough to efficiently use all that horsepower will also pose transport problems [3].

Drones and robots may reverse this trend to bigger and bigger tractors. The need to accomplish more with an hour of labor has always been a major reason for buying a larger tractor. But with driverless tractors, one person can monitor the work of several small tractors that can accomplish the same tasks with less soil compaction and a better match-up of horsepower-to-tillage-tool. I often see 500hp tractors pulling light tillage tools, tools that could be drawn with a 100hp tractor, because that is the only tractor the farmer has available for the job. Using a large tractor for light work is not fuel efficient: Moving 25 tons of steel around a field takes significantly more fuel than moving a tractor weighing five tons.

Drones are already being used to map fields and monitor crops for disease, weeds, insects, and nutrient deficiencies. They can also be equipped to spray fertilizers or crop protectants, and programmed to work in swarms [4]. Drone technology is being driven by agricultural applications. "Precision agriculture accounts for approximately 80 percent of the known potential commercial market for UAS" (Unmanned Aerial Systems) [5].

Drones could make a significant contribution to the health and well-being of the world's small and subsistence farmers. Small farmers in the underdeveloped world often spray their fields by walking through a one hectare (2.5 acre) field with a backpack sprayer, dispensing toxic spray with a side-to-side motion from a wand held in the right hand. Over 90 percent of them wear no protective garments or face protection as they walk forward, often barefoot, through the area just sprayed, against all rules of safe pesticide use [6,7,8]. His health is endangered, as well as the health of his family if he does not shower and change clothes before entering his home. According to a 2004 study cited by Wikipedia [9], developing countries account for 25 percent of worldwide pesticide use and 99 percent of deaths related to pesticides, a tragedy of inadequate government regulation, education and enforcement.

Now picture instead a farmer standing at the edge of his small field with a smart phone, controlling the motions of a small drone equipped with a small spray tank and boom to safely spray his field. Drone manufacturer DJI has developed such a drone. Called Agras MG-1, the company says it will carry a 22- pound payload, and can cover 7-10 acres per hour, scanning the terrain in real time and automatically adjusting its height above the ground [10]. Using ultra-low-volume spray nozzles, this drone could spray 10 or more acres per load. Drones are not just for the large farmer: In many applications they will be the great technology equalizer for the small farmer versus the big farmer.

Robots milk cows and monitor the health of livestock. Robots are being developed that can pick apples, measure the quality of a head of lettuce and pick it, and many other jobs normally requiring human hands and judgement. Development of these types of robots is accelerating because of the chronic shortage of agricultural hand labor, and in the current political climate, that shortage is reaching the tipping point. Either more foreign workers are let in, at least temporarily, or crops that cannot be "robotized" will cease to be grown in the U. S., moving to less developed countries where labor is cheap, and people are willing to bend their backs and get their hands dirty in order to put food on the table and a roof over their heads. It is a shame that in the U. S., employers needing seasonal workers and willing to pay wages of $15 per hour or more cannot attract the homeless or unemployed to do agricultural hand work. In Santa Barbara County, California, strawberries, broccoli, lettuces and other crops valued a $13 million were plowed under in 2016 due to a lack of harvest labor [27].

URBAN FARMS

Growing produce on vacant lots, or abandoned warehouses, or in shipping containers is attracting attention of entrepreneurs these days, both growers and suppliers. Freight Farms of Boston, Massachusetts, converts used shipping containers into grow boxes for $80,000, and as of June, 2016 had installed over 60 "boxes" in 22 states and two Canadian provinces. The containers are equipped with LED lights, climate controls, and water plus nutrient circulation systems. The company says each box has the "growing power of two acres of farmland" for growing greens such as lettuce. They can be set up anywhere there is space available—under bridges, in parking garages, vacant lots, etc. Individuals and companies buying them sell their greens to restaurants and others that put a premium on fresh, local produce [11].

Hydroponics are also being put to use to grow greens in old warehouses or other unused buildings, and in multi-story buildings constructed to optimize "vertical farming", a term coined by Professor Dickson D. Despommier, Ph.D, of Columbia University. He authored the book, *The Vertical Farm: Feeding the World in the 21st Century*, published in 2010. Vertical farms didn't attract a lot of interest until the Fukushima disaster of March, 2011, in Japan. Japanese consumers were wary of radiation contaminated produce from their own farms, so the Japanese government encouraged the development of indoor/vertical farms. Toshiba and Panasonic have since become leaders in indoor farming [12].

U.S. cities are beginning to view their vacant lots as potential vegetable plots. New York has 7300 acres of vacant land in nearly 30,000 parcels. Detroit is estimated to have 20 square miles—12000 acres. Cities with more than 100,000 people have 19-25 percent of their land area unused [13,14]. Not all vacant lots would be suitable for urban farming, of course, but many could, and some are, being used for vegetable production. In 2013, Philadelphia's mayor estimated his city had 40,000 vacant lots. Urban farming was taking place on 750 pf those parcels, accounting for 350 new farms [15]. (Getting classified as a farm by the USDA is easy— "any place from which $1,000 or more of agricultural products were produced and sold, or normally would have been sold, during the year' [16].)[44]

Studies have shown getting vacant lots cleaned up and used for some purpose, even if just to grow grass, reduces crime. Vacant lots left to grow weeds and accumulate garbage attract drug dealers and other criminal acts. "A 2016 study by the University of Pennsylvania's Urban Health Lab showed that fixing up vacant lots reduced nearby gun violence by five percent" and saved taxpayers $26 in reduced costs due to gun violence for every dollar spent on cleanup [17].

Vertical farms, warehouse farms, rooftop farms, and vacant lots—can they grow enough produce to make a difference? Perhaps, but such methods are expensive compared to large open fields, and the market will be limited to those restaurants and individuals who are willing to pay a premium for fresh, local produce. Hydroponic growers who eschew pesti-

---

[44] Obviously, many farms are part--time or hobbies. A full-time farm begins at about $250,000 gross sales, of which, hopefully, about 25,000 will be net income. There are about 210,000 farms in the US that have sales at or above $250,000, and they account for 80 percent of the country's food and fiber production [16].

cides and synthetic nutrient sources want to label their plants organically produced, but organic growers are opposed, and I think they have a valid argument. Plants grown indoors under LED lights and fed a nutrient solution in an artificial soil that has no microbiota runs counter to everything organic growers say results in nutritious food. Do we know everything a healthy soil supplies a plant? Hydroponics can supply all the known plant nutrients and grow seemingly healthy plants, but does the soil biota supply a nutritional edge that we can't measure?

Indoor hydroponic growers claim a heathier product because there is no exposure to outdoor pollutants, insects, or bacterial sources such as wild animal feces or contaminated irrigation water. But I think it is only a matter of time until we see headlines such as, "Listeria Contaminated Produce from ABC Vertical Farm Sickens Thousands." Also, water molds, such as *Pythium* or *Phytophthora,* can infect the nutrient circulating system and destroy an entire crop in a short time. And insects, such as aphids, whiteflies, and mites, are the bane of indoor growing systems [18]. Agricultural systems are seldom perfect for long. Farming is full of surprises.

California and Arizona produce nearly 100 percent of the lettuce consumed in the US. Lettuce consumption in the US averages about 25 pounds per person per year, and is produced on about 282,000 acres [19]. To replace those acres with indoor hydroponic facilities would take the equivalent growing space of 141,000 shipping containers. New York City had a population of 8.55 million in 2015. If consumption is 25 pounds of lettuce per person yearly, total yearly New York demand would be 213.75 million pounds, or the production from about 5,000 California acres or 2,500 shipping containers. Probably doable in shipping containers or warehouses, but at tremendous initial investment and higher growing costs [18].

FUTURE GMO POSSIBILITIES

The genetic manipulation of plants to enhance yield, nutrition and insect and disease control is still a young science. We may someday have wheat or other crops that will get some of their nitrogen from the air as leguminous plants have done for millennia. Regarding drought resistance, research under the direction of Jill Farrent, professor of molecular and cell biology at the University of Cape Town, South Africa, is studying "resurrection plants"--plants that revive from an apparent dead state when rehydrated--with the intent of transferring the trait to food plants. She says all plants have the genes to induce this inactive state, but only turn them on in the seeds. Tricking some food plants to turn them on in response to drought conditions is her goal [20,21].

A new area of research emphasis in pest control is RNA interference. An RNA (ribonucleic acid) molecule resembles a portion of one strand of DNA (deoxyribonucleic acid) except that the nucleic acid uracil substitutes for thymine in DNA. Double stranded RNA is common in viruses, but only present during cell division in other life forms.

There are many types of RNA. They are programmed to carry out specific functions and orchestrate the work inside the cell. Messenger RNA (mRNA), for instance, unwinds a portion of DNA that codes for a specific protein, then copies the instructions and carries them to the ribosome which constructs the desired protein. Interfering with these instructions causes the construction process to fail. Making a useful interference RNA (RNAi) involves first identifying proteins in a pest that are unique to that pest and essential to its survival. A double-stranded RNAi is then constructed that matches the gene that codes for that protein. The RNAi is then put into an insect bait. Or a plant can be modified by genetic engineering to produce the double stranded RNAi [22].

Since double-stranded RNAs usually only exist in viruses, the immune system of a bug ingesting the bait or plant tissue senses the invasion of a troublesome virus and proceeds to chop up the RNAi and anything that matches it in its genome, killing the bug. If the pest is a weed, researchers have demonstrated that a spray containing an RNAi construct can penetrate a plant's leaves, bind to a gene essential to the weed's survival, thus turning it off and killing the weed. [22]. Researchers visualize such sprays helping plants survive drought or diseases as well as insects. RNAs do not survive long inside or outside a plant cell. Such a spray could be the perfect pesticide—protecting the plant then going away in 3-4 weeks [22].

Monsanto is experimenting with an RNAi that can kill the *varroa* mite that is the bane of beekeepers. The RNAi would be put in sugar water used to feed bees. Consuming the RNAi has no effect on the bees, but is fatal to the *varroa* mite. Currently beekeepers use pesticides to do that job, but killing the mite without also killing the bee is tricky [22].

Monsanto is a leader in RNAi research, with a number of potential products in the pipeline. Monsanto calls these products "Biodirect". Bayer and Syngenta are also working on RNAi products. If pending mergers are approved by regulators, Monsanto's products will soon be rolled into Bayer's product pipeline, and Syngenta's will be a Chinese product. China's state-owned China National Chemical Corporation, known as ChemChina, is buying Syngenta. With that purchase, China becomes a major player in the agricultural technology market, including genetically modified seeds [23].

Grain yields on Chinese farms are significantly lower than those on U.S. farms, and Chinese leaders are trying hard to correct that deficiency [23]. For years, representatives of Chinese seed companies have been roaming the U.S. Corn Belt, seeking superior technologies, even surreptitiously digging up samples of newly planted GMO seeds from farmer's fields and sending them to China[24].

As always, these new uses for RNAs has its detractors.

One expressed worry is that manufactured two-stranded RNAs might match a DNA stretch in humans and turn off some of our genes. Proponents counter that RNAs don't make it past our saliva and stomach acids. And we have been eating plant, animal and virus RNAs for thousands of years without getting our DNA destroyed. Besides, any plant protector or enhancer will have to be rigorously vetted before allowed into our food supply.

"Turbocharging a new Green Revolution" is the title of a July, 2011, news release by researchers at Cambridge University in England [25]. Twelve institutions across four continents launched an effort, funded by Bill and Melinda gates and others, to transform C3 photosynthesizing grain plants into C4 photosynthesizers (see Chapter 4, Note 4, for an explanation of C3 vs. C4). It is believed C4 capability could increase wheat and rice yields by 50 percent or more while using less water and nitrogen per unit of production. For instance, wheat, a C3 plant, requires two to three pounds of nitrogen to produce a bushel of grain (60 pounds) while corn, a C4 plant, uses a little over one pound of nitrogen to produce one bushel (56 pounds). As is abundantly evident, giving the major food grains C4 ability would go a long ways towards meeting the food needs of 2050 and beyond. In December of 2014, researchers in the Philippines working under the auspices of the International Rice Institute (IRRI) successfully transferred enough C4 photosynthesis genes into rice to give the plant a rudimentary C4 capability [26].

The technologies described in this section are but a small sample of the enhancements to our abilities to grow food that can be delivered if technologies are judged by the results produced and not by the process by which they were developed. For the past 30 years, the world's peoples have been fed a constant diet of misinformation, fear and doubt about genetically engineered plants and animals by NGOs such as Greenpeace, while money pours into their coffers because they are "protecting" the public from "frankenfoods". Their proclamations are promulgated by a technology illiterate media that always "leads with stories that bleed". Compounding the problem are labeling laws requiring GMO statements on food labels, implying danger when none exists. No credible evidence of harm to humans or meat animals has been documented since introduction of GMOs into the food supply in 1996. We need to apply these technologies if the world is to be adequately fed in 2050.

CHAPTER 9 REFERENCES

1. Soliday, Robb. "Mapping the way to better yields." Wheat Life, February 2013, pp. 24-27.

2.Bunge, Jacob. "On the farm, data harvesting sows seeds of mistrust." Wall Street Journal, Feb. 26, 2014, p. 1,14.

3.Wehrspann, Jodie. "Tractor Engines, Gain More Horsepower." Farm Industry News (on the web), March 1, 2010.

4.Scherer, Colleen. "It's a Bird, It's a Plane, No, It's Swarming Ag Robots?" Agri-Times Northwest, April 15, 2016, page 9.

5.Precision Agricultural Economics" published on the Farm. com website, and reprinted in Wheat Life, June, 2015, p. 13.

6."Pesticide Use in Developing Countries". The World Bank. New Ideas in Pollution Regulation. Undated, about 2005.

7."Pesticides and Health Hazards. Facts and Figures." Pestizid Aktions-Netzwerk e. V. (PAN Gemany). 2012.

8.Williamson, Stephanie. "Pesticide Issues in Developing Countries." Symposium on pesticide reduction in agriculture, Zurich Sept 3, 2015.

9.Goldmann, Lynn. "Childhood Pesticide Poisoning. Information for Advocacy and Action." Published May, 2004, by the Chemicals Programme of the United Nations Environmental Programme. www.who.int

10.Rice, Alison. "Crop Dusting Drone Flies." AgWeb.com, as reported in Agri-Times Northwest, Dec. 18, 2015, p. 9.

11.Mims, Christopher. "Farming Inside the Box." The Future of Everything, issue 2, June 2016. Dow Jones and Company, Inc., Wall Street Journal Supplement.

12.Shayon, Sheila. "The Vertical Farm: A Chat with Dickson D. Despommier, Ph.D." The Next Economy, Sustainable Brands Issue in Focus, Feb. 10, 2017.

13.McPhearson, Timon. "Vacant Land in Cities Could Provide Important Social and Ecological Benefits." The Nature of Cities (blog), August 21, 2012.

14.Davidson, Kate. "Detroit has tons of Vacant Land. But Forty Square Miles?" April 18, 2012. http://mediad.public-broadcasting.net/p/michigan/files/styles/x_large/public/vacanthome_detroit_davidson.jpg

15.Vinnitskaya, Irina. "What Cities Can Do with Vacant Lots." Arch Daily (website), January 26, 2013.

16.Pastor, Rene. "What's in a word? USDA's Definition of Farmer Raises Hackles and Concerns." February 14, 2013. https://www.farmpolicyfacts.org/about-farm-policy-facts/

17.Moore, Martha T. "Remaking Vacant Lots to Cut Crime." The Pew Charitable Trusts / Research & Analysis / Stateline. January 6 2017.

18.Kaiser, Cheryl and Erust, Matt. "Hydroponic Lettuce." University of Kentucky Cooperative Extension Service. December, 2012.

19.National Agricultural Statistic Service. Lettuce Statistics, 2016.

20. Wikipedia. "Jill Farrent." April 2017.

21. Giles, Frank. "TED Talks Take on Agriculture Innovation." April 17, 2017. Find at ted.com/topics/agriculture.

22. Regalado, Antonio. "The Next Great GMO Debate." MIT Technology Review, September/October, 2015. https://www.technologyreview.com/s/540136/the-next-great-gmo-debate/

23. Stevenson, Alexandra; Bray, Chad; Tsang, Amie. "Chem-China Deal for Syngenta Reflects Drive to Meet Food Needs." The New York Times, February 3, 2016. https://nyti.ms/1Kpjrwq

24. Genoways, Ted. "Corn Wars." New Republic, August 16, 2015. http://www.newrepublic.com/article/122441/corn-wars

25. Hibberd, Julian. "Turbocharging a New Green Revolution." Department of Plant Sciences, Cambridge University, United Kingdom. July, 2011.

26. Bullis, Kevin. "Supercharged Photosynthesis: Advanced genetic tools could help boost crop yields and feed billions more people." 10 Breakthrough Technologies, March/April, 2015. Massachusetts Institute of Technology.

27. Papenfuss, Mary. "Immigration Crackdown Expected to Increase Crops Left Unharvested in California Fields." The Morning Email. Huffington Post. June 26, 2017.

CHAPTER 10.
AGRICULTURE AROUND THE WORLD: HOW WE WILL FEED 10 BILLION

By 2050, predictions are that earth's population will be 9.7 billion, plus or minus 300 million, and by 2100 population will stabilize at 11.2 billion. These predictions assume fertility rates continue to decline and eventually reach the replacement level of 2.1 children per woman. Presently the world fertility rate is 2.5 children per woman, but varies widely between rich and poor countries. The average rate for the 48 least developed countries is 4.3 children per woman. In Africa, where poverty is most prevalent, the rate is 4.7. In South America, poverty is less severe and the rate is 2.15. North America and Europe have rates below the replacement level, 1.86 and 1.6, respectively [1].

It is a well-established fact that as incomes collectively rise, average fertility rates fall. The predictions in the preceding paragraph assume the impoverished peoples of the world will gradually see their living standards improve. It is also an established fact that as household income rises, demand for meat and dairy also rises. By 2050, meat consumption is expected to rise 73 percent and dairy consumption by 58 percent over 2010 levels [2].It is an oxymoron that, while rising incomes reduce the fertility rate and results in less mouths to feed, demands for higher quality nutrition puts more demand on land resources.

Can we feed all these people in a sustainable and environmentally friendly way? Yes, if we are willing to embrace the technologies described in previous chapters, and apply them in ways that are appropriate for the small farmers in least developed countries as well as farmers in developed countries. No-till and other conservation practices must be applied worldwide to preserve and sustain the soils of the world. Synthetic fertilizers and crop protection chemicals will need to be used on most of the world's cropland to get maximum yields. Low-input, low yield organic farms can sustain the soil resource, but they cannot produce enough food to sustain the current population, much less the projected population of the future. As quoted in Chapter Three, "Even with the best organic farming practices available, even cutting back our diets to minimal, vegetarian levels, only about four billion of us could live on what the earth and traditional farming supply" [3]. The rest of us (now 3.3 billion [1]) owe our existence to nitrogen taken from the atmosphere by the Haber-Bosch process. Or, stated differently, nearly one-half of the nitrogen that is a building block of protein and DNA in everyone's body was, on average, produced from the atmosphere synthetically. Unless major crop plants (wheat, rice, corn, etc.) are somehow engineered to take most or all their nitrogen needs from the air as leguminous plants do, all future population increases will be dependent on the Haber-Bosch process.

That is not to say organic farming is unimportant. Natural supplies of nitrogen and natural ways of protecting plants should be used when available and practical, and conventional farmers are doing that when returning plant residues to the soil, growing cover crops when land would otherwise be idle, fertilizing fields with manure from on farm or near farm livestock operations, and using university generated IPM (Integrated Pest Management) programs that prioritize natural pest control, using synthetic pesticides only as a supplement. But NGOs and pundits who insist the world's people can be fed using organic methods exclusively are being irresponsible.

Farmers in the developed countries have been employing soil-conserving techniques with increasing success since the 1950s. No-till is the culmination of those efforts, and where it is applied erosion is virtually eliminated. In 2014, estimated area farmed using no-till worldwide was nearly 309 million acres, or about nine percent of global arable land [4]. Over 90 percent of those acres occur in the highly developed farming areas of three continents—South America, North America, and Australia-New Zealand [5]. Nearly every country in the world has some acreage under no-till, but adoption in Europe has been slow, and very slow among the subsistence farmers of Asia and Africa. Using computer simulations, Rosegrant, et al, [13] predicts 70 percent of the world's rain-fed farmers will have adopted no-till by 2050 [page 49] and that practice alone will increase farm output 41 percent in Eastern Europe and Central Asia, 31 percent in Sub-Saharan Africa, and 35 percent in South Asia [page 71].

Rolf Derpsch, et al, did an extensive evaluation of no-till practices country by country in 2010 [5]. The authors found no-till or other direct seed practices[45] being used on farms of all sizes, from half hectare (1.2 acre) farms in China to farms with thousands of acres, not only in North and South America, but in Kazakhstan, Russia, and Ukraine. Africa has a low rate of adoption, but the concept is being intensely promoted by the FAO (United Nations Food and Agriculture Organization) and other government and non-government organizations. Africa's malnourished, overworked, erosion depleted soils must be rejuvenated to meet the needs of Africa's growing population, and many of the continent's governments are beginning to step up to the challenge with agronomic research and extension programs.

The widespread adoption of no-till in Brazil was sped

---

[45]The authors consider seeding machines that seed and fertilize in one pass but disturb most of the top two to three inches of soil to be a conservation (direct seed) tillage practice but not no-till. I personally disagree with that distinction.

up because the country's machine manufacturers produced equipment not only for large, powerful tractors but also for animal traction and manual operation [5]. Derpsch, et al, states "there are about 100,000 small farmers using no-till farming systems" in Brazil employing Brazil-manufactured specialized machines. These machines are being exported around the world and will be an important asset to the world's small farmers.

Derpsch, et al, concludes, "The wide recognition of no-till farming as a truly sustainable system should ensure the spread of the no-till technology and the associated practices of organic soil cover and crop rotation, as soon as the barriers to its adoption have been overcome, to areas where adoption is currently still low. The widespread adoption globally also shows that no-till farming cannot any more be considered a temporary fashion craze; instead largely through farmers' own effort, the system has established itself as a farming practice and a different way of thinking about sustainable agro-ecosystem management that can no longer be ignored by scientists, academics, extension workers, farmers at large as well as equipment and machine manufactures and politicians.

"With adequate policies to promote Conservation Agriculture/No-till, it is possible to obtain what is called the triple bottom line-- economic, social and environmental sustainability-- while at the same time improving soil health and increasing production...It has been proven that with CA (Conservation Agriculture) the erosion rates can be brought to levels below the soil formation (rate), which makes the system long-term sustainable." No-till pioneer Carlos Crovetto has been using no-till on his farm in Southern Chile continuously since 1978, on slopes up to 18 percent. Erosion has been virtually eliminated, and by 1997 he claimed to have had added one inch of topsoil, and increased soil organic matter from 1.7 percent to 10.6 percent in the top 5cm (2 inches) of soil [6]. Adding one inch of soil in so short a time seems a bit exaggerated. I expect when the organic matter he is measuring is fully decomposed, he will have added approximately one-tenth of an inch of soil. The point is, conservation tillage, especially no-till, when all plant residue is returned to the soil, can build new soil faster than it erodes away.

The advantages of no-till have been pointed out a number of times in this book. Derpsch, et al [5], summarizes them quoting from a paper presented in Hanover, Germany in 2009 [7]:

1. 96% less erosion

2. 66% reduction in fuel consumption

3. Reduced CO2 emissions

4. Enhanced water quality (less runoff, less nutrient leaching)

5. Higher (soil) biological activity (increased soil health)

6. Increased soil fertility (from increased organic matter)

7. Enhanced production stability and yields (drought less damaging)

8. Incorporation of new areas into production (marginal land productively farmed)

9. Lower production costs

To this list can be added the sequester of carbon, as explained in footnote 3, Chapter two.

Photo 7. Ray Reser direct seeding garbanzos into last seasons' wheat residue. Near Walla Walla, Wa. (Photo by Author.)

244

No-till has its naysayers in the environmental movement, especially because of its reliance on herbicides such as Roundup for pre-planting weed control. Some also contend it is a lower-yielding practice, pointing to research such as that of Pittelkow, et al [8]. These researchers analyzed 610 studies that compared no-till with conventional tillage in 63 countries and 48 crops. They concluded that, overall, no-till yields less, but results were variable and no-till can produce superior yields under certain conditions. They recommend caution in introducing this practice to "resource-poor and vulnerable smallholder farming systems."

I conclude Pittelkow, et al's study is an example of research perhaps well done but with irresponsible conclusions, for the following reasons. (A) No-till can have a long learning curve among researchers as well as farmers. Each soil type, each crop, and each kind of seeding equipment has its own learning curve. No doubt much of the research examined by Pittelkow, et al, suffered from lack of know-how by those conducting the experiments. (B) Putting no-till on eroded, nutrient and organic matter-deficient soil typically farmed by resource-poor farmers will rev-up the soil biota who will consume the available nutrients at the expense of the crop, and if the experimenters didn't' compensate for that phenomenon, no-till will yield less for the first, perhaps ten, years. (C) Farmers big and small in the Americas are having great success with no-till; there is no reason small landholders in Asia and Africa can't do the same.

Africa has great agricultural potential. Most people, I think, do not visualize the immense size of the continent. Africa can swallow up all of the U.S., China, India, and most of Eastern and Western Europe. The amount of undeveloped and under-utilized arable land is huge. The so-called Guinea Savanna Zone stretches from Guinea on the West coast eastward to the Ethiopian border, then south through Uganda to Mozambique, then west to the Atlantic coast of Angola, touching some 25 countries. The savanna lands encompass nearly one-and- one-half billion acres of which nearly one billion is considered farmable. Less than one-tenth of that land (98 million acres) is presently cropped. It is one of the largest underused agricultural land areas in the world [9]. For comparison, The U. S. has approximately 390 million acres of cropland, and another 415 million acres of pasture and rangeland [10].

The restraints on developing this land and other lands in Africa are many. Most Important is the failure of most countries to provide unconditional title to the land; approximately 80 percent of land in Africa is communal. Communal land is at risk in many cases of being appropriated by governments and sold in large tracts to foreign governments seeking to insure future food supplies for their peoples. China, Saudi Arabia and South Korea are some of the countries that have already made large investments in Africa. And Europe is looking towards Africa as a source of biofuels [17].

In order to have the incentive to improve their holdings, to plant trees and make other long-term investments, and to be able to provide collateral for loans, land holders need clear title that can be passed on to descendants. This is a political problem that needs to be addressed by government. Government also needs to subsidize research and extension services to small landholders, most of whom have little formal education.

Another major obstacle to land title is tribal customs. Land is generally divided up among the male members of an extended family. If a husband dies, the wife is often left landless, even though she is the one who has most likely been doing the farming. One-third of Africa's subsistence farmers are women, yet extension workers work primarily with the husbands, who may or may not pass production tips onto the wife. One of the keys to raising the incomes of Africa's subsistence farmers is developing programs that work directly with women farmers. Women supply approximately 50 percent of the agricultural labor in Sub-Saharan Africa (all lands south of the Sahara desert, which envelops the Arab countries bordering the Mediterranean from the Atlantic to the Suez Canal). "If women farmers could access the same productive resources as men (i.e. improved seeds, fertilizers, crop protectants, and financing), they could increase yields on their farms by 20-30 percent, lifting 100-150 million people out of hunger" [12].

The Guinea Savanna is not considered prime farmland, but neither was the Brazilian *cerrado*—the new world complement to the Guinea Savanna—50 years ago. Then the unexpected happened.[46] In 1972, Russia's wheat crop failed. Russia had always depended on their wheat crop to feed their livestock as well as their people. In past years when crops failed to meet domestic needs, Russia's leaders slaughtered livestock to save grain for bread. But wheat was plentiful and cheap in the wheat exporting democracies of the West, so the Soviet Politburo decided to save their livestock and buy wheat. They bought massive amounts of wheat from the U. S., later termed "The Great Grain Robbery" by pundits. The U.S. government held massive stocks of wheat in storage because of price support programs that loaned farmers money on their crops, then foreclosed on the crops when the loans could not be paid back. This program had kept millions of family farmers in business since the Great Depression, but the massive amounts of government-owned grain kept a lid on prices worldwide, as it would be sold whenever market prices rose a small amount above farm loan price.

Earl Butz was the Secretary of Agriculture in 1972, in Richard Nixon's administration. Republicans had railed against the government control of farm prices for years, and Butz saw the chance to get rid of the price-depressing surpluses. The Soviets bought millions of tons at bargain prices. Farm

---

[46] The following four paragraphs tell the story as I remember living it.

prices soon began to rise. By the end of 1972 wheat had doubled from its decade-old depressed price of $1.30-$1.50 per bushel. Then 1973 brought unfavorable worldwide weather for crops, and the cushion of surpluses had disappeared. Panic buying by importers ensued, and by the end of 1973 (my year as president of the Washington Wheat Growers), wheat had doubled in price again. Farmers were ecstatic. It was like wheat selling for $20 per bushel in 2017 instead of the present $4.50 per bushel.

Prices for soybeans, corn, and other grains and pulses enjoyed similar price increases. Soybeans were in such short supply that Richard Nixon did the unthinkable for a Republican, free-market President: He put an export embargo on soybeans that had already been sold to Japan to reserve adequate U. S. domestic supplies. The Japanese were understandably furious. The embargo was lifted after only five days, but limits were put on how much could be shipped on existing sales contracts. To Japanese buyers, the reputation of the U.S. as a dependable supplier had been irreparably damaged.

What does this story this have to do with the Brazilian *cerrado*? The Japanese, alarmed that the American President could deny them access to the U.S. soybean supply, vowed to diversify their supply in the future. In the following years, Japanese investors poured money into Brazil and other South American countries with undeveloped agricultural potential. With this investment money and governmental incentives, Brazilians and not a few North Americans began developing the poor grazing lands of the cerrado. They were helped by a public research firm, *Empresa Brasileria de Pesquisa Agropecuaria* (Brazilian Agricultural Research Corporation), which has become, in modern times, the world's leading tropical-research institution. To create farmable land out of the *cerrado*, *Empresa* concentrated on four things. First, the soils were too acidic to grow good crops, so the farmers hauled lime to the fields, two or more tons per acre. Next, they went to the African savanna and brought back a promising grass that they crossbred with native grasses and came up with a variety that yielded 8-10 tons per acre, much more than the native grasses. The pastures of the *cerrado* mature a beef animal in 18-20 months whereas 30 years ago it took four years. "Brazil increased its beef exports tenfold in a decade, overtaking Australia as the world's largest exporter" [11]. Regarding soybean production growth, Brazil accounted for 17 percent of world exports in 1973 and 40 percent 12 years later, even though the world market was almost three times larger in 1985 [14].

Embrapa had to modify the soybean plant to make it productive on acid soils and adapted to a tropical climate. They also created a new strain of rhizobium bacteria that would efficiently infect the roots to produce nitrogen for the soybean plant in acidic soils. Next they shortened the time it takes for the soy plant to reach maturity, so that two crops can be grown in one year. Brazil now surpasses the U.S. in soybean production, and Brazil is currently only using one-eighth of its 988 million acres of arable land, land that excludes the destruction of any rain forest [11].

Can this "Miracle of the *cerrado*" [11] be transferred to Africa? Many people think that it can, and hopefully without the 5,000-50,000 acre farms that blanket much of the *cerrado*. Had policies been in place to distribute land and finance inputs to Brazil's poorest farmers and would-be farmers, development of the *cerrado* would have eliminated much of the country's poverty.

Thailand followed a different path. Agricultural land distribution over the last half-century in Thailand's sparsely populated Northeast area followed a path that limited farm size and significantly reduced poverty. Both Brazil and Thailand concentrated on developing export markets for their new farmers. For Brazil it was soybeans, corn and other grains: For Thailand it was cassava. The governments of the Guinea Savanna lands should heed the lessons of the *cerrado* and Thailand's Northeast lands if a productive, poverty-reliving development is to occur.

Theoretically, the world could probably be fed without the technologies described in Chapter nine if untapped arable lands in Africa and South America are fully utilized, and lands devoted to wildlife in Europe, North America and elsewhere are devoted to food production. I don't think that is a result anyone wants. But with these lands in reserve, the world is in no danger of running short of calories.

No book on agriculture these days would be complete without at least some mention of global warming. That the world is warming is undeniable. Who or what is causing it I will leave to others to decide. I do know we have been releasing, since the 1850s, increasing amounts of carbon dioxide that was taken out of the atmosphere millions of years ago and stored in coal, oil, and natural gas. This release has to be at least partly responsible. What effect global warming will have on the food supply is positive or negative depending on who you talk to. One expected result is that extra CO_2 will enhance photosynthesis.

In any event, crops will have to be protected against weeds, insects, and diseases, mostly with synthetic products or innovative breeding. Organic farming methods are fine as far as they go, but feeding the world with organic methods exclusively is impossible—there will never be enough organic fertilizer to maintain yields, and pest control will be hit and miss.

When no-till and other soil-conserving methods are universally applied, our soil resource will not only be maintained but will be improved for future generations. Returning crop residues and avoiding excessive tillage builds organic matter, which is the key to maintaining soil health. And soil organic matter is an important CO_2 sink, storing 5 tons of carbon for every one percent organic matter. There are about 3.7 billion acres of cropland in the world [15]. Raising the organic matter level on all those acres one percent (entirely possible, see Ch. 2, Notes 2-1 and 2-2, and Ch. 4, note 4-2) would remove 18.5 billion tons of carbon from the atmosphere, equal to nearly six percent of the atmospheric carbon increase (300 billion tons) since 1700 [16].

Barring some man-made or natural disaster, such as nuclear war or an asteroid strike, the world's farmers can adequately and sustainably feed the world in 2050 and beyond, providing politicians will provide a supporting role and critical Luddites cool their rhetoric. Let farmers be farmers. They are problem solvers. They are innovators. They are environmentalists. In the 19th century, the cotton gin, the reaper, the threshing machine, and the steel plow came from farm shops. In the 20th, they survived a devastating Dust Bowl and a Great Depression with pure grit. Then the sons went off to war and the daughters built the machines of war, a winning combination. After the war, many went to college on the GI bill and became engineers, doctors, lawyers, entrepreneurs and agricultural experts. They helped build an interstate road system and send a man to the moon. As farmers, they taxed themselves and formed commodity commissions to support research and help market their crops. They tackled the problem of soil erosion, and from their shops came no-till seeding machines and better soil-conserving tillage tools. The problem of how to control erosion was conquered. Now it needs to be universally applied.

Farmers are the best judges of what technologies will best conserve and sustain productivity of our soils. But they need a stable government that respects property rights, and a financial system that   provides credit at reasonable rates to finance the tools of production, and a safety net when nature deals a bad hand. Reward them adequately and they will find a way to feed the world sustainably with nutritious, safe, plentiful food.

"When tillage begins, other arts follow. The farmers, therefore, are the founders of civilization."
—Daniel Webster

CHAPTER 10 REFERENCES

1.World Population Prospects: The 2015 Revision. United Nations Department of Economic and Social Affairs/Population Division.

2. "Major gains in efficiency of livestock systems needed." News release, De. 14, 2011, Rome. Food and Agriculture Organization of the United Nations. www.fao.org/news/story/en/item/116937/icode

3.Hager, Thomas. Alchemy of Air. 2008. Three Rivers Press.

4.Kalaugher, Liz. "No-till farming alone could cut yields." Environmentalresearchweb Oct. 23, 2014.

5.Derpsch, Rolf, et al. "Current status of no-till farming in the world and some of its main benefits." International Journal of Agriculture and Biological Engineering. Vo. 3, No. 1. March, 2010.

6."Stubble over the soil means No-Till forever." No-Till Farmer. Brookfield, Wisconsin. De. 1997, pp. 6-7.

7.Friedrich, T.; Kienzle, J; Kassam, A. H. "Conservation Agriculture in Developing Countries: The Role of Mechanization." In: Paper presented at the Club of Bologna meeting on Innovation for Sustainable Mechanization. Hanover, Germany, Nov. 2, 2009b.

8.Pittelkow, Cameron M., et al. "Productivity limits and potentials of the principles of conservation agriculture." Nature 517, pp. 365-368. Jan.15, 2015. Published online Oct. 22, 2014. doi: 10.1038/nature 13809.

9.World Bank. World Development Report 2008: Agriculture for Development. World Bank, Washington, D. C.

10.USDA. 2012 Census of Agriculture: Land Use.

11.Cremaq, Piauj. "The miracle of the cerrado." The Economist. August 26, 2010.

12.Zeigler, Margaret: Steensland, Ann. 2016 Global Agricultural Productivity Report. Global Harvest Initiative, Washington, D.C. Oct. 2016, p. 40.

13.Rosegrant, Mark W., et al. Food Security in a World of Natural Resource Scarcity. International Food Policy Research Institute, 2033 K Street, NW, Washington, D.C. 2014.

14.Faminow, Merle D.; Hillman, Jimmye S. "Embargoes and the Emergence of Brazil's Soyabean Industry." Agriculture Economics Department, University of Arizona, Tucson. The World Economy. Vol. 10, issue 3, pp. 351-366. Sept., 1987.

15.Vieru, Tudor. "NASA to Map 3.7 Billion Acres of Cropland Around the World." Softpedia News, January 30, 2014.

16."What is the Carbon Cycle?" Soil Carbon Center, 2004 Throckmorton Plant Sciences Center, Kansas State University, Manhattan, KS 66506. Undated.

17.Kariuki, Julius Gatune. "The Future of Agriculture in Africa." Boston University, The Pardee Papers, No. 15, August 2011.

18079196R00142

Made in the USA
San Bernardino, CA
28 December 2018